The MEMORY of ALL THAT

The MEMORY of ALL THAT

George Gershwin, Kay Swift, and My Family's
Legacy of Infidelities

Katharine Weber

Crown Publishers
New York

Portions of this work were previously published in different form:
"A Decent Family": "Oy Tannenbaum" in the *New York Times,* December 17,
2005; "A Child's Christmas in New York" in *Half/Life: Jew-ish Tales from
Interfaith Homes,* edited by Laurel Snyder (Brooklyn, NY: Softskull Press, 2006).
"The Fire That Time": "The Fire That Time" in the *New York Times,* June 4,
2006. "Subject: Sidney Kaufman": "The Loves of His Life" in *The Other Women,*
edited by Victoria Zackheim (New York: Grand Central Publishing, 2007).
"The Memory of All That" and "Ganz": "The Memory of All That"
in *A Few Thousand Words About Love,* edited by Mickey Pearlman
(New York: St. Martin's Press, 1998), "In a Painting, Gershwin Packed the House"
in the *New York Times,* August 30, 1998, and "The Memory of All That,"
liner note essay for *Fine and Dandy: World Premiere Recording*
(Bronxville, NY: PS Classics, 2004).
See page 267 for additional credits.

Library of Congress Cataloging-in-Publication Data
Weber, Katharine.
The memory of all that: George Gershwin, Kay Swift, and my family's legacy of
infidelities / Katharine Weber.—1st ed. 1. Weber, Katharine, 1955—Family.
2. Authors, American—20th century—Biography. 3. Gershwin, George,
1898–1937. 4. Swift, Kay, 1897–1993. I. Title.
PS3573. E2194Z46 2011
813'. 54—dc22   [B] 2011003023

ISBN 978-0-307-39588-7
eISBN 978-0-307-88859-4

Printed in the United States of America

Book design by Lauren Dong
Jacket design by Jean Traina
*Jacket photographs: All courtesy of the author except George Gershwin's
1934 self-portrait with Andrea Warburg, used by permission
of the Ira and Leonore Gershwin Trusts.*

10 9 8 7 6 5 4 3 2 1

First Edition

For Nick
O.L.I.H.T.S.

Warburg Family Tree

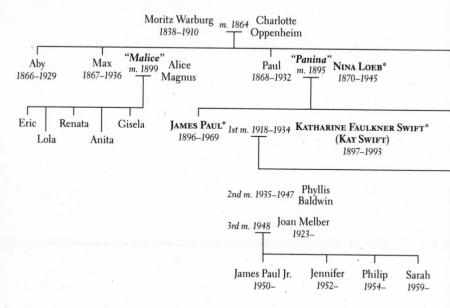

Moritz Warburg *m. 1864* Charlotte
1838–1910   Oppenheim

Aby	Max	*"Malice"* Alice	Paul	*"Panina"* **Nina Loeb***
1866–1929	1867–1936	*m. 1899* Magnus	1868–1932	*m. 1895* 1870–1945

Eric   Renata   Gisela   **James Paul*** *1st m. 1918–1934* **Katharine Faulkner Swift***
Lola   Anita   1896–1969   **(Kay Swift)**
                                                   1897–1993

2nd m. 1935–1947 Phyllis
                   Baldwin

3rd m. 1948 Joan Melber
              1923–

James Paul Jr.   Jennifer   Philip   Sarah
1950–   1952–   1954–   1959–

Loeb Family Tree

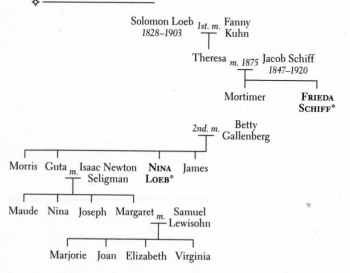

Solomon Loeb *1st. m.* Fanny
1828–1903   Kuhn

Theresa *m. 1875* Jacob Schiff
                   1847–1920

Mortimer   **Frieda
Schiff***

2nd. m. Betty
          Gallenberg

Morris   Guta *m.* Isaac Newton   **Nina**   James
               Seligman   **Loeb***

Maude   Nina   Joseph   Margaret *m.* Samuel
                                 Lewisohn

Marjorie   Joan   Elizabeth   Virginia

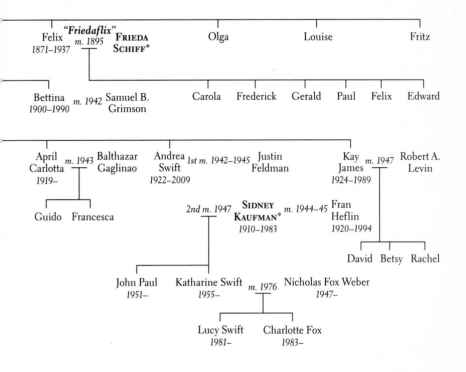

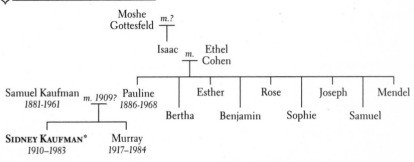

Gottesfeld Family Tree

*Names in boldface appear on more than one tree.

Shippen/Swift/Dorr Family Tree

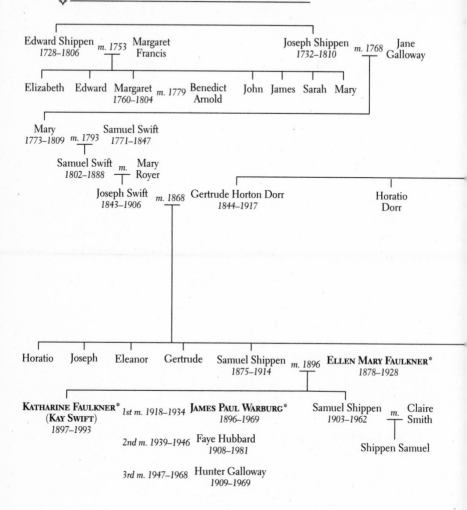

Edward Shippen
1728–1806
m. 1753 Margaret Francis

Joseph Shippen
1732–1810
m. 1768 Jane Galloway

Elizabeth   Edward   Margaret
1760–1804
m. 1779 Benedict Arnold   John   James   Sarah   Mary

Mary
1773–1809
m. 1793 Samuel Swift
1771–1847

Samuel Swift
1802–1888
m. Mary Royer

Joseph Swift
1843–1906
m. 1868 Gertrude Horton Dorr
1844–1917

Horatio Dorr

Horatio   Joseph   Eleanor   Gertrude   Samuel Shippen
1875–1914
m. 1896 **ELLEN MARY FAULKNER***
1878–1928

KATHARINE FAULKNER*
(**KAY SWIFT**)
1897–1993
1st m. 1918–1934 **JAMES PAUL WARBURG***
1896–1969

Samuel Shippen
1903–1962
m. Claire Smith

Shippen Samuel

2nd m. 1939–1946 Faye Hubbard
1908–1981

3rd m. 1947–1968 Hunter Galloway
1909–1969

* *Names in boldface appear on more than one tree.*

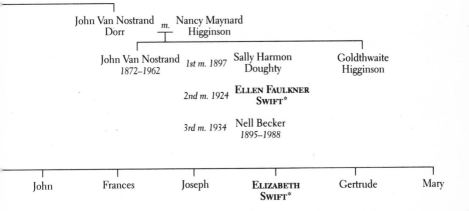

John Van Nostrand · m. · Nancy Maynard
Dorr · Higginson

John Van Nostrand · 1st m. 1897 · Sally Harmon · Goldthwaite
1872–1962 · Doughty · Higginson

2nd m. 1924 · **ELLEN FAULKNER**
SWIFT*

3rd m. 1934 · Nell Becker
1895–1988

John · Frances · Joseph · **ELIZABETH** · Gertrude · Mary
SWIFT*

Faulkner Family Tree

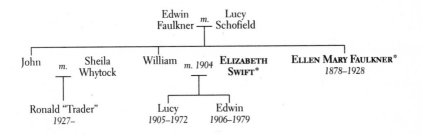

Edwin · m. · Lucy
Faulkner · Schofield

John · m. · Sheila · William · m. 1904 · **ELIZABETH** · **ELLEN MARY FAULKNER***
Whytock · **SWIFT*** · 1878–1928

Ronald "Trader" · Lucy · Edwin
1927– · 1905–1972 · 1906–1979

I think it is all a matter of love;
the more you love a memory, the stronger and stranger it is.

—Vladimir Nabokov

Contents

The MEMORY of ALL THAT

We Saw the Sea

WE ARE WALKING INTO THE OCEAN. HE IS HOLDING ME in the crook of his left arm and I cling awkwardly to the soft expanse of his chest where I am squashed against his cold skin and his disconcerting chest hair. He wades deeper into the black water that laps against my thighs, and I am afraid, afraid of him and afraid of the ocean. He strides through the waves, a father going into the ocean with his little girl, and over his shoulder I see my mother in her blue seersucker shorts and her dark blue sleeveless shirt standing on the wet sand at the hem of the tide, taking photographs, her face masked by her perpetual Leica as she frames her picture of a devoted father holding his happy child.

She takes the picture of her husband and her little girl, the devoted father and his happy child enjoying this moment of going into the ocean on this perfect summer day. This is a day we won't forget, a moment we have not forgotten, because she is taking, she has taken, this photograph, the evidence of this afternoon, this spot of time in one of many summer days spent in the funny rented house on Luchon Street at the end of the block facing the dunes. Remember that summer? she will ask me from time to time for the next forty years. Remember that summer, the one after the summer of John's heart operation, the summer we rented the Lido Beach house with the kitchen upstairs, and you had that terrible sunburn, remember the lady across the street who put polish on the nails of her brown standard poodles? What were their names? Coco and Chanel. You remember everything, don't you?

He strides purposefully away from the shore, his enormous black swim trunks billowing under me like seaweed. He is as purposeful as the polar bears I have seen at the zoo, the ones who dip into the water, swim in a circle and clamber out, only to repeat the activity relentlessly. They have to do it. They don't know what else to do. He is wading deeper into the ocean, turning momentarily sideways to brace against the occasional wave that breaks against us, as if this slow march toward the horizon is a requirement, as if he doesn't know any other way to be at the beach with his child, any other way to go into the water with his little girl. He doesn't know what else to do.

I have never seen my father run, I have never seen him throw a ball, I have never seen him sit on the ground, I have never seen him in a bathing suit before, and now he is carrying me into the ocean, and I am seven years old and he is fifty-two, and this is the summer we are renting the beach house at the end of Luchon Street, facing the dunes, the house with the kitchen upstairs and the dog-smelling shag carpet, and the sour piano on which my grandmother, my mother's mother, the one we call Ganz, teaches me to play a new chord each time she visits. The sea air has ruined the soundboard, she diagnoses. My father is working at his office in the city and is only here on weekends, like a guest, and he sleeps in the room we call the guest room, downstairs, next to the room where my brother sleeps, and I share the upstairs bedroom, with its twin beds, with my mother. We are wading deeper into the ocean and a wave smacks me in the face and I am afraid and I cling more tightly to his unfamiliar arms and chest, and he says, Oh ho, are you afraid? Do you want to go out?

I say, Yes, I want to go out, looking over his shoulder at the beach, where my mother is now sitting on the blanket beside my brother, who wears a pith helmet and digs in the sand between his spindly legs. It is the summer after the summer of his heart surgery at the Mayo Clinic, and everyone says he is fine now, but where they cut open his skinny chest is a long red caterpillar of an incision which my mother gaily calls his zipper, but I am never supposed to bring it up at all. I am supposed to act as if it isn't there, even though it is disturbing and irresistible to look at, even when she calls it his zipper, which makes me worry that he could come unzipped.

MY MOTHER is angry at me the week before our family drives to Rochester, Minnesota, for those interminable days I spend interrogating my Magic 8 Ball under the folding card table in the dingy apartment next to the hospital while everyone is preoccupied with the before, during, and after of my brother's heart operation. (Is he going to die? *Don't count on it, Ask again later, Cannot predict now.* Is he going to die? *Outlook not so good.* Outlook not so good that he will die or outlook not so good that he won't die? *Reply hazy, try again.*) The day before his seven-hour surgery, my father lets John sit in his lap behind the wheel of our car, even though he is nearly eleven, too old to sit in a lap but too young to reach the pedals, so he can steer the car down the street, so he can tell himself, I drove the car! And so my father can tell himself, I am a devoted father who let his son drive the car before his heart operation.

I don't mean to make my mother angry the week before we

set off for Rochester in our aqua-and-white Buick (ours because somebody who owned movie theaters had rented a lot of Yugoslavian movies my father imported, but then he couldn't pay the money he owed, so instead, one day my father came home with this car and a Georg Jensen stainless steel cutlery service for twelve, and my mother said, Oh, Sidney). She is upset with me because of a concerned telephone call from a neighbor, a call she says put her on the spot (whatever that means), which is how she finds out that I have told the girl next door (while riding our bicycles, shouting it over my shoulder as we careen in giddy training-wheel laps around Fairway Close, the circle of eight houses where we live in Forest Hills Gardens) that we are driving to the Mayo Clinic in Rochester, Minnesota, because my brother has a hole in his heart.

I am embarrassed by my confusion about whether this Mayo has anything to do with the other mayo, mayonnaise (which my brother likes very much, and so I will not taste it until I am twenty-two years old), the way I am slightly confused about whether Castro Convertibles, which are advertised with a catchy jingle on the radio, have anything to do with Fidel Castro and Cuba. *Who was the first to conquer space? It's incontrovertible! The first to conquer living space is Castro Convertible! Who conquers space with fine design? Who saves you money all the time? Who's tops in the convertible line? Castro Convertible!* This conquering space, does this have to do with the space race, and Sputnik? Aren't the Russians friends with Castro? Is a convertible sofa anything like a convertible car?

My mother informs me that what I have done, this terrible deed of telling our neighbors about the hole in his heart, is just like twisting a knife in someone's back. I am ashamed that boasting about how my brother has a hole in his heart is like twisting a knife in his back, making another hole in him, because it feels as if she knows this about me, that I, her stuttering six-year-old daughter who cannot bring herself to ask for clarification on the Mayo issue, am capable of stabbing people in the back with a knife, and not just stabbing them, but twisting the knife. Maybe I am. *Outlook not so good.* I had not known it was supposed to be a secret, but now I have learned that when somebody has a hole in his heart, it is always a secret.

I say, Yes, I want to go out. He lunges forward, deeper into the ocean, triumphantly crying, as if this is all my idea, as if he is catering to my whims. Okay, then, we will go *out, out* to sea! He slides us toward the horizon into deeper water, and I am not sure he is even standing on the bottom anymore, because it feels as if we are being lifted by the swells. A small airplane dragging a banner chugs across the sky, from the direction of Point Lookout. *Get the fastest tan that anyone can!* A second airplane follows, dragging another banner. The advertising planes always fly from Point Lookout, past Lido Beach, past Long Beach, and then where do they go? I never see these airplanes fly back the way they came. They are forever flying from left to right. *Tan, don't burn, get a Coppertone tan!*

I try to convey the urgency of my desire, try once more to correct this misunderstanding, No, no, I want to go in! And he says, Fine, if you insist, we will go *in, in* to the sea! And he moves us into even deeper water, and he begins to sing in his tuneless way, *We joined the Navy to see the world, and what did we see? We saw the sea.* This is one of two songs that my father sings, recklessly off-key, when he is in a good mood, the other one being about a ukulele lady who might cry or sigh or love somebody else by and by. The faraway lifeguard in his sunglasses, his nose a white beak of zinc oxide, is perched on the top of his high laddered chair. He cannot see that we are in danger. He will never come to rescue us. He isn't even looking in our direction.

Does he memorize where everybody is? Will he notice when we have gone all the way out to sea?

The Atlantic isn't romantic and the Pacific isn't what it's cracked up to be, my father hums under his breath as the unromantic Atlantic laps at my chin and gets in my mouth each time I open it to try to speak. I keep getting slapped in the face by waves and he doesn't notice. My eyes are stinging, and I want to cry, but I can hardly speak or breathe and I keep swallowing seawater by mistake, and closing my eyes doesn't make anything different.

I cling to him but I am afraid of him, and I am afraid we will drown before he understands me, and he jumps up so we are lifted with the next swell and then he asks me again, Do you want to go out now? and I say, Yes! Yes! I want to go out! And like a crazy person, he answers merrily, Then out to sea we will go! Now we go even deeper, and now he is really treading water, and I don't know how we will ever get out of the ocean if he will only go deeper and deeper, away from dry land, no matter what I say. We will drown, I will drown in his arms, we will drown together, the devoted father with his sunburned child in his arms frolicking happily at the seashore on this perfect summer day, a day we will never forget, a moment nobody will ever forget, because this spot of time is captured in the photograph my mother has just taken of the two of us, the devoted father and his happy child enjoying this moment of going into the ocean on this perfect summer day, that summer we rented the Lido Beach house, at the end of Luchon Street, facing the dunes. The dogs were named Coco and Chanel. Coco had blue toenail polish and Chanel had pink toenail polish. I have no memory of the moment we turned back, no memory of the relief of being put down to stand dripping on the sand, no recollection whatsoever of not drowning.

A Decent Family

MY FATHER STOPPED SPEAKING TO ME A FEW DAYS AFTER my twenty-fourth birthday, for reasons that grow only more inexplicable over time. It made no sense, but beyond writing him a note a year and a half into the silence to tell him I was expecting a baby, I didn't attempt reconciliation. He was silent when Lucy was born in October of 1981. Even then, it did not occur to me that I would never see him again. I well remembered the seven years in my childhood when he refused to speak to his younger brother, Murray, when there had been a bitter falling-out over a coffeepot.

My father had presented his mother with an elaborate silver tea-and-coffee service which was possibly meant for hotel use and which might in fact have been used by a hotel (it wasn't new) before it materialized as an element in one of his strange business deals. He was very proud of this ornate silver set, which now graced his mother's Brooklyn dining room. And then she had given the coffeepot from the set to Murray's wife. Why did my father stop speaking to his brother instead of his mother? It was she who gave away the coffeepot and she who refused his demand that she get it back. My father thought she had no right to give the coffeepot away, especially not to his brother's wife, whom my father disdained. He was insistent that the coffeepot should be returned to its rightful place on her sideboard with the rest of the set, which she had no right to break up, and his mother was equally insistent that the set was hers, and what she did with it was none of his business. What was at stake for my father was clearly not that ugly silver object. He chose to see this as a personal rejection, a statement of preference. His mother had always been hard on him and soft on Murray. He would never be the one she loved more. (My cousin Stephanie, Murray's daughter, knows a completely different version of the silver coffeepot story: the silver coffeepot belonged to her mother in the first place, and my father's unreasonable desire to possess it was the source of the conflict.)

But in more recent years my uncle Murray had been promoted from persona non grata to close family member. He lived in our house in Forest Hills Gardens for a period of time after his marriage ended in 1974, up in the guest room on the third floor. He was given to witty remarks like "We who are about to dine salute you" on his way out to dinner. At this time he was rather minimally employed, having some connection to a Queens auto shop dedicated to replacing broken carburetors with slightly less broken carburetors. (Kaufman Auto Supply, founded by my grandfather Sam Kaufman, had once been a thriving business on Bedford Avenue in Brooklyn, but now the only evidence it had ever existed was the occasional stray miniature Kaufman Auto Supply screwdriver in the various desk drawers I rummaged.)

Murray was pleasant and easygoing. His humor was a lighter version of my father's. "Where do you think I should go to replace the broken lawn sprinkler?" my mother asked him. "A haberdasher's, of course!" he replied. His presence was an intriguing contrast to the awkwardness of conversation with my father, who frequently offered only silence if my questions or remarks didn't interest him. In this time period, my mother and

Murray were alone together in that big house a great deal. It occurred to me that my mother would have been much happier married to Murray.

When I had my learner's permit, my father advised me that contrary to what I had learned from my requisite hours at the Rite-Way Auto School ("Learn to drive the Rite Way!"), there were many occasions when a driver needed to keep one foot on the gas and the other foot on the brake. I turned to my easygoing uncle Murray for driving lessons. We spent hours together in his gold Maverick, crisscrossing the streets and highways of Brooklyn and Queens, parallel-parking on side streets in Flatbush, navigating the Queens Midtown Tunnel, cruising on the Brooklyn Queens Expressway.

I assumed that my own rupture with my father was, at worst, another one of those biblical, seven-year Kaufman edicts. Surely this schism would inevitably resolve itself when he got over his anger at me. Nothing changed when my daughter Lucy was born, but still, I thought perhaps by the time she turned five or six the relationship would have tempered. But in July of 1983, when Lucy was not yet two, just weeks after the birth of her younger sister Charlotte, my father died.

My father stopped speaking to me for reasons that had to do with his blatant unfaithfulness to my mother, some of which I had witnessed throughout my childhood and adolescence. On the night of my twenty-fourth birthday, he declared that he planned to divorce her. After a two-hour rant to me and Nick, my husband of three years, about my mother's deficiencies (which included an aversion to sex, and among the many complaints he enumerated that night was the claim that the last of the "four times" in their thirty-one years of marriage he ever had sex with my mother was when I was conceived), we finally went to dinner.

My father never acknowledged that it was my birthday, even when, unbearably, in the course of our gloomy meal at Seafare of the Aegean, there were three occurrences of birthday candles and singing waiters at other tables. Maybe Nick and I had been wrong to cancel our plan for my birthday dinner in New Haven in order to accept my father's last-minute invitation to meet him for dinner in the city. I had assumed that his summons had been prompted by his desire to celebrate my birthday with me, but that was probably wishful thinking on my part. Did he even remember that it was my birthday? I was certainly wrong, as it turned out, to take him at his word about his intention to divorce my mother.

Taking him at his word was something I should have learned by then never to do, and I am not sure even now why I hadn't accepted this, after all the lies and misrepresentations, all the broken promises between us. Why did I persist in being so literal-minded over the years?

My EARLIEST memories of my father are filled with my own desperate anxiety about keeping up with him, about satisfying his expectations that I understand him, no matter how obscure his remarks or actions. When I was in elementary school, I was doing my homework one evening when my father appeared in my bedroom doorway and said, "A man walks into a bar and asks for something. The bartender pulls out a gun and says, 'Your money or your life!' The man thanks him and walks out. Why?"

My failure to recognize that the man had hiccups was clearly a disappointment to my father, who simply turned and walked away. That moment was a more devastating failure for me than had been losing the fourth-grade spelling bee a few weeks earlier, when I omitted the second *o* in *chocolate*. On another occasion not long after, I redeemed myself while driving with him when I knew what a contestant on a radio show did not—that the word for a group of islands was *archipelago*.

His Talmudic riddles were often simply unfathomable, like his query about why you never buy ink, the answer being because ink is something you borrow. But more often his questions did have answers, if you paid close enough attention to understand the likely direction of what he was actually asking. What travels around the world while staying in a corner? A stamp. If there are three cups of sugar and you take one away, how many do you have? The one you took away. When is a door not a door? When it is ajar. When is a car not a car? When it turns into a driveway. I was twelve the day I thrilled myself by immediately recognizing the answer to his sudden demand, out of the blue, while we were shopping for bargain-priced, random useless objects at his favorite store, Job Lot Trading Company on Vesey Street in lower Manhattan, that I explain this number sequence: 14, 34, 42, 72, 96. These are express stops on the Seventh Avenue IRT subway line in Manhattan.

Throughout my childhood, the nerve-racking quiz show challenges whenever I spent any time with my father were tempered by a powerful sense I got from him that the two of us were superior beings who dwelled in a realm beyond my disappointing mother and brother. We were in league together. Not only was it important to have the answers to my father's questions, it was also important never to show confusion, or fear, which would irritate him and might cause him to lose interest in the conversation. Of course he expected me to keep up. Of course he depended on me to know all the answers. Even when I was very young, he rarely explained anything directly or showed awareness that my experience didn't perfectly match his experience.

He counted on me to observe and understand everything he said or did when we were together. How could I let him down?

I AM five years old, sitting on the bench seat close beside my father in our aqua-and-white Buick, the one that always felt borrowed because he got it as part of a deal, on a mission to get the best Christmas tree we can find. We drive and we drive, until we are at last in his old Brooklyn neighborhood, on Liberty Avenue. We park in front of a corner lot with colored lights strung along the top of the chain-link fence. The lot is filled with stacked Christmas trees, each trussed with twine into a tight bundle. Dozens more unfettered trees of all sizes, short needled, long needled, some fat with heavy branches, others oddly thin and bare, are leaning in rows, and the frozen air has the magical smell of Christmas, fresh balsam and fir.

My father has cautioned me to remain very quiet, and we have worked out in advance how I am to signal to him which trees are the good ones without revealing our preferences to the tree man. We pick our way across the slushy lot until we are among the trees. It is very cold. There is fresh snow on the top layer of trees. The tree man sees us.

He has a long black beard and wears a round fur hat, and he is bundled in a big coat that looks as if it has been made from dead animals. His dark eyes meet mine and I look away, embarrassed, certain that I have already done the wrong thing. I reach up for my father's hand but he is no longer beside me, and I turn to locate him, then trot after him, playing my part of the little girl here to select a Christmas tree with her father. The tree man has a large knife stuck into the leather belt that holds his coat around him, and a moment later I see him use it to slash at the twine binding a tree in order to shake it open for a customer.

"What do you think of this one?" my father asks, standing an enormous tree upright. I shake my head. It's the wrong kind, with long, sharp needles. I like the denser kind of tree that has short needles. People who get those long-needled trees are the same people who decorate with white lights and tinsel but no ornaments, or with no lights but only one kind of ornament, just shiny purple balls all the same size, like a department store. My father props up another tree. Too short, and it has a bald patch on one side. He tries again. This one is absurdly tall and thin, with stunted branches. We search through the trees, now demanding that the tree man cut the cords on some of the bundled ones, which he does with a flourish of the knife.

Finally, we come to one tree that is perfect, proportioned gracefully from top to bottom, with boughs full of short, dense needles, just the right height for our living room. I recognize in an instant that this is the one. My father thumps it hard on the ground to test for freshness. The tree man exclaims in protest, but there is no shower of needles to betray a dried-out tree. All his trees are fresh, the tree man says indignantly. What do you think, I would sell trees that are not fresh? I give you a good tree. My father looks to me for approval. I nod. This is the tree that will be perfect when it is hung with the Christmas ornaments from the trunk in the attic, from the intricately figured metal spheres from Germany and the striped Murano glass candy canes from my mother's childhood Christmas trees, to the stuffed felt mice dressed in evening clothes that my mother's mother has given me. The tree man is hovering impatiently.

My father says something I don't understand. The tree man counters with something else I don't understand. My father says something dismissive and makes a gesture with his hand. The tree man shouts something. My father shouts something back and now I recognize the language used for arguments with his mother. He is arguing with the tree man. I am worried because the tree man has that knife. My father lets the tree drop back against the stack of trees where we found it, and reaches for my hand. I don't know what to do. I am disappointed. He takes my hand and we start to walk away. The tree man grabs our tree and walks beside us awkwardly, holding the tree in his arms and shouting some more. My father mutters something. Now we are at the entrance to the lot. Here is our car. The tree man is following us and he is still talking. Are we leaving without a tree? I fight to hold back my tears. My father says something. My feet are frozen from walking through slushy puddles in my leaky snow boots. The sky is white with cold, and my teeth are chattering.

The tree man is trussing up our tree with twine, still shouting, almost talking to himself. My father lets go of my hand to get out his wallet from his pants pocket, while shouting more angry, unfamiliar words, and now he is shaking his finger at the tree man. The tree man leans the bundled tree against our car and puts out his hand, saying something in a more conciliatory tone, and my father matches him, repeating his words, and suddenly counts out some money into the gnarled hand, shaking his head in disgust. The tree man *tsks* to himself and tucks the money away into a pocket, shaking his head in matching sorrow over this unfortunate transaction.

My father tells me to get into the car, which I do, while the tree man and my father together hoist our tree onto the roof of the car and tie it down with twine, which they run through the interior of the car several times. I feel very important, scrambling to take the ball of twine when it is handed in the window to me on one side by my father and passing it through to the other side into the hands of the tree man, who looks into my eyes again for an instant and smiles briefly.

When they are done, my father says something to the tree man, who shrugs and replies, *Zei Gezunt,* before he turns away to deal with another customer. Driving away, slowly, because of the tree, which is not very aerodynamic, my father explains to me what a *goniff* is (the tree man), and what *hondling* is (bargaining to get a fair price for our tree from the *goniff*). Because we are in the neighborhood, we stop to get knishes at the store where my father's cousin Morry used to work, where the people behind the counter still know my father, so they give us extras. We eat the knishes on the way home. A hot knish—that is the taste of Christmas.

JUST A few weeks earlier, on my fifth birthday, the November day that was also my first day of kindergarten owing to New York City public school rules, my father told me that his present to me was his promise to build a playhouse in our backyard the following spring. I was excited, and could hardly wait to set up housekeeping in my playhouse. The very word *playhouse* was so playful and domestic and personal. I imagined my playhouse clearly. I knew exactly how it would look where my father and I had located it in the backyard, near the old apple tree. But then it was winter, and after that he was away on business trips that lasted months, and time passed. A lot of time passed. I would have forgotten all about it if my father had not brought up the playhouse intermittently, until finally, when I was twelve, and really no longer remotely interested in a place to have imaginary tea parties for my stuffed animals or a secret clubhouse with my friends, who were few, construction began.

Assisted by Jake LaMotta, my father began to build my playhouse, working several Sundays in a row. He had become friendly with the retired boxer through an acquaintance, a film producer named Peter Savage, whose distinguished silver temples made him look, I thought, like Veronica Lodge's father in the Archie comic books. Peter was recruited on a couple of occasions to pitch in on this haphazard carpentry project, too. He was helping Jake write his memoir, which would be published three years later with the title *Raging Bull*. My father was very eager to option the half-written book for a movie, which was possibly the reason he kept inviting Jake over to help with the playhouse. Plus, Jake might have been down on his luck, but he was a powerful man who knew how to mix cement and lay concrete blocks. I heard my father tell Jake that the huge pile of lumber in our backyard had "fallen off the back of the truck" on its way to the set for *A Man Called Adam*, a film with Sammy Davis Jr. which my father was involved in financing.

Despite a lot of talk about who should play him on the screen (my father had Marlon Brando in mind, and Jake was on board with that), like most of my father's movie deals, it never happened. Thirteen years later it would be Martin Scorsese's *Raging Bull* movie, not my father's, that would hoist LaMotta out of his career doldrums.

They worked for several weekends in a row, erecting the foundation and frame of a much too large and elaborate structure in our backyard, during which time I was often expected to play for long hours with Jake's seven-year-old daughter, even though she was so much younger than I it was more like baby-sitting. She often didn't feel well, and was usually wearing party dresses as if headed for a destination that was not our house. Presumably, her mother dressed her for these outings with Jake on the assumption that the afternoon would hold some more festive activity than sitting on my bed looking out the window, watching our fathers while they maneuvered concrete blocks and two-by-fours and sheets of plywood, with much hammering and sawing and swearing, when they weren't taking breaks to sit at the kitchen table eating enormous sandwiches and drinking beer (Jake) and Dr. Brown's Celery Tonic (my father) and making plans for the movie my father would make about Jake's life.

Jake's little girl wasn't willing to play outside. She worried that her frilly outfits might get dirty. But she didn't like books, didn't play cards, and wasn't interested in board games. She did like brushing her hair while looking in the mirror on my closet door. Yet neither of us contradicted Jake when he would call up the stairs at the end of the afternoon, "All good things must come to an end," when it was time for them to leave, as if this time we had spent together was a good thing.

The playhouse was abandoned, half-built. My father left for one of his extended disappearances overseas (with an itinerary that I would learn, decades later, the FBI knew much more about than we did). My father's plans for a *Raging Bull* movie faded away and Jake LaMotta and his tedious child were never seen again. The playhouse roof leaked from the start, being only partly shingled, and within a year the wood frame began to warp and rot, and the plywood floor began to delaminate and bulge in disturbing broken blisters. By the time I left home when I was sixteen, the latchless, cockeyed door had become immobilized by swales of dead leaves filling the interior. The playhouse had been used just once, for a clandestine interlude during a ninth-grade planning meeting about a class trip to hear Donovan at Madison Square Garden. A few of the most advanced and sophisticated among us went into the backyard to share a joint along with some swigs from a bottle of Boone's Farm strawberry wine.

✧ ✦ ✧

MY FATHER's broken promises to me also included invitations to accompany him on several marvelous trips to scout locations for major films he was on the verge of signing, as one of the first completion bond guarantors in the film industry. My father claimed to have invented the concept of film completion bonding, a form of production insurance that guarantees completion on budget and within schedule, though nobody else has ever given him this credit. His claim of a perfect record was maintained by his habit of breaking his contracts on productions that seemed on the verge of going over schedule or budget.

Just days before each of these scouting trips would have occurred, when I had read the script and studied up on the location, my father was betrayed. Inevitably, there had come, just in time, the discovery that the marvelously talented director or producer or writer who had seemed to be my father's closest friend, this film being only the first of what would most certainly be a series of projects together, had now revealed his true colors, and was in fact a despicable charlatan of the lowest order, a poseur, a worthless, inept, backstabbing, swindling fraud.

There were two different promised cars, well before I had my driver's license. I was so lucky, so privileged! One was a tantalizing yellow Jensen-Healey that had been used in a movie called *Brannigan,* which is one of the numerous films over the years on which my father claimed to have worked as an executive producer or an associate director or an associate producer or one of those other production titles nobody can clearly explain; his name is not in the credits.

When I was in high school, I was promised summer production assistant jobs three summers in a row on films my father was involved in—one had a location in Alaska—but something always went wrong with the production schedule, the funding, or with my father's relationship with the director. As the start dates grew closer and closer, if I asked about the promised jobs or tried to make any summer plans one way or the other, my father would become angry. I was supposed to be grateful for his good intentions and all his efforts on my behalf and stop nitpicking about the details. Did I want to be just like my mother; was I that rigid and inflexible? Obviously, I just didn't understand the film business and probably wasn't suited for it if I required from him as much mindless scheduling precision as my disappointing mother, the woman he called a zombie, the woman who let him down because when they were in a supermarket together, when he asked her to get some butter, she returned with only a stick of Land O' Lakes butter in hand. My father wished he had a wife given to more passionate response to the bounty of a supermarket, a wife who would have returned to him laden with ripe exotic fruits, caviar, mare's milk, a tin of pickled lark's tongues, and a tub of the finest Normandy butter. He told me that he wished my mother were "a more feminine creature" who dressed better. He called her a demanding infant because from year to year she persisted in being curious about his plans for Thanksgiving and Christmas.

When I was thirteen, the one time I ever made any kind of trip alone with him, my father left me with a film crew on location in a wilderness in Northern California for five days. It was the summer after I had been hospitalized for two months with a life-threatening bout of pancreatitis, and this trip was a reward for the misery I had endured. After this experience, I cannot explain why I thought I ever wanted those phantom production assistant jobs on movie sets. We arrived on the set, he introduced me to the first crew members we saw, took my small green overnight bag out of the backseat of the rented car, set it on the ground at my feet, and then he drove away.

I soon learned that nobody was expecting me and no arrangements had been made. Not very many people had ever heard my father's name before, and at first it was unclear if he actually did have anything to do with this movie, but then someone figured out who he was. I was shown to an empty bunk in a partitioned area in the women's crew house, a primitive lodge that reminded me of Girl Scout camp, where I would rather have been.

The production manager, a cheerful woman named Donna who walked around whistling "If You Knew Susie Like I Know Susie," showed me where meals were served and found a blanket for my bunk, because the nights were cold and there was no heat. She gave me assignments. (The movie was a Civil War–era Western called *Cain's Cutthroats,* for which my father wrote the production bond. Maybe.) I helped out on the set by laying authentic campfires, and holding props as a gunfight scene in a saloon was blocked (the guns were surprisingly heavy, nothing like the pair of hollow six-shooters I had worn in holsters at age five, during the interlude when I wore a fringed vest and a cowboy hat and only answered to "Wyatt Earp"). I delivered messages from the office to the crew and the horse wranglers. Mostly, I waited on John Carradine, who could barely hold a mug of coffee because his shakes were so bad, so I would sit beside him holding his coffee for him until he wanted another sip. I was told to encourage him to eat something, a doughnut from the craft table, anything, but he never wanted food, and between scenes he would just sit on a rock or a tree stump, away from everyone else, suffering with his eyes closed.

Every night I stayed in the lodge after dinner with the cast and crew watching the dailies projected on a bedsheet, which reminded me of Girl Scout camp rainy day activities. The first night I was there, the dailies featured a gang rape scene on a pool table. Over and over, take after take, the female lead was forced backwards onto the pool table, her high-necked bodice was ripped in exactly the same motion, down and to the right, to expose her breasts in precisely the same way with each take, and then she was held down by three men while the fourth one raped her. I had sat among these men at dinner. (The female lead, an actress for whom this was apparently a career peak, since her subsequent credits list parts like "party guest" in a 1976 movie called *Chesty Anderson, U.S. Navy,* did not eat with everyone else in the main lodge, but would go through the cafeteria line and take her tray to her trailer.) A wildly swinging stained-glass chandelier suspended over the pool table was kept in motion by somebody's hand reaching into the frame to push it at the start of each take as "Action" was called and the clapper board was pulled away. Even at thirteen I recognized that this was not going to be a good movie.

I had no idea when my father was going to come back for me. The location was a deteriorating dude ranch that felt abandoned, and I really wasn't even sure where I was. I had no mental map of the state of California. I felt entirely alone, and it didn't occur to me to try to communicate with anyone about my situation. My brother was at his year-round boarding school in New Hampshire (he spent five years there; the first time we visited him, the Thanksgiving of his first year, as we arrived there was pandemonium because his classmate Temple Grandin was up on the roof of the main house, having climbed up there, as she tended to do, to get a better view of the clouds in the sky).

With me away on this wonderful adventure in California with my father, my mother was free to go off with a bird-watching crony to an Audubon camp on an island in Maine.

When I went to Girl Scout camp in upstate New York for a few weeks each of the two previous summers, my mother diligently provided everything on the checklist, including name labels sewed into every piece of my clothing. This was a huge undertaking for her, as nobody had ever shown her even rudimentary sewing skills when she was growing up; the Warburg family had a household seamstress taking care of everything she wore. My mother had no idea how to sew, and was made apprehensive by the sight of a needle and thread. In preparation for her Audubon camp experience, I took over this task, cutting the "Kathy" off the "Kathy Kaufman" labels that were in abundant supply and sewing the "Kaufman" labels into all her clothing for her, resisting the impulse to duplicate her regrettable decision to sew, with her Frankenstein's monster stitches in black carpet thread, name labels into all the toes of my white crew socks.

I GOT very little sleep those nights on location with *Cain's Cutthroats*. I didn't dare use the shared bathroom, which required opening closed doors and walking through two rooms in which people were sleeping, and instead crept outside to the dark bushes. I slept in my clothes in the filthy bunkhouse, in the lower bunk of the rickety bunk bed in that partitioned corner. Every night there were different people having sex in the upper bunk. I concluded that they were different people from the sound of their voices, but I had no idea who they were, or how they could think it was okay to have sex in the upper bunk when a thirteen-year-old was sleeping in the bottom bunk. Each night, as the mattress above me bounced rhythmically against the sagging support springs, and the bed frame squeaked, the entire double-decker bed frame rattled and skittered as if we were in steerage quarters on a ship sailing a stormy sea. Though my heart was pounding and I was peculiarly, excruciatingly mortified, I lay very still under my mildewed blanket and pretended to be deeply asleep. I didn't know what else to do.

My father came back for me, unannounced, after five days, just appearing one morning at breakfast, as if this had been the agreed plan. Where had he been, and what had he been doing? These were not questions I could ask. We drove down the Pacific Coast Highway in silence, back to the Westwood motel where I would spend most of the remaining week of this trip at the pool, reading through the accumulation of movie scripts that covered every surface in our motel suite, getting food from the vending machines in the corridors, while my father was wherever he was, all day every day.

One afternoon we drove to Malibu, where there was a brunch gathering at the beachfront home of a movie producer friend of my father's. There were perhaps a dozen people eating and talking and sitting around. I was the only child. After a while, with nobody to talk to, I went out to walk on the beach. After maybe an hour of skipping stones into the surf, I got cold and went back inside, where I discovered my father engrossed in a game of chess with the host's girlfriend—a terrifyingly beautiful, tanned, blond bombshell in an aqua bikini. I had never seen him play chess before. It was like a scene from a movie, James Mason playing chess with Marilyn Monroe.

Most of the people at the party were gathered around, watching them. Their game went on and on. When my father shook his head and declared it a draw, everyone applauded. I felt as if we had all been watching them have sex. A little while later, as we were leaving, the bombshell, who may have only been a few years older than I was, took my arm and told me how lucky I was to have such a wonderful father.

The day before I flew back to New York, my father was suddenly interested in how I had been spending my time, asking me what I had seen and done since returning from *Cain's Cutthroats*. He was exasperated that I had not somehow organized for myself a tour of Hollywood, perhaps stopping for lunch at the Brown Derby Restaurant after a morning at the La Brea Tar Pits, before taking in a movie at Grauman's Chinese Theatre. Did I want to be like my mother, unimaginative and willing to settle for whatever was closest at hand rather than seeking out the choicest experiences? He proposed a day trip over the border so I could fly home having done something more than just lurk around the motel.

We drove to Ensenada, where he indulged my desire to acquire pottery birds and massive quantities of fireworks, the two most prominent items for sale at the sides of the road. On the way back, in a crowded market in Tijuana, a man approached us and muttered something to my father with the word *puta,* and then took out some money and made an unmistakable gesture in my direction. Did he think I was a prostitute? My father turned and walked away, heading, without a backward glance, to where we had parked the car. I trotted after him, my pleasure in this rare day we had spent together suddenly evaporated. Our silent drive north was interrupted only when the border patrol officer asked if we had anything to declare as we left Mexico. My father replied, "Just a few trinkets for the little girl."

I flew to New York the next morning with a carry-on bag stuffed with my pottery birds and my fireworks—a heady mix of Roman candles, M-80 salutes, cherry bombs, pinwheels, and bottle rockets. I had to change planes in Chicago. My flight was canceled and I had to fly to New York on a different airline that left from another terminal. The only person who seemed to notice a solitary thirteen-year-old girl lugging a clinking bag of Mexican pottery and explosives through O'Hare Airport was a sailor in uniform who followed me with offers of an ice cream soda. In New York, my mother forgot to meet my flight, or my father forgot to tell her about it. I took a taxi to the house. I became frightened of my fireworks and a few days later I buried them in the backyard. I gave the only unbroken pottery bird to my mother, who would from time to time remind me about my memorable trip. What a marvelous adventure it must have been (but what a shame you didn't take any pictures, she would always add), the time Daddy took you to Hollywood and you got to spend all those days on the set of a movie!

JUST TWO years before my father stopped speaking to me, there had been the biggest broken promise of them all, an invitation to meet him for lunch, which would have been our first and only occasion of having lunch alone together since the *Cain's Cutthroats* trip, let alone since I had become an adult, since I had married. There had been some lunch and dinner invitations from him before this, which I had always hoped would be just the two of us, but each time there had been a third person, one or another of the miscellaneous women who floated through my father's life. Several of these bizarre encounters (who was being shown off to whom?) had taken place, strangely enough, at Max's Kansas City, the hip downtown bar and restaurant frequented by people like Andy Warhol, not people like Sidney Kaufman. I had somehow believed this time it would be different—this lunch would be just the two of us, a celebration of his gift of a magnificently generous cashier's check he would hand over for the down payment on the eighteenth-century Connecticut farmhouse in which I have lived all these years from then until now.

Although the plan had been agreed to only hours earlier, my father simply vanished on the day we were supposed to meet at his office, which, owing to his having canceled and rescheduled twice, was now the day before the closing. I spent frantic hours making calls from the pay phone on Sixth Avenue in front of his office building, trying to locate him at his lawyer's office, his banker's office. I phoned my mother at home in Forest Hills, but she had no idea where he was or when he had left the house. She had suggestions, and not much sympathy. What did I want her to say or do about it? she snapped, taking a grim satisfaction in my panic. Welcome to her world. I spent much of the afternoon in the building's lobby, asking the desk man to ring my father's office from time to time, though he would have come through the lobby to get there, unless he had been there all along and wasn't answering his telephone, before I finally gave up and took a train back to New Haven.

I was devastated, fearful we would lose the house, but also, I was confused that I had fallen for the fiction of a Sidney Kaufman magnificent gesture all over again. I had looked forward to our lunch, and had believed that it was actually going to happen. I had envisaged the wonderful ceremonial occasion of it, a celebration that Nick and I were buying our first house. What a rare and tender moment this would be, what a loving and loved feeling I would have on this day with my father.

Was it a setup? Had he wanted to prove to himself that I would trust him, that I would take him at his word that his offer and his invitation were genuine? Was this how he treated everyone? Or did he have some scheme for coming up with the money that had gone wrong, and so he went into hiding because he just didn't have the money and just couldn't face me? Had I once again been too literal-minded? Had I inadvertently called his bluff by accepting his offer as if it were genuine?

There was never an explanation for what happened that day (the unfinished playhouse having been a harbinger of his inability to make good on the offer of any kind of house). I never had lunch alone with my father again, and the money, which was subsequently wired into our account with an hour to spare before the closing, surely came from my mother's Warburg inheritance. She didn't really understand or track her income very well, and always called the U.S. Trust checks that appeared miraculously in the mail (she never noticed that they arrived quarterly) "manna from heaven." She wanted no credit for that wire, preferring that I believe my father had actually come through.

I SUPPOSE it isn't entirely inexplicable that I chose to take my father literally once again on the night of my twenty-fourth birthday, the last time I ever saw him, when he said he was planning to divorce my mother, "though leaving her will be tantamount to murder." This was why he wanted to warn us, to warn Nick and me of his plans; she would need our support. I wanted to believe it. I had longed for this moment. My birthday wish as I blew out the candles on my cake, that my parents would divorce, was the only wish I ever made, year after year, going back as far as I could remember.

And so, the day after that grim birthday dinner, when it seemed I had at long last gotten my wish, Nick and I did as he asked and phoned my mother at their house in West Hollywood. They had moved to this residence only a couple of years earlier, because of a theory that after he underwent surgery for esophageal cancer my father needed to spend more time in the

Southern California climate for his health. (In fact, in the remaining years of his life he spent more time in London and New York than he ever spent in that house.)

I had been disappointed when they chose this prosaic if pleasant ranch house over the Richard Neutra Bonnet House just up the hill, which they had also considered but had found too small. Andrew Dice Clay was probably disappointed, too; he soon moved into the house next door to my parents on Metz Place, which shared a common driveway, and for several years he and my mother would have vicious shouting matches about issues of his emptied trash cans left rolling around, and the idling motors of cars perpetually sitting under my mother's living room window while his large coterie of friends and associates came and went at all hours. It is possible he got material for his routines from my mother, who was not known for demure, ladylike murmurs under circumstances like these.

We phoned her to break the news of my father's intentions, just as he had asked, and to offer support and encouragement about his decision, pointing out to her all the ways her life would improve, all the reasons why this was a good thing. She was bizarrely complacent about this, and was not especially receptive to anything we told her. She said she would wait to discuss it with Sidney when he arrived.

When he got there a day later and heard from my mother about our telephone call, he was shocked and furious. We were lying! He denied completely ever having said one word to us about a divorce or anything like it, and he was outraged at our audacity and our interfering fabrications. My mother somehow accepted his explanation that this was our insane mischief, and nothing was going to change.

My father telephoned our house, the Connecticut farmhouse he had by then probably convinced himself he had generously given us, in a fury. He denounced me for my high-handedness, going to my mother as I had with this "story" about him. I said that he was only thinking of himself, first telling us in painful detail about his reasons for wanting a divorce, asking us to get involved, and now, with this apparent change of heart, denying the whole thing. I called him selfish, which enraged him in a new way. Perhaps it shamed him. He replied, "That's it. I am through with you. I can no longer have you in my life. That was your smart remark for the day, for the week, for the lifetime."

Nick, my partner in this crime, tried to intervene by reasoning with my father, as I stayed on the extension, listening to my father's voice for the last time I would ever hear it. But my father shouted at Nick for his intrusion into this situation, and said his defense of me and our outrageous behavior was "jejune." Then my father uttered the parting words which don't require advanced psychoanalytic training to parse: "Ours was a decent family until you entered it."

I should have recognized that his rant the night of my twenty-fourth birthday was not about what it seemed to be about at all. My father would never divorce the recipient of those manna-from-heaven checks. Why would he? He had always done whatever he pleased without consequence. He had never been faithful to my mother, not even in the first years of their marriage. I do think he loved her, especially in their first years together, though there is little evidence that she was one of his big loves. Their marriage was tragic.

MY MOTHER was a very nonstandard person possessed of an original mind and a wonderful sense of humor. She took great pleasure in some things (Fred Astaire, nature, her own ability to whistle with perfect pitch, pets, games, sports, photography, small children, Broadway show tunes, and nostalgia for most aspects of her cherished childhood), but she was terrified of much else (financial paperwork, bills, sex, left turns in busy traffic, cooking, social encounters requiring her to dress like a grown-up woman, lightning, being shouted at by my father, unexpectedly spicy food, her son's future, and very put-together women to whom my father would be attracted).

In many ways she lived like a child who had been unfairly forced into adulthood. Even so, she could have had a much better life than the one she had. A brief first marriage at a young age had failed in a humiliating and confusing way. Soon after that, she thought she was romantically involved with the African-American actor Gordon Heath until he made it clear to her that while he adored her, he was a homosexual. When I reflect on some of her closest friendships throughout her life, it is evident to me that she could probably have led a much happier and more fulfilled life without a husband, among women.

My mother grew up in Manhattan, the daughter of Kay Swift and James Paul Warburg. She knew so little about her heritage that when Florence Guggenheim Straus told her that the two of them were the only Jews in the Brearley School's sixth-grade class, she was stunned. This was the first that Andrea Swift Warburg had heard about being Jewish. Her mother's Swift family Episcopal traditions were all she knew. The family name notwithstanding, James Paul Warburg spent his life trying to "get off the anthill" of his "Our Crowd" family. He was proud to fit in with his WASP Harvard friends and colleagues, and would have three Protestant wives.

Although my mother descended on both sides from fantastically interesting and accomplished people, she had little personal ambition to make her mark on the world. She was privileged in many ways, but she was also deprived of much experience, having grown up in strange, swaddled splendor, protected from the world. She was dressed and fed by servants, with few opportunities to make any choices or decisions for herself. As a child, she was unaware of the Depression and she had no idea why there were men selling pencils and apples on street corners.

My mother spoke to me almost daily about her childhood. Her descriptions of Warburgian household splendor made it clear to me that she grew up in a fairy tale that had ended. But her recollections of family gatherings at Great-uncle Felix's grand house at 1109 Fifth Avenue (today it's The Jewish Museum) inevitably included her father's characterization of that branch of the family as "show-offy," and impressions of the Warburg cousin whose face was said (by our branch of the family) to resemble a vacuum cleaner. My mother never wasted an opportunity to refer to Uncle Felix's house as The Jew Mu.

As an adult, my mother had no interest in what most people would consider the usual trappings of wealth, and she avoided situations where her origins had any meaning. She aspired to live in a very ordinary way, and was at her most comfortable with ordinary people who had no idea about or interest in her background. Even as a child, my mother craved ordinariness. When she was ten, she and her younger sister, Kay, made a break for freedom from Mademoiselle, a tutor who took them on French conversation walks in Central Park twice a week. That afternoon they strapped on their roller skates and took off. Their goal was a Madison Avenue lunch counter, where the two little Warburg princesses fulfilled their hearts' desire—baloney sandwiches and Coca-Colas—while the police searched for them in Central Park.

MY FATHER was genuinely charmed by my mother when they met. She was beautiful and bright, funny and quirky, a poor little rich girl. He loved seeing himself with her, a Kaufman born to impoverished immigrants in Brooklyn keeping company with a coddled Warburg princess. The Warburgs had been significant patrons of New York's Henry Street Settlement House (Lillian Wald had counted Andrea's grandmother Nina Loeb Warburg among her greatest supporters), while my father's family, the immigrant Kaufmans and Gottesfelds, had been the very people for whom this charity was intended.

Sidney's mother had been a garment worker, the Triangle Waist Company being the last sweatshop where she found employment, finishing buttonholes, before she left factory work at the end of 1909 because she was pregnant with him. After the Triangle factory fire of 1911, the Solomon and Betty Loeb Memorial Home in Hartsdale (Solomon and Betty were Nina's parents) provided places for some of the survivors of that fire— most of them immigrant women like my father's mother—to convalesce.

My mother had her reasons for being attracted to my father. There was something deeply appealing and familiar about him, from the shock of dark hair rising over his high forehead to his beaky nose and intense, brooding looks (he was not the man some girls think of as handsome). He had started out a smart Jewish boy from the streets of Brooklyn, the child of poor Eastern European immigrants who kept a kosher home and lived by old traditions in their Williamsburg neighborhood. He always insisted that a Kaufman cousin was the pickle seller depicted in *A Tree Grows in Brooklyn*. He grew up to be a man whose ambitions and talent had taken him from those modest origins to the exciting realm of not just absorbing culture but contributing to it. He would find opportunities to make a name for himself in show business. He was a man with an aura of importance. Which is to say that Sidney Kaufman looked and sounded and felt like a faint echo of the man whose presence had overwhelmed my mother's childhood and changed her family—George Gershwin.

The first time my parents went out for dinner, for some reason she told him at great length about her favorite toy when she was a child, a miniature grocery store that was a Christmas gift from her father's aunt Alice and uncle Max Warburg in Hamburg. It had perfect tiny wax vegetables and fruits, and little wooden crates, and a little striped awning that cranked out. There was a grocer in a white apron. And then my father told my mother that he was born in the back of a grocery store just like that, in Brooklyn, and the grocer in the apron cranking out the awning was his father, Sam.

MY PARENTS were married at City Hall with no family present in July of 1948. My father was thirty-eight and my mother was twenty-six. It was a second marriage for both. Was it doomed from the start? What kind of match was it, when my father dreamed of being somebody and my mother dreamed of being nobody? Their honeymoon consisted of a trip to stay in a primitive cabin on a lake in upstate New York, where my father needed to be anyway. The expenses were covered, since it was the location for a documentary film about fly-fishing for which he was the director. (I never knew my father to have any knowledge about or interest in fly-fishing.) That was all I knew about their honeymoon, until a Sunday lunch gathering some fifteen years ago at the home of our wonderful friends and neighbors Nancy Lewis and her husband, R. W. B. Lewis.

There I met Michael Roemer, a filmmaker and Yale colleague of Dick Lewis's, who in the course of conversation heard me say something that prompted him to ask if by any chance my mother was Andrea Warburg and my father Sidney Kaufman. When I said that was right, he replied, "I went on your parents' honeymoon with them!" Conversation came to a halt.

He described their honeymoon with some embarrassment. He had tagged along at my father's invitation, accepting a small job as part of the crew, without really understanding the plan. He found himself staying in this romantic, primitive little cabin with them, having to walk through their bedroom to get to the only bathroom, averting his gaze so as not to stare at my mother, whom he called very beautiful and very shy. He could still see her in his mind's eye, lying there in that bed, with a certain look on her face. (Where did the rest of the crew stay? Why did this weird situation persist without remedy?) Michael reiterated how awkward the whole circumstance had been, and how young and unsophisticated and foolish he had been. Michael's wife, Barbara, grew more and more unhappy about this conversation to which the entire table of guests was listening avidly, and at that moment she developed a migraine that required their immediate departure.

There wasn't actually very much more to the story, I learned, when I met him for coffee in New Haven a couple of years ago to learn more. Michael Roemer was a German émigré of twenty when he went on my parents' honeymoon with them. Having been sent to England at age eleven in the *kindertransport* program during the war, he had only arrived in America in 1945, to go to Harvard. He was in New York to see if he could find employment on a film, and someone introduced him to Sidney. That summer, he was a sort of Sidney protégé of the moment. Michael admired my father's erudition and assured knowledge about everything. He knew everyone. Sidney Kaufman was a man who seemed to be someone who could make things happen.

At first he believed everything Sidney said. Sidney put him on a weekly salary that was enough to live on, and they began to meet in order to work on a screenplay together. But these meetings, many of which took place bizarrely in a room at the Surrey Hotel on East Seventy-sixth Street, which my father liked to book so they could sit by the rooftop pool and swim laps, consisted of my father holding forth, either at the Surrey or during long walks along the East River, while the younger man listened respectfully, and very little screenplay writing ever actually occurred. Then came the strange honeymoon trip, the memory of which haunted Michael all his life. By the end of the honeymoon, the honeymoon was over.

My father had introduced Michael to the producer Louis de Rochement, and that relationship was to bear fruit, as Michael would work for him for several years, before he left to make his first film, *Nothing But a Man*. He only crossed paths with Sidney once more after they parted ways, he told me, at the Venice Film Festival in 1965, when he was there with *Nothing But a Man,* which won two festival awards. My father was staying at the elegant Hotel Des Bains on the Lido, the *Death in Venice* hotel, and Michael saw him there, eating lunch at a table on the terrace, and approached him to say hello. Sidney was strangely unfriendly to him, and the conversation was awkward and brief. Michael hesitated, and I asked if my father was with someone, a woman, a woman who was not my mother. Yes, Michael said. I'm sorry. Don't worry, I said, but tell me this, did she have one arm? He nodded.

I BELIEVE my mother convinced herself that this marriage to my father was her only chance of success as a wife and mother. By the time I was born in 1955, four years after my brother's birth in 1951, they had been married for seven years, and, if my father's regrettably explicit rant had even the semblance of truth, their meager sex life had more or less ended with my conception. Throughout my childhood, my mother was fearful of my father's anger. She never felt entitled to demand faithfulness or much of anything else from him. He came and went as he pleased, he lived his life, bankrolled by her family money (it is my impression that with all his film plans and deals, and all his businesses incorporated in Delaware and the Cayman Islands which made his estate a rat's nest of misdirection and shell corporations that fronted other shell corporations, each of which had impressive stationery naming him President or Executive Director, every nickel he ever made probably cost her a dime). My mother's only demands were questions about his travel plans, which irritated him, and in any case he never answered her truthfully. She never confronted him, and she always gave him whatever he wanted. Why would he ever change their arrangement? The person he divorced, instead, was me.

The Fire That Time

MY FATHER'S MOTHER WAS A TINY, QUERULOUS, BORSCHT-making woman whom we visited in Brooklyn. She did not die in the Triangle shirtwaist factory fire of 1911. She couldn't have died in the fire; she wasn't there. She had stopped working at the Triangle Waist Company as a button-hole finisher a little more than a year earlier, because she got pregnant with my father. So it wasn't really a close call, but to my father it was a dramatic brush with death, and that is the way it was always presented to me—Grandma could have died in that fire on March 25, 1911, when the Triangle Waist Company, which occupied the top three floors of the new ten-story Asch Building, a block east of Washington Square, went up in flames.

The fire, probably ignited by a cigarette butt, spread swiftly through the crowded sweatshop, accelerated by the machine oil–soaked floors and tables, fed by bundles of shirtwaists and scrap materials that littered the work areas. The firemen's ladders reached only as high as the sixth floor. The lifesaving nets were useless. Some sixty workers, most of them young women, jumped to their deaths. Most of the nearly six hundred workers on the premises that afternoon survived by fleeing down the stairs or crowding into the elevators, which made a few trips before the smoke and heat rendered them inoperative.

The 146 workers, most of them women, who did die on March 25, 1911—the women who jumped from the ninth floor to the cobbled pavement below, the teenaged girls who burned to death on the wrong side of doors that were locked or opened inward, the ones who died when the single, hideously inadequate fire escape buckled and sheared off the building—they were all just like my grandmother. They were girls fresh off a boat, making their way, learning English, learning to be Americans, learning to be New Yorkers, working long hours bent over needles and bobbins and sewing machines in sweatshops of every size, from makeshift one-room workshops in tenement flats to enormous factory operations set up in converted warehouse lofts, like the Triangle premises on the top floors of the new, ten-story Asch Building at the corner of Greene Street and Washington Place, a veritable skyscraper standing where a row of elegant townhouses, one of them the birthplace of Henry James, had been demolished to make way for industry.

As the granddaughter of Pauline Gottesfeld Kaufman, I descend from someone who did not die in that fire. This is my legacy, my heritage. She didn't die in the fire, but she could have. Tens of thousands of other people's mothers and grandmothers were also not there in that particular sweatshop on that particular day. In this sense, tens of thousands of young immigrant women survived the Triangle fire, and went on living their new lives in America, and had children and grandchildren and great-grandchildren. We all share that heritage, that same brush with history and fate.

Over the years, I have spent quite a bit of time at Washington Place and Greene Street, gazing up at the top three floors of the former Asch Building, now unpoetically renamed the Brown Building, which today houses labs and classrooms for New York University. Standing on that corner, or sitting on the curb on the other side of Greene Street, as often as I have done it, each time visualizing the events of that March day in 1911, I have always been moved to tears.

One morning in the late spring of 2001, I walked in the door of the Brown Building, and although there was a security guard, I flourished an expired Yale faculty ID with authority and signed in without challenge. The elevator required a key for the ninth floor, so I climbed the stairs. Two flights up, I realized where I was, and had to stop, just to feel the echoes of the past in that stairwell, where people died.

The ninth floor was, in 2001, a partitioned warren of laboratories and offices. I gazed out the second south window in from the corner, then enclosed in a corner office. This was the window from which so many people jumped that day, including an unidentified man, immortalized in Robert Pinsky's poem "Shirt," who gallantly helped several young women up onto the windowsill so that they could jump, helping them, in Pinsky's words, "As if he were helping them up to enter a streetcar, and not eternity." The third woman he assisted to her death put her arms around his neck and kissed him before she jumped. He jumped after her. I stood there trying to see with the eyes of a panicked sleeve setter, trying to imagine the pandemonium, the fear and the flames and the noise and the smoke and the unbearable heat—trying to imagine the unbearability of everything that would lead you not to hesitate to make that leap.

I thought of my grandmother coming to work each day in this building, and I tried to imagine her working the sewing machine, driving buttonholes into the blank cloth, one after the other, from top to bottom of the back of a nearly finished shirtwaist, moving down the placket until the piece was done and put on her pile, then reaching for the next shirtwaist, thrusting the next blank placket under the sewing machine needle, to begin again. Her sewing machine was one of 288 Singer machines mounted on those long tables that ran all the way from the Waverly Place end to the windows fronting onto Washington Place, on the ninth floor of the Triangle Waist Company.

The young women who spent ten or twelve hours a day bent over those machines in order to earn, on average, less than two dollars a week were mostly Yiddish and Italian speakers. Packed together in tight rows at those whirring, clacking, chugging sewing machines, they sat there with few breaks or even much conversation, shoulder to shoulder on those long benches, running the thin linen fabric under the machines as fast as they could, flipping the piece, turning the armhole, finishing the seam, each worker making her part of the whole, the sleeves, the plackets, the pleated fronts, the collars, the cuffs, sewing as fast as they could, trying to keep up, trying to get ahead, in this same place where I now stood alone in the quiet hum of a laboratory.

In my childhood, my father told me the story of the Triangle fire several times, always prefacing his remarks with the words, "Your grandmother was a great lady." My grandmother died when I was twelve, and I have no memory of her ever mentioning the Triangle fire, though she did once tell me, prompted by nothing that I can recall, as we ate squares of her lemon sponge cake (how I have tried without success to duplicate that dense, eggy creation) at her blue-and-white enamel-top kitchen table, about an altercation with a policeman.

I realized many years later, when I was immersed in the Triangle fire doing research for a novel, that this probably signified her participation in the massive New York shirtwaist workers strike of 1909. The policeman took her roughly by the arm to arrest her, she grabbed him by the hair, they struggled, she broke free and ran away, and after a few blocks, when she could duck down an alley and catch her breath, she realized that she was holding something tight in her fist—a clump of his hair. "I was a tiger," she told me, and I wasn't sure what she meant, but I believed her. I had seen her win shouting matches with my father by tearing out clumps of her own hair and brandishing them for emphasis.

She sewed on buttons and mended my clothes with astonishing speed and skill when we visited her in Brooklyn. If she spotted a loose button or a torn seam, out would come the needle and thread, and she would fix the trouble in an instant while I stood there in the garment, holding still, as if she were a doctor stitching up a wound.

As she threaded the needle and bit the thread and began to whip it through the shoulder of my shirt or the hem of my pants in a blur of efficiency, she might say something about having worked with a needle and thread and earned a living sewing, from the time she was a young girl in Skala, the village of her childhood, though she never told me anything else about her childhood. When she was born, Skala, in eastern Galicia, was part of the Austro-Hungarian Empire; it was part of Poland after World War I; after World War II, it was part of the Soviet Union; since 1990, Skala on the River Zbrucz—as it is now known—has been in Ukraine.

After his mother's death, my father brought her ancient Singer sewing machine in its wooden cabinet into our house. It sat undisturbed for years in a nook on a stair landing, a poignant reminder of the determined, stubborn, admirable woman who arrived at Ellis Island in 1900 and earned her living with a needle and thread and a sewing machine so long ago.

In the summer of 2003, on tour for my third novel, I found myself in the Family History Library in Salt Lake City, the world's largest genealogy library, founded by the Church of Jesus Christ of Latter-day Saints. With the help of a volunteer, I located the 1910 Brooklyn census. Here, on Stagg Street, on a day in July, are the entries in a copperplate hand for Samuel Kaufman, grocer, born in Rowno, Poland (crossed out) Russia (today, Poland), arrived in 1905; his wife, Polly (surely a mishearing on the part of the census taker on the doorstep of "Pauline" uttered in a Yiddish accent), born in Skala in Austro-Hungary, arrived in 1900, and here is my father, Simon, as he was called on his birth certificate but nowhere else, born in the USA, aged four months. Until I saw this document, I had not known if they met in New York or on the ship that brought them here. The census page also revealed that they were married in January of 1910, just three months before my father's birth. When I pointed this out to my helper, she laughed and said, "Oh, we see that often in family research. You know what they say—babies come after nine months, except the firstborn. The firstborn can come at any time."

Pauline Gottesfeld arrived at Ellis Island with her mother and father, Ethel and Isaac Gottesfeld, and her younger brothers, Samuel, Benjamin, and Joseph, and her sisters, Bertha, Sophie, and Esther. (There was another sister, Rose, who either died young or perhaps for whatever reason stayed in Skala. There was another brother, too, named Mendel. There is no record of their arriving in America with the family, and their names are not mentioned in Joe's obituary in 1944.) The family may have emigrated because of a fire. Although records are scant, because of the devastation of the Jewish population of Skala (between the world wars because of the violent raids of the Cossacks crossing over the river from the east, and then during World War Two the Nazis succeeded in eradicating the remaining Jews of Skala), there are numerous references to "the Great Fire of Skala" in 1899. This was a catastrophic fire that swept the town, which apparently precipitated a wave of immigration to America by Skala families whose homes and businesses had been reduced to cinders.

I know nothing of the first years of the Gottesfeld family in New York City, but there is no question that they found their way with alacrity. I believe that Pauline, born in 1885, was the oldest of the seven Gottesfeld children. My father often remarked that his mother had only had the equivalent of a third-grade education, and none of it in America, having arrived at fifteen, already an experienced seamstress, and so she went to work immediately in one sweatshop after another, here sewing overcoat linings, there sewing ladies' foundation garments, working a series of these jobs for nine years, helping to support her family, helping to earn the money the family needed to put a brother and a sister through law school. Her last job in the needle trades was at the Triangle Waist Company.

Employment at the Triangle Waist Company, though we now regard it with a contemporary gaze of horror, was actually a step up for those garment workers. Cramped and noisy as it was, it was a modern factory that was a more comfortable and efficient place to do piecework for good money (if you could work fast without error) than any of the dark, cramped sweatshops all over the Lower East Side, where it was harder to work as efficiently and make as much money for a day's work.

Pauline's sister Esther, born in 1893, and her brother Ben, born in 1896, having arrived in America as children, grew up with the advantages of New York City public schools, and they both went to law school and became practicing attorneys. Ben, a graduate of St. John's University Law School, had an office in Brooklyn near Borough Hall for many years. Because my father stopped speaking to him after Pauline died in 1968, convinced that Ben, the executor and "Court Street shyster," had looted her estate, I have only a single dim recollection of Ben, at a Passover Seder when I was four or five. He is sitting beside my grandfather Sam Kaufman (who died when I was six), the two of them down at one end of the table in their yarmulkes, each wearing a tallis, mumbling the prayers at top speed from a Hagaddah, in alternating turns, making a conversation of their determination to complete the unabridged reading of the Passover service while the rest of us eat dinner.

Esther, who attended St. Lawrence University and Brooklyn Law School, practiced in New York for a few years until she followed her rabbi husband, Nathan Lublin, who moved from a Bronx synagogue to Manchester, New Hampshire. She was admitted to the bar in New Hampshire on October 2, 1928, the sixth woman ever to be admitted to the New Hampshire bar and the first Jewish woman.

Their brother Joe owned a garage in Jamaica, Queens, and was dedicated to the Saratoga Spring Cure and Convalescent Home, the Herzl Nordau Society, and the Greater New York Benevolent Society, according to his *New York Times* obituary, which appeared in 1944 when he died at fifty. The *Times* notes that his charity work may have killed him: "Mr. Gottesfeld's enthusiasm for the benevolent work he was doing was said by friends to have contributed to the decline which led to his death."

In 1923 their brother Sam was convicted of participating in what a *New York Times* headline called a "Huge Liquor Plot," and spent a few years in prison as a consequence of his involvement in a conspiracy to defraud the government in a complex scheme involving the switching of water for whiskey in a large whiskey shipment from a bonded Seagram's warehouse to Greece. He was one of seven men convicted of the plot. "Had the plans of the conspirators gone through," the *Times* reported, "it was said they would have made at least $5,000,000." When he got out of prison, Sam started over with an abbreviated name, Gotty, and a ladies' hat shop, Gotty's, in Jamaica, Queens. Ten years after his conviction, he was elected president of the Master Group of Retail Milliners.

In my childhood, a fire destroyed the hat shop, which had not been very profitable, and I overheard my father talking with his brother Murray about the probability that this had been caused by "Jewish lightning." Soon after the fire, my father brought home several dozen wooden hat blocks, no two alike, some of them scorched and blackened. They were crammed onto the shelves of mystery in our attic, that repository of relics and secret artifacts, where they loomed creepily forever after, a secret miniature Easter Island row of primitive tribal gods. They had an acrid, corky odor of fire. I was halfway convinced they were actual heads of dead relatives that had been transmuted by fire into these forms.

Samuel Kaufman arrived at Ellis Island with forty dollars, the story goes, and at first he worked as a pack peddler selling pants all over the Lower East Side, before he got a pushcart, switched to fruit, sold fruit on Delancey Street, and saved his money to open a store. At some point he crossed paths with Pauline Gottesfeld, the possessor of five more years of American experience and much better English. She walked to work each day from the family apartment on Orchard Street, or was it Hester Street? Maybe she bought an apple from his cart.

Or maybe they met in Williamsburg, Brooklyn. According to my recent discovery of a City of New York "Certificate and Record of Marriage" for Samuel Kaufman and Pauline "Gotesfield," Sam was living on Graham Avenue, five blocks from Pauline's address on Montrose Avenue, at the time of their marriage on June 20, 1909, which is six months earlier than the marriage date recorded in the 1910 census. Perhaps they had a reason to keep their marriage secret until my grandmother became pregnant with my father and stopped working. Which of these documents, each in its own way inaccurate, tells the true story? I will never know.

By 1910 they were on Stagg Street with their little grocery store, and by 1920 they owned the building, and then they owned a few more buildings on Ten Eyck Street, and by 1925 they were the proprietors of Kaufman Auto Supply on Bedford Avenue, a business that prospered for some twenty years before being bought out by Pep Boys Auto, their biggest competitors. (Inevitably, my father believed his family had been swindled by Manny, Moe, and Jack.) Part of the campus of Medgar Evers College occupies the ground where Kaufman Auto once did business, if family mythology is reliable.

I don't know precisely when my grandparents left the Lower East Side for the grocery store on Stagg Street in Williamsburg, but moving on was a natural next step for them, as it was for hundreds of thousands of immigrants who began their American life on the Lower East Side. The Diaspora that began when they fled their homelands in the late nineteenth and early twentieth centuries was completed as they left the Lower East Side, many for the comfort and prosperity of uptown or the New York suburbs, others for similarly improved situations in cities across the country. Isn't this why so many subsequent generations have such a sentimental and romantic sense of the Lower East Side? It is where we are all "from."

Immigrants from places like Italy or Scandinavia or the British Isles could stay in touch with their ancestral lands; they could make plans for returning to their home villages, and many did. But those who had fled Czarist Russia, those who had survived the pogroms and upheavals of Eastern Europe, people like my grandparents—Sam Kaufman went AWOL from the Czar's army, into which he had been conscripted when he was rounded up on the street one day in Rowno, when he was repeatedly forced to eat rabbit, which was trayfe—they had no way to go back, nowhere to go back to. Their shtetls were vanishing even as they were leaving, and so they set sail across the ocean with a different sense of the journey, a sense that with only darkness at their backs, the only possibilities and opportunities life could offer lay straight ahead.

So many second- and third-generation American Jews cannot name with certainty even the country of origin of their forebears, let alone the region or the city or town where their ancestors lived. We know remarkably little about the daily lives of our ancestors just one or two generations back in the Old World; often we don't know even their professions, or their original names. (I have no idea about Sam Kaufman's family, and do not know the names of his parents or any siblings other than one sister, Jeanette. My father claimed that Albert Shanker, the longtime head of the teachers' union, was a Kaufman cousin.) Among the few photographs from my father's family, there is a perplexing portrait of an elderly Orthodox Jew with long white hair and a long white beard, labeled "Civil War Veteran," but I have no idea how he is related, if at all, to Sam Kaufman, who arrived on these shores forty years after the Civil War ended.

In my tenth-grade social studies class at Forest Hills High School, I was given a then-popular American history textbook that had the phrase "melting pot" in the title. For those of us who descend from the resourceful men and women who got themselves here from Eastern Europe in the last decades of the nineteenth century and the first decades of the twentieth, some of the flames under that melting pot were those of the Triangle fire, because it is our fire, just as the Lower East Side is where we are from.

I continue to spend time on the corner of Washington Place and Greene Street. Now that I have written my Triangle fire novel, with its told and retold versions of those moments, I am no longer certain if I am being moved by history, or by the knowledge that my grandmother who worked here for long hours, six days a week, finishing buttonholes for the Triangle Waist Company at a Singer sewing machine on the ninth floor, was spared a terrible fate because she got pregnant with my father, though I am convinced that my grandmother would have been among the survivors of the Triangle fire if she had been working at her machine that day. Perhaps I am deeply touched because of my heritage—a grandiose Kaufman sense of personal history and its phantom connection to historic events.

Looking out that window on the ninth floor for the first time on that afternoon when I climbed the stairs, gazing down at the same sidewalk and cobbled street that were there in 1911, I could imagine a moment of crazy optimism, a moment when you might think that maybe you could survive the fall, if you were extra lucky, if you fell just right. Optimism is what got my grandmother and my grandfather here. It's what got hundreds of thousands of immigrants here. They possessed a willingness to believe that against all odds, having survived the atrocities in their homeland, they could survive the dreadful ocean crossing in steerage, that they could arrive with nothing and soon enough have something, and that, with enough determination and hard work, they could make their way, they could survive, and then they could do better than survive, they could thrive.

I opened the window and leaned out, and I looked down. It is a very long way down to the pavement below, but if it feels like no choice anyway, if only darkness and flames are at your back, you leap. And you hope.

Subject: Sidney Kaufman

MY FATHER WAS THE QUINTESSENTIAL UNRELIABLE NAR-rator. He was the hero of all the stories he told about himself. Sometimes he triumphed, other times he was wronged, but each recounting of his many exploits was an illumination of his superior intelligence and his impressive moral stance on the important issues of our times. He had been everywhere and done everything and met everyone. Sidney Kaufman knew how to solve the world's problems, yet he had become inexplicably exhausted and cynical before I was born. For someone so brilliant and formerly ambitious, his professional identity was strangely slippery and uncelebrated, with little to show in the way of actual accomplishments. The man who knew everyone and everything was unrecognized by the world and unknowable to me.

There was an incomprehensible disconnect between the cosmopolitan life my father had apparently once led and the way he sat around the house in his bathrobe and didn't leave until noon for his office in the city, which was as cluttered with cascades of unpaid bills and debt-collection notices as were several jam-packed rooms in our house. Unopened mail, some of it many years old, could be found in both locations, interleaved among the hundreds of movie scripts that were heaped everywhere, along with tilting piles of newspapers and magazines in which were important articles my father was saving for future projects. (Whenever I needed three brass fasteners for my school reports, I would simply extract them from the nearest movie script.) It was all part of my father's grand plan for a panoply of movies that were always imminently in development. His mind was replete with extensive schemes for success. I searched the credits of every movie I ever saw in the fruitless hope of spotting his name.

None of the good friends or famous colleagues about whom he spoke so vividly seemed to be around anymore. Despite their frequent references to rollicking parties and intimate friendships, my parents had a nearly nonexistent social life and almost never left the house together. On one rare occasion, when I was seven, people from the fabled past appeared in the present, when Kate and Zero Mostel came to our house for dinner. In order to reserve them all for himself, Zero reached into the basket of dinner rolls on the table and licked each one before putting it back, while everyone laughed uproariously.

My maternal grandmother, who had known the Mostels for years, was also there that night, and after dinner she played the piano while everyone sang a song she made up on the spot about my brother and me, which featured the refrain "John is eleven, and Kathy is seven," which Zero sang with gusto, at one point picking me up and whirling me around the room. After I had gone upstairs to bed, the music continued, and I could hear peals of laughter when Zero sang, "Lookie, lookie, here comes nookie walking down the street!" But later that evening, according to my mother, Kate said something insulting to my father. They never saw the Mostels again. Sidney, my mother often cautioned me, had sensitive feelings that were very easily hurt.

✧ ✦ ✧

MY FATHER's frequent and mysterious business trips throughout my childhood were a relief, because when he was away my mother didn't have to pretend he was coming home for dinner night after night, which often meant that we waited for him until it was apparent that he wasn't going to appear, no matter what he had told her when he went into the city, no matter what she preferred to believe. He liked to cook, having learned by the age of eight to prepare meals for himself and his baby brother, Murray, while their parents worked in the grocery store, and my mother barely knew how to cook anyway, and was especially terrified of cooking for him and enduring his inevitable scorn of her feeble culinary skills. She wasn't even good at making school lunches. Sometimes my sandwich bread was splotched all over with green mold. Once, instead of a can of juice, she accidentally put a can of tomato paste into my lunch box.

On nights when my father said he was coming home to have dinner with us, my mother made no preparations, did no shopping, and somehow, as if all previous experience was forgotten, on each of these nights she expected him to provide dinner for his family. When he hadn't shown up by eight or nine o'clock, which was the case most times, we were like a band of neglected hungry children, my mother being the oldest child, the one who knew how to light the stove, and we would forage in the kitchen and end up eating scrambled eggs or French toast. I concealed these invalid menus from my friends at school, who seemed to eat roast chicken or meat loaf at six o'clock every school night, right after their fathers came home from work. My father never left the house early in the morning like those fathers, either. When my father was away, and there was no question that he was supposed to come home and make dinner for his family, it was much more relaxing. Every night we ate at six o'clock, one of my mother's three very basic meals—spaghetti with sauce from a jar, broiled chicken, or steak with Le Sueur canned peas and a lot of Tater Tots—with the television on.

When I was nine, my father left on a trip in his usual fashion, which is to say he didn't know when he would leave until the day before his flight to London, and he didn't know when he would return, and he was irritated by my mother's questions about his plans. He would be in London, Rome, Berlin, and Zagreb. Other destinations would no doubt evolve. What difference did it make? If he made up an itinerary he couldn't possibly know yet, would that make her happy?

When we hadn't had any calls or letters from him in over six months, I began to hear my mother provide different explanations to her friends and relatives, explanations that were contradictory and that contained definite lies. How could she tell her father that she had spoken to Sidney on the telephone, and he was in London, and would be back home with us soon, when I knew she had not heard from him for a very long time and had confided in a late-night phone call with her sister, my aunt Kay, that she had no idea where he was and was very worried, but this was a secret nobody else knew?

My father returned one spring afternoon without notice, behind the wheel of an old powder-blue Renault, as if he had driven back from Europe, having been gone by then for nearly eighteen months. Neither his disappearance nor his return was ever mentioned, now that he was back. While he was away, I had stopped being able to go to sleep at night, and had developed the habit of roaming around the house on a frantic mission I couldn't help. I lurked like a burglar, spying on my mother while she read to my brother, spying on my mother while she read alone in her bed, spying on my mother after she turned out her light and listened to the radio in the dark, the tinny sound of a Yankees game from the West Coast, or the sonorous voice of Long John Nebel, the only sounds left on which to eavesdrop.

I went upstairs to the third floor and investigated the attic like a secret agent, rummaging the stuffed shelves and stacked boxes and mothball-smelling steamer trunks for clues, searching for the truth. I took the lid off a cardboard shoe box that was wedged on a low shelf between a broken green radio and a broken brown radio, and discovered a round pink plastic case with a hinged clamshell lid which, when opened, revealed not the face powder compact it resembled but a strange round, brittle rubber object, like nothing I had ever seen before. This mysterious item was disturbing to me, though I didn't know why. It was beigey pink, like the flesh of a creepy doll, and slightly domed, with a thick rolled rim like the mouth end of a balloon, but it was hard like an old pencil eraser or a worn-out Pennsy Pinkie ball, and its thin surface was crazed all over with tiny cracks, like an antique china cup. When I picked it up and tried to flex it, a gaping crack opened up across the middle, a horrifying wound, and I closed it back inside its clamshell. Also in the shoe box was a folded, dried-out tube, like petrified toothpaste, which I unrolled and flattened until I could make out the unfamiliar word *spermicidal.*

I discovered a hatbox filled with letters. There were dozens of letters my father had written to someone named Beatrice, tied in a bundle. There was a matching bundle of letters Beatrice had written to him. I read them like a novel, night after night. They had begun their romance in 1937, or at least that was the date of the first saved letter, when she was married to someone else, though her husband was coincidentally also named Sidney, and the letters continued through the time period when my father talked about someone named Fra, and then he started mentioning my mother, and at a certain point Beatrice married someone named Paul, and they kept writing each other through the year we lived together as a family in London on Rutland Place. There were some letters addressed to him there. Had I picked them up from the cold checkerboard marble floor of the foyer when they had been pushed through the brass letter slot?

The newest letter in the hatbox, from Sidney to Beatrice, was dated 1963, just the year before my nocturnal inspections of this collected correspondence. His letters to her were tender and ornate in their declarations of love and passion. He quoted poetry. This was a side of my father I didn't know at all, and I thought perhaps my mother didn't know it, either. I had certainly never come across any letters like this in any of her desk drawers or anywhere in the house. In a big paper clip, there were dozens of receipts for hotel rooms over the years for Mr. and Mrs. Sidney Kaufman, from 1937 to 1963. His last letter to Beatrice was about how desolate he had felt alone at the motel after she left, and how he had accidentally backed his car over a little black kitten and killed it, and how he sat on the ground beside the dead kitten, crying for all his losses. The letter was smeared in places, as if he had cried while writing to her in his familiar, angular fountain-penned hand.

All of her letters were typed, on onion-skin paper. Her language was elegant, concise, surprising, and vivid. I read and re-read their letters night after night, carefully putting each letter back into its proper envelope, preserving their order, putting them precisely where I found them before creeping back to my room, where I would lie in my bed and go over and over the words and sentences in the letters, still not sleeping but exhausted and content to lie still under my covers.

One day, when I was sprawled on the living room rug, half watching a Jimmy Stewart movie on television while doing homework, when the credits scrolled at the end of *Mr. Smith Goes to Washington,* I spotted the screenwriting credit for Beatrice's first husband, Sidney Buchman. I asked my mother as casually as I could, at dinner that night, if she had ever heard of him, saying I had recognized his name in the credits of an old movie on television that afternoon—wasn't he someone Daddy knew?

She replied, Oh yes, and you know Beatrice, that book editor who shares Daddy's office? She used to be married to that guy, a long time ago. But he was a son of a bitch, she added. He went to jail during the witch hunts.

When I was thirteen I met Beatrice. My father took me to his office one day and introduced me to her there, saying, awkwardly, "This is Beatrice. She could have been your mother." She was very pretty, very tailored, and crisp. She wore a beautiful striped blouse tucked into a wide leather belt cinched around her waist. Her straight skirt was wrinkled from sitting at her desk. My mother did not own clothing like this. The only times she dressed up were for very rare special occasions, not for regular days.

My mother's most frequent kind of dressing up was in her Girl Scout leader uniform, which she put on to go to meetings with other Girl Scout ladies, now that she had become the Cookie Chair for all of Queens, the same year I dropped out of Girl Scouts. She had been an unusual troop leader. When our Junior troop made a trip to the World's Fair in nearby Flushing Meadow Park, my mother had led us all through a hole in the parking lot fence to avoid paying admission.

Beatrice chatted with me, looking into my eyes in a knowing way. She knew a lot about me, she said. What she didn't know was how much I had already come to admire her, how I had studied her letters to my father and soaked up all their wit and originality, all her elegant turns of phrase, her wandery associative style, how I had begun to imitate her physical writing traits as well, her use of dashes to break up long sentences, her habit of double spacing to begin new paragraphs, which she did without indenting. We three had lunch together that day. She asked me about my writing and listened seriously to my shy, hesitant answers. My father seemed proud to show me off to her, and to show her off to me. I felt disloyal to my mother, but thrilled to have been admitted at last to his secret world, his secret life.

I began to meet her for lunch, just the two of us, every few months, starting then, when I was thirteen. This went on for years. She was an editor of nonfiction. She had a Ph.D. in physics and edited science and medical books, as well as political books and biographies. When I was sixteen, she told me I ought to write a book about my grandmother and her romance with George Gershwin. Nobody would ever be able to write about her the way I would write about her someday, Beatrice said.

We talked about novels. She told me about novelists I should read and I wrote down their names and then I read their novels. John Dos Passos. Conrad Aiken. Theodore Dreiser. Sherwood Anderson. Thornton Wilder. May Sarton. Booth Tarkington. Guy Endore. Djuna Barnes. Herman Wouk. Mary McCarthy. D. H. Lawrence. Joseph Heller. All these books were readily available on the shelves in our house, it turned out, most of them my father's old hardcovers. Beatrice and my father had very similar taste, or perhaps she had his taste, or he had hers.

I didn't set out to keep our lunches secret from my mother, but she never asked me one thing about who I was meeting or why a thirteen-year-old was dressing nicely to go alone into the city (which required a long walk to the subway and then a ride on the E or F train to Midtown) for a lunch date. This was how my father did it! It was that easy to conduct this clandestine relationship in plain sight. It seemed my mother was as oblivious to my involvement with Beatrice as she had been to my father's carrying on with her over the years. More likely she knew perfectly well all about Beatrice and what he had been up to with her, and what I was up to with her, but feigned obliviousness was her way of dealing with it, as with so many other troubling aspects of her life.

My mother certainly never mentioned my father's attempts to have her meet Beatrice in 1946, two years before they married, when she was visiting her mother in California and Sidney sent her a letter from Brooklyn in which he said, "Beatrice wrote me recently and asked about you. I hope you will call her. You may find the 'contact' very pleasant if you keep it from becoming too murky. I'd rather like you to try." (My best guess is that my mother ignored this peculiar invitation.)

Though we never spoke of it, I assumed that Beatrice reported on our encounters to my father. I hoped she did, because she made me feel precocious and clever and I wanted him to see me that way. And I sensed through Beatrice a view of my father I didn't know: She spoke with fond familiarity of his intellectual passion and his accomplishments, telling me I should be proud of him. Her reverence for Sidney, even the way she said his name, was fascinating. My father and I shared this wordless bond, our secret Beatrice connection.

WHEN I requested my father's FBI records in 1992, I hoped there would be something quite specific and concrete in those files, some enormous central revelation of a fact or circumstance to explain why for all the years I was growing up I always had the feeling that my father had a secret life. He was clearly a man on a mission, but what mission, for whom? I wondered for many years if my father was, in actual fact, a spy. Perhaps he was a double agent. A triple agent! I wanted it to be true. That would have explained everything.

I half expected the FBI documents to reveal a second family somewhere else, another wife and other children about whom even Beatrice had been ignorant. I was prepared to learn about these children, my mysterious secret half-siblings. It would have been a relief, an explanation for the feeling I had throughout my childhood that *we* were Sidney Kaufman's other family, while meanwhile his real family was somewhere else, living their lives contentedly in some other city or even on some other continent, having no idea we existed, having much more certainty than I did that Sidney Kaufman (if that was the name by which they knew him) was singularly devoted to them as a husband and father. For the nearly nine years it took for the FBI to honor my Freedom of Information Act request for my father's records, I really believed there was a chance that the Federal Bureau of Investigation could explain my father to me at last.

I was confident that the FBI had compiled records on my father because of his anti-Nazi activities in the 1930s, combined with his having been sympathetic to Communism (though he was never an actual Party member) before Stalin disappointed so many dreamy idealists of his generation. He once told me he had written a column for the *Daily Worker* in the 1930s under an assumed name. What name? I asked, my curiosity piqued. What difference does it make? was his only reply.

My father knew countless people in show business who were politically active in the 1930s and then subsequently blacklisted in the 1950s, from Sidney Buchman to the Mostels to Ring Lardner Jr. He knew three of the Hollywood Ten very well—John Howard Lawson, Edward Dmytryk, and Herbert Biberman—and was acquainted with all of them.

Sidney Kaufman managed to cross paths with just about

every left-wing émigré in New York and Hollywood, from Ernst Toller, Max Reinhardt, Salka and Berthold Viertel, and Luise Rainer, to Erwin Piscator, Geza Herczeg, Mady Christians, Irmgard von Cube, Fritz Lang, and Gabriel Pascal. My father had an affinity for this European set, and wherever he went he was drawn to them and was well received by them. He spoke their language figuratively and literally (his Yiddish-speaking childhood household made it possible for him to get by in Polish, German, and Russian).

I was certain that my father's personal and professional connections before, during, and after the war had just about guaranteed FBI investigation as a Communist sympathizer at the very least. But I had no idea how extensive his FBI records actually were.

Some 648 pages of FBI files concerning Sidney Kaufman were released to me in 2000. There are at least 800 pages in my father's FBI and CIA records, probably more that are still classified in field offices I didn't specifically identify in my request, but at least 152 pages have been deemed, even now, to be exempted from disclosure for reasons having to do with national security. (The Federal Bureau of Investigation definition of "national security" covers their perpetual concealment of the identities of informants.)

Why exactly did the FBI have Sidney Kaufman under surveillance from 1936 to 1972? This is where it all began, in this first memo to J. Edgar Hoover:

SIDNEY KAUFMAN
INTERNAL SECURITY–C

In a report dated December 5, 1936, confidential informant [redacted] reported on a weekly fifteen minute broadcast by the captioned individual entitled "Cinema Comment." Informant stated that Kaufman spoke for four minutes on the theoretical subject of the arts and motion pictures, then for about eight minutes he delivered what informant described as extremely clever Communist propaganda in the guise of a review of a Soviet picture, "Son of Magnolia," which was currently showing. Informant stated that no one unfamiliar with Kaufman's Communist Party affiliations could have suspected that this was Party propaganda.

The FBI tracked my father's movements over the next thirty-six years. If my father's life is a series of snapshots, the FBI are the shadowy figures lurking at the edges of the pictures of Sidney Kaufman in his various apartments and offices, Sidney Kaufman sailing on the *Queen Elizabeth* in 1958 with a redacted female companion who was not my mother, Sidney Kaufman in what should have been privileged conversations with his attorney, Sidney Kaufman lying about his travel destinations to his wife, the woman to whom numerous "pretext phone calls" were made by the FBI over all those years.

My birth is mentioned in a memo to J. Edgar Hoover about my father's whereabouts: "His travel in Europe had been interrupted on 11/1/55, by a cable informing him that his wife had entered a hospital (she subsequently bore a baby on 11/12/55)."

It is clear that the FBI read our mail, checking up on individuals with whom my father corresponded even casually. They collected information on each person in his address book. How they came to possess his address book (or copies of the pages) is redacted. Did they burglarize his office and rifle his desk, the way I so often burglarized my own home, perpetually ransacking drawers in the hope of finding family secrets and their explanations? Or did they break in to our house and photograph every page of his address book with a Minox camera while we slept in our beds? Perhaps the FBI had a mole in his office. He had a series of secretaries over the years, not all of them women he also slept with. Was there a secretary who made copies of every page, doing her patriotic duty for the FBI, while my father was at lunch? Could it have been the implausibly named Miss Trout? Was the enduring Miss Misk who "did the books" for my father's various companies actually a mole?

Ludicrously, the FBI devoted energy to analysis of individuals in the pages of his address book such as Balthazar Gagliano, an Italian musician living in South America with no apparent connections to the Communist Party, even collecting data on Gagliano's unpaid utility bills at his former home in Tampa, Florida, without apparent awareness that his relationship with their subject was simply that he was married to my mother's older sister, April.

It is abundantly clear that the FBI tapped our telephones at home and in my father's office. They investigated each bank transaction underlying his business deals. (They were frequently perplexed by the discrepancies between overheard conversations and this financial data.) They scrutinized our magazine subscriptions (making note, for instance, that we received *National Guardian,* "a radical leftist publication supportive of the Rosenbergs"). They questioned my father's friends and associates and possibly our neighbors.

Although all informant names are redacted when the FBI releases records of individuals whom they have investigated, enough facts and details about some of the informants in my father's files were left un-effaced that I have been able to identify a number of them with absolute certainty, and I am fairly confident about the identities of a few others. Many of these informants were friends. They had all become former friends before I was born.

Perhaps this begins to explain a strange feeling I had in my childhood, a sense of how much my parents had loved all the wonderful important friendships they had once had, combined with my awareness that all of these relationships had pretty much vanished without explanation in the years around my birth. It is perhaps hard to imagine now that one's circle of close and like-minded friends would evaporate this way without one person warning my parents or explaining the self-preserving necessity of avoiding further contact. Even devoted friends might have chosen distance after being questioned by the FBI in that frightening time period of 1950s Red-baiting. If it was apparent that the most casual, ordinary social interactions with my family would lead to another visit from the FBI and perhaps questions not just about Sidney Kaufman but also about the political beliefs and activities of these involuntary informants who chose to continue the relationship with a known subversive, it makes sense that so many relationships would just wither to nothing at this juncture, without rupture, without animus, just a graceful fade to black.

Grace and Byron McGrath, for example, both of them stage and screen actors, were very close friends of my parents before I was born. They had a son, Dennis, about whom I heard endless wonderful, hilarious stories throughout my childhood. I never met them, because they moved to Salt Lake City (where Grace, a Mormon, was from) the year after my birth. But there was zero communication with them—no calls, no letters, no talk of visits—and they might as well have died. This is just one of many examples of vivid friendships that evaporated in this time period for no apparent reason. In my father's FBI records, there is no question, despite the blacked-out names, that the McGraths were the married actors who moved to Salt Lake City with their young son in 1956. There are pages of information about my father's beliefs and professional activities from this informant, clearly Byron, who was characterized as "extremely cooperative" about providing information on the Subject by the Salt Lake City FBI office. No wonder they were never seen or heard from again.

It is evident that the FBI made informants of bankers, travel agents, airline reservation offices, Consolidated Edison, and New York Telephone. There were the countless "pretext phone calls" to our house from FBI agents posing as Realtors or business acquaintances. Most invasively, the FBI eavesdropped on my father's meetings with his attorney, Isidore "Gibby" Needleman, who was himself a much bigger target for scrutiny than was the elusive yet ultimately inconsequential Sidney Kaufman.

GIBBY NEEDLEMAN roomed with my father at Cornell, in the Ithaca boardinghouse at the top of a windswept hill where the Jewish students were relegated (the way my father told it). His wife's name was Edith, and they were both short and wide, and I thought they were relatives. He expected hugs and kisses from me despite his abhorrent cigar reek. Gibby had functioned at one time as the legal counsel to the Amtorg Trading Corporation, which, to quote the FBI, "is a New York corporation organized to act as an exclusive buying and selling agency in the United States of the Soviet Union and is operated by the Russian Government. It is registered with the Department of Justice under the terms of the Foreign Agents Registration Act."

Amtorg (the odd name, which seems like a Russian word or something spelled backwards, is derived from the words

American Trade Organization) was in fact established in 1924 by Armand Hammer as a means of conducting international trade between America and Russia. Amtorg was the only conduit for any Russian imports or exports in the United States. The FBI assumed it was a front throughout the Cold War era for Soviet intelligence operations in the United States. Nothing has ever linked Gibby Needleman to specific espionage activities of any kind, but for this reason the FBI labeled him a probable Soviet agent for most of his life (he died in 1975 at the age of seventy-three). Attorney-client privilege has a crime or fraud exception. Thus, throughout my father's FBI records there are numerous summaries or transcriptions of attorney-client conversations between Gibby and my father, clearly based on recordings. (More than one redacted name is followed by ["phonetic sp., Yiddish-sounding"].)

MY FATHER's FBI records were significantly augmented by an erroneous conflation with a different Sidney Kaufman, also born in Brooklyn, who served in the International Brigades in Spain from July 1937 through February 1939.

The Sidney Kaufman who went to Spain in 1937 was not my father. This other Sidney Kaufman was born in 1914, while my father was born in 1910. The Sidney Kaufman Papers in the Abraham Lincoln Brigade Archive (part of the Tamiment Library & Robert F. Wagner Labor Archives housed in the Bobst Library at New York University) contain letters and postcards Sidney Kaufman wrote home to his sister from Spain. My father had no sisters, only his younger brother, Murray, born in 1917, the seven-year gap between them occurring because their mother's pregnancy in the intervening years had ended with a stillbirth. So my father had no sisters unless we count that stillborn baby, a girl, my father told me several times, starting when I was six or seven.

His sister was born dead, he told me, because his mother spent her days on her hands and knees, scrubbing hallway floors and stairs in the tenement buildings they managed in exchange for their tiny apartment over their grocery store on Stagg Street in Williamsburg, Brooklyn. Pauline Gottesfeld Kaufman worked too hard through the pregnancy and she lost the baby in the eighth month. The stillborn child, my father explained, was kept preserved in a large bottle of formaldehyde in the doctor's nearby office, where Sidney and Murray were brought, from time to time, to have a look at their sister.

When I traveled in China a few years ago, I had the recurring sense, while walking through street markets, each time I caught sight of large jars holding preserved ginseng roots floating in liquid, that this was what my phantom aunt (I think of her as Miriam) looked like in her cold, watery deadness. Could there be a shred of truth to this fable of her preserved, vitrine existence in a doctor's office? Why wouldn't they have buried her? Why would parents expose their sons to the horror of their dead sister in a jar? Why would my father tell me about it? The contents of those jars in the Chinese ginseng sellers' stalls were, in any case, exactly what I knew she looked like in his story.

The other Sidney Kaufman had been a merchant seaman in New York when he volunteered to fight the Franco forces with the Abraham Lincoln Brigades. He served in World War II as a cook on a troop ship in the South Pacific, and was a lifelong member of the Marine Cooks and Stewards Union, as well as the International Longshoremen's and Warehousemen's Union. The FBI repeatedly identified this Sidney Kaufman as a member of the Communist Party, or CP, as the FBI calls it, based on information supplied by numerous redacted informants.

It seems absurdly inept that the FBI could have their left-leaning Sidney Kaufmans from Brooklyn conflated. Presumably there are as many references to the wrong Sidney Kaufman in that other Sidney Kaufman's FBI records as there are in my father's records. This confusion was finally noted by an FBI memo investigating my father's passport application in 1955, when his claim that he had never before left the country didn't match the FBI's knowledge of Sidney Kaufman's travels in Spain and France, although they had also been simultaneously tracking my father's entirely domestic activities for nearly twenty years.

MY FATHER had a sense of history, but more than that, he had a grand if not grandiose fascination with his own role in the great pageant of time. He reminded me more than once that as a young child he had stood on a Brooklyn street corner watching Civil War veterans march in an Armistice Day parade (he claimed that Buffalo Bill Cody, leading the parade, patted him on the head). He saw himself as a character in a movie of the sort he was always trying to produce. (One of his unrealized lifelong quests was to make a film based on *The Surprising Adventures of Baron Munchausen*.) He not only tried to seize opportunities with the vigor of an immigrant, but was also obsessed with trying to portray European culture on the screen for American audiences. He relished being an insider, someone in the know, a person of note who knew other people of note in film and theater circles, a man who made things happen. He relished equally being an outsider, being the self-made Brooklyn boy born in the back of that grocery store on Stagg Street, someone with extra appreciation for the finer things in life because he knew what it was to have found his own way from nothing to something.

Although many of my father's stories about himself are unverifiable, the FBI records provide evidence that some of his self-mythologizing was nearly accurate, especially when it came to his strange military career. The song he sang when we waded out to sea was true; my father did in fact join the Navy—four weeks after he joined the Army. His Naval commission was being processed when he was drafted by the Army, and nothing could be done in time to speed up the Navy or reason with the Army, into which he was inducted at Fort Meade on November 6, 1943, as a private, at age thirty-three. He was issued all the standard uniforms and gear, had the usual medical evaluations and received all requisite vaccinations, and then he went through the first weeks of basic training. When his Navy commission came through, he was honorably discharged from the Army, on December 6, 1943, so that he could immediately be commissioned into the Naval Reserve as a lieutenant (junior grade).

My father was unable to persuade the Navy doctors that, having just received full vaccinations from the Army, it was unnecessary and in fact undesirable for him to have the identical vaccinations all over again, and so he had to submit to a full course of duplicate injections. Plagued all his life by a painfully dysfunctional gut, he would often blame the Army and the Navy for having made him "sensitive." On the other hand, he got to keep all of his free GI gear, and in my childhood he would brag about how he had gotten something for nothing from the Army. He was especially proud of his indestructible two-buckle Army combat boots, which he wore on those weekends of work on my playhouse with Jake LaMotta, gleefully mentioning their provenance each time he put them on. The shaving mirror from his Army kit was the perfect duck pond for my model farm when I set it up on the Ping-Pong table. My mother sent me off to Girl Scout camp with his corroded Army canteen, which gave water a taste like mildewed canvas.

Why was Sidney Kaufman cleared for a Navy commission, and, subsequently, work in the Office of War Information (producing radio broadcasts for the armed services), and work in the Office of Strategic Services (making training and propaganda films), if the FBI had by then spent eight years amassing a file about his activities and links to the Communist Party? It's possible he simply slipped through, owing to the volume of wartime security clearances. Perhaps because he was processed by the Army and then the Navy, each branch of the service assumed the other had performed the background check. Or perhaps Hoover's FBI didn't share this sort of information with the armed services.

Having first become the object of FBI interest in 1936 because he was accused of conveying Soviet propaganda in the guise of a movie review on the radio, it is no small irony that during the war my father was employed in the OWI and the OSS creating and disseminating propaganda.

In my childhood, a significant number of my father's friends and associates were left-leaning people with whom he had worked in the OSS. In his FBI records, many of those OSS contacts are identified as subjects with their own files, under investigation for suspected sympathy to Communism if not actual membership in the Communist Party. One of my father's OSS cronies with an FBI dossier of his own was the journalist Harold Weisberg, a onetime State Department intelligence analyst. While he wrote stories for the *Wilmington Morning News* and the *Philadelphia Ledger,* he and his wife, Lil, ran a poultry farm in rural Maryland. He believed that the FBI was watching him, and this is confirmed by numerous reports in my father's records whenever "[name redacted], see BUfile # [redacted], a journalist and chicken farmer living in Frederick, Maryland," visited our house. He also believed that the government was deliberately sending military flights at low altitudes over his farm in order to make his chickens nervous and reduce their egg productivity, thereby damaging his livelihood.

Harold Weisberg often stayed in our Forest Hills house for weeks at a time while researching what became his obsession, the assassination of John F. Kennedy and the multitude of errors and omissions in the Warren Commission Report. While America mourned, in my house this terrible event was discussed with irritable cynicism from the first hour. The day of the Kennedy assassination, my third-grade class had been listening to a music appreciation program on the radio, which was interrupted with the news from Dallas that the president had been shot. Sam Kandel, the boy who sat in front of me for much of elementary school because of the alphabet, said he was sure President Kennedy was probably only shot in the leg. A moment later there was an announcement over the PA system sending us all home twenty minutes early. I ran home, crying without really knowing why, because all the teachers and the crossing guard lady on Ascan Avenue were crying, and found my father, who was agitated but not sad like everyone else, watching Walter Cronkite on television saying that word had just come, the President of the United States is dead, President Kennedy is dead.

Walter Cronkite kept taking off his black-framed eyeglasses, which were just like my father's, and then putting them back on again. My father declared with vehemence, "I won't be surprised when that son of a bitch Lyndon Johnson emerges as the mastermind of this." (My father usually erupted with a counter-story in the same way whenever I told him anything I had learned in school. Earlier in the week, when I had described my part in the third-grade Thanksgiving play, he had told me the Pilgrims gave smallpox-infested blankets to the Indians. I learned years later that he was wrong, though there were smallpox blankets used during the French and Indian War.) Our housekeeper, Kitty, was crying in the kitchen and I went in there to sit on her lap and we listened to the radio together.

The first of Harold Weisberg's many books on the Kennedy assassination, which he self-published in 1965 when no mainstream imprint would touch it, was *Whitewash: The Report on the Warren Commission Report*. An obtuse and colorless writer obsessed with facts, he was dogged and thorough if nothing else, and is still regarded as the "dean of assassination researchers." Although I disliked his perpetual soggy cigar and its aroma, which wafted at dawn from the attic bedroom where he stayed and worked, I liked Harold. Owlish behind his round glasses, he took me seriously, and would ask me respectful questions about the imaginary families I drew with the grease pencils he brought me each time he came to stay in our house. While Harold was around, he would sit with me on days when I came home from my nearby elementary school for lunch. While I ate my sandwich and drank my milk, we chatted about his theories about the grassy knoll, the possible second gunman, Lee Harvey Oswald's murder of Officer Tippit, and the missing three frames of the Zapruder film.

In our correspondence shortly before he died at eighty-eight in 2002, he told me that those metal tins of grease pencils he gave me each time he visited, being too broke to have anything else in hand when he came to stay in our house for weeks at a time, were leftovers from a large supply he had stolen from the OSS.

MY FATHER lived like a spy. But the closest Sidney Kaufman ever came to anything resembling a Top Secret mission was an

OSS project in 1944 that turned into a comedy of misunder-
standings. Harold Weisberg confirmed the story exactly the way
my father told it: In the middle of the night, Sidney Kaufman
was dragged out of bed and arrested by military police connected to the G-2 War Department staff, charged with the trea-
sonous offense of carelessly leaving the very highest level of Top
Secret documents lying in plain sight on his desk. He attempted
to explain that these documents were in fact props for a training
film on the correct procedures for handling and safeguarding
Top Secret documents. The documents were merely ordinary
maps and aerial photographs of a shopping center in Van Nuys,
California, all without any wartime significance whatsoever,
which had simply been stamped with the Top Secret designation for use as props in the training film.

Just look at them—it's obvious that these are not actual Top
Secret documents, my father reasoned with the arresting offi-
cers who had handcuffed him while he was still in his pajamas.
You'll see right away that these maps and photos are just movie
props, not Top Secret documents at all. This outrageous suggestion was out of the question and in fact constituted a further
security breach. He should have known the arresting offi-
cers were not cleared to look at documents with this officially
stamped designation! My father was taken to a holding cell, and
it was the next afternoon before someone with sufficiently high
rank and security clearance could be located to look at the prop
documents and authorize his release.

Another OSS story verified to me by Harold Weisberg concerned a training film about ship maneuver strategies to avoid
mined harbors. The film was shot in the Chesapeake Bay in
1944, with a Navy ship zigzagging on cue as if entering and
leaving potentially mined waters. The film was in the process of
being edited when Sidney was in New York soon after, visiting

his parents in Brooklyn. He passed by the Brooklyn Navy Yard, and seeing Navy ships maneuvering in the harbor, had the idea to stop and shoot some additional authentic footage for the training film with the 16 mm. camera he happened to have with him.

Both the Williamsburg and the Manhattan Bridges had pedestrian walkways which would ordinarily have provided the perfect vantage point, but for precisely this reason, these had been covered, for wartime security. He found his way instead to an adjacent waterfront pier, and as he stood on the pier filming the Navy vessels, a small military plane flew low overhead, circled around, and buzzed over him again, even lower. It circled back, and this time, as it flew even lower, a sandbag was dropped perilously close by. As my father put away his camera and began to backtrack to his car, a military Jeep rolled up, and two soldiers detailed to patrol the Navy Yard demanded to see his identification.

Sidney wasn't in uniform, but his OSS badge quickly identified him, and the two soldiers both started to laugh. What the hell was that sandbag? Sidney asked them. Who was the genius in charge of that maneuver? He could have killed me! The soldiers told him he should leave immediately or he would be killed, in fact. That was Rear Admiral Monroe Kelly who dropped the sandbag, and he had radioed the shipyard's security office from the air to say he was going to kill the son of a bitch civilian spying on his shipyard, if he could catch him once his plane landed at Teterboro Airport and he was driven back to Brooklyn.

WHEN THE FBI finally began to release pages of my father's records in a series of mailings to me, I had a number of communications about the material with Harold Weisberg, in letters and phone calls. He anticipated correctly that the FBI had documented my father's affair with Martha Dodd Stern.

Daughter of William Dodd, the American ambassador to Germany between 1933 and 1937, Martha was a divorcée whose romances had already included Carl Sandburg and Thomas Wolfe by the time the Dodd family arrived in Berlin. A pretty young woman of twenty-five with few apparent scruples, she quickly became a Nazi enthusiast, and had at least two love affairs with high-ranking Nazis (one of them was Luftwaffe Colonel General Ernst Udet, Baron Von Richthofen's rival flying ace in World War I).

In her 1939 memoir, *My Years in Germany,* Martha described her giddy delight driving through German streets with her family in their official automobile. "We saw a lot of marching men, in brown uniforms, singing and shouting and waving their flags. . . . The excitement of the people was contagious, and I 'Heiled' as vigorously as any Nazi. . . . I felt like a child, ebullient and careless, the intoxication of the new regime working like wine in me."

Martha's introduction to Adolf Hitler was arranged by Ernst Hanfstaengl, a German businessman with an American mother who moved back and forth easily between his American Sedgwick and German Hanfstaengl worlds. The son of a renowned art publisher, Ernst was an intimate of many in the Third Reich's inner circle. He was eager for Martha to meet Hitler, saying, "Hitler needs a woman. Hitler should have an American woman—a lovely woman could change the whole destiny of Europe. Martha, you are the woman!"

The day of her introduction to the Führer, Martha prepared to charm him. "Since I was appointed to change the history of Europe, I decided to dress in my most demure and intriguing best—which always appeals to the Germans: they want their women to be seen and not heard, and then seen only as appendages of the splendid male they accompany—with a veil and a flower and a pair of very cold hands."

Although she later distanced herself from her early enthusiasms for the Third Reich, she was aglow at her encounter with Hitler, who kissed her hand twice. Reflecting back on this encounter, Martha wrote, "Hitler's eyes were startling and unforgettable—they seemed pale blue in colour, were intense, unwavering, hypnotic. Certainly the eyes were his only distinctive feature. They could contain fury and fanaticism and cruelty; they could be mystic and tearful and challenging. This particular afternoon he was excessively gentle and modest in his manners. Unobtrusive, communicative, informal, he had a certain quiet charm, almost a tenderness of speech and glance. . . ."

When Hitler didn't call or write, Martha grew disillusioned with the Third Reich and set about changing the history of Europe in a different way. Her next boyfriend, Boris Vinogradov, was a Soviet intelligence official stationed in Berlin. Martha quickly became a Soviet agent working on assignment for the NKVD, the secret police agency that became the KGB, passing embassy secrets to the Russians until she left Germany.

Back in New York at the end of 1937, when her father's diplomatic appointment ended, Martha was assigned to the Soviet Station there and given the code name LIZA. She also met Sidney Kaufman within days of her return; possibly they were introduced by the German playwright and political activist Ernst Toller, with whom my father worked on several unrealized film projects. Martha and Sidney were soon living together in his penthouse apartment at One Sheridan Square. Harold told me that my father boasted to him about Martha waking up in his bed on the day of her wedding to Alfred K. Stern, which took place in September 1938.

During the war, Martha Dodd is believed to have recruited individuals in the OSS for the Soviets. She was an active Soviet agent until 1953, when the Sterns (Martha had recruited Alfred, who also became Soviet agent) fled the U.S. to avoid arrest. They had liquidated all their assets and were clearly never coming back. They lived the rest of their lives in Communist countries, with an interlude in Cuba. Martha died in Prague in 1990.

My father's FBI records include a memo to Hoover dated January 30, 1956, concerning letters of December 1955 that had been omitted from a report out of concern that the contents could jeopardize "the Mocase." This was the Bureau name for the case they were building against the Soviet espionage ring of that name, which would culminate in indictments in 1957. The ring had included Martha Dodd Stern and Alfred Stern until they fled in 1953, as well as Jack and Myra Soble, who were both sent to prison in 1957. The Sidney Kaufman memo reads:

Referenced San Francisco letters set forth that the subject and MORROS have entered into a business deal in which KAUFMAN will buy from MORROS, the American distribution rights to the picture "Night in Venice" for $2,500. In Yugoslavia, KAUFMAN paid $1,000 down for the film.

While in Yugoslavia, KAUFMAN advised MORROS that at one time KAUFMAN had been the common-law husband of MARTHA DODD. He said he had lived with her and had slept with her for about a year and a half in New York City. MORROS asked if it were true that DODD was a Communist. KAUFMAN stated that it was not true; that she was a Leftist. She didn't know. She was very poor and was sex crazy. MORROS noted that KAUFMAN always called MARTHA DODD by that name and never by her married name.

A subsequent 1956 memo to Hoover concerning Sidney Kaufman follows up on his Martha Dodd connection with a report on a strange turn of events that took place two months after her marriage to Alfred Stern:

The 11/23/38 issue of "Variety" magazine, a New York theatrical publication, on page four, reported that "SIDNEY KAUFMAN, film and radio scripter, last week served summons answerable in the NY Supreme Court on ALFRED K. STERN . . . alleging he was badly assaulted by STERN without provocation in the public offices of Metro last Wednesday (16th). KAUFMAN, who headquarters in the MGM Press Department, is demanding $25,000 damages. STERN refused to comment on the complaint thus far. He recently married MARTHA DODD, daughter of ex-Ambassador (to Germany) WILLIAM E. DODD."

. . . The complaint alleged on 11/15/38 Defendant STERN entered the premises on 1540 Broadway, third floor, whereat he assaulted the plaintiff and used violent abusive names. The plaintiff was seeking $25,000 damages. The defendant's attorney made various motions for dismissal of the complaint in particular alleging that the suit should have been brought in New York County (Manhattan) rather than in Kings County (Brooklyn) because of the fact that the plaintiff did not reside in Kings County. In answer to this motion KAUFMAN filed an affidavit in which he alleged that he did reside at 1150 Bedford Avenue, Brooklyn, and was employed on the faculty of the New School for Social Research, that he had only temporary residence at the Barbizon Plaza Hotel and also at 1 Sheridan Square, both Manhattan. KAUFMAN alleged further that his legal voting address was 1150 Bedford Avenue.

By order of the court the action was transferred to New York County, and subsequently it was discontinued on stipulation of both parties to the action on 3/10/41.

ALFRED K. STERN is a principal in the MoCase (Bufile 100-202315).

Had Stern just learned of Martha's involvement with my father up to and including their wedding day, or had there been another, more recent liaison? What else could possibly have prompted the assault on my father?

MY FATHER joined the Navy, but he didn't see the world. His entire military service during the war was stateside. He didn't leave American soil until 1955, the year of my birth. His passport application for travel to Belgrade and Berlin that summer, to obtain North American distribution rights for a number of Yugoslavian films, was the subject of numerous memos and reports in his FBI records. First he was denied a passport because they thought he was the other Sidney Kaufman, and then, when that confusion was addressed, he was investigated further because FBI surveillance of his meetings with his attorney had brought to light his plan to meet with Berthold Brecht's widow (the FBI called him "Barthold Bracht, a Communist writer") in Berlin.

Boris Morros, a Paramount producer, had become a Soviet agent (codename, FROST) in 1934. He became a counterspy informing to the FBI in 1947. This question about Martha being a Communist was clearly a test to see if Sidney knew she was working for the Soviets. But it is also possible that Sidney, who met with Morros in Yugoslavia in 1955 in the course of his first travel outside the United States (the trip that was cut short by my birth in November), did in fact know that she was not just a Communist but was also an actual spy. Perhaps he was feigning ignorance to Morros, whom he presumably did not suspect of being a Soviet agent, let alone a counterspy reporting to the FBI.

Morros knew perfectly well the answer to his question about Martha, given that he had first met with her and Alfred at their Ridgefield, Connecticut, home in December of 1943 in order to obtain funding in the form of a $130,000 investment from the Sterns, to finance the Boris Morros Music Company, a sheet music publishing venture that would serve as a front for espionage activities. Stern ran the office, where they were able to give legitimate employment to other Soviet agents in New York. It didn't go well. They quarreled when Morros published sheet music for the hit song "Chattanooga ChooChoo" over Stern's objections (he really didn't like the name of the song). The company was disbanded, but because Morros paid Stern back $100,000 of his investment, the Soviets took this as a sign of Morros's integrity, and he was able to continue to operate as a double agent. Ultimately it was the information he passed on to his FBI handlers that led to the indictment of the Sterns.

Boris Morros led a vertiginous life. A talented musician in Russia, he was Piatigorsky's first cello teacher. At Paramount he was a musical director for nearly a hundred movies and worked with many Paramount stars, Bing Crosby among them. Films he produced include *Second Chorus* (1940) with Fred Astaire and Paulette Goddard, and the 1939 Laurel and Hardy movie *Flying Deuces*. His *Night in Venice* deal with Sidney ran aground when it became apparent that Boris did not actually own the rights to the film, and unlike the Sterns, Sidney did not get his money back until many threats of legal action led to a settlement. Forever after that, Sidney referred to Boris as "a swindler."

I well remember struggling when I was a child to take

telephone messages whenever Boris Morros called the house looking for my father. His thick Russian accent made it difficult for me to write down phone numbers accurately, and I was too embarrassed to ask him to repeat himself more than once. Was "vun" the same thing as "one"? "I am heppy to give you numbers to write down," he would say. "You hev pin? Vunderful." Ironically enough, I imagined I was speaking to Boris Badenov, the Russian spy from *Rocky and Bullwinkle*.

HAROLD WEISBERG also told me that in the late 1950s my father had an affair with Moura Budberg, aka Countess Budberg, aka Maria Ignatievna Zakrevskaya, aka Countess Benckendorff, aka the Baroness von Budberg-Bönningshausen. The FBI references her twice in my father's records. She was thought to be a double agent for both the Soviets and for British intelligence. Known for her affairs with Maxim Gorky and H. G. Wells, she was a screenwriter and a literary agent in London. Sidney introduced her to Harold Weisberg, whose assassination books she represented in Europe, though their business was severely hampered because almost every piece of mail they exchanged was either damaged by tampering or vanished altogether. Purely coincidentally, when my husband and I went to the village of Glandore in County Cork on our honeymoon in 1976, we stayed in a flat adjacent to Shorecliffe House, presided over at the time by a marvelous Danish woman, Estrid Good, whom my husband had come to know when his parents had rented a cottage from her three years before. The flat where we spent those two weeks was called "The Dacha," an unusual designation in West Cork. Estrid explained that she had built it for her good friend Moura Budberg, who intended to retire to Glandore, but Moura had died in 1974, before construction was completed.

✧ ◆ ✧

BEYOND THE vague beliefs asserted by all the redacted informants that he was a Communist sympathizer, according to FBI records, Sidney Kaufman was named by at least three actual Soviet agents—Boris Morros, Elizabeth Bentley, and Jacob Golos—as "an individual sympathetic to the CP and otherwise connected to individuals, organizations, or activities connected to the CP." Memos concerning the FBI investigations of Joris Ivens (a Dutch filmmaker and left-wing activist) and Harry Magdoff (a political activist thought to have been a Soviet agent, one of the Perlo Group) note that my father appeared in the address books belonging to both. Sidney Kaufman's ability to create a false aura of authority and engagement was apparently persuasive even to Soviet agents.

The FBI had yet another preoccupation with my father. In 1955, consequent to that same first trip to Yugoslavia, a man who had struck a distribution deal with my father died unexpectedly. In lieu of payment, for some strange reason, he was offered 1,700 East German typewriters. The question of just what exactly Sidney Kaufman was doing with these typewriters threads through the FBI's Kaufman memos over a period of years. What was he up to? Was he trying to sell them without having legally imported them? Given that the "Made in East Zone of Germany—USSR occupied, Rhine Metal" stamp on the back was not a selling feature in the United States in 1955, was he removing these labels? If so, "This, of course, is a violation of the Tariff Act of 1930, coming under the primary investigative jurisdiction of the FBI inasmuch as the typewriters have been cleared from customs."

He gave ten typewriters to the office of the Yugoslavian consulate. Why? "Subject told NEEDLEMAN he hoped they would like them and want to buy more." The 1,700 typewriters of Sidney Kaufman, like *The Five Hundred Hats of Bartholomew Cubbins,* were a feature of my childhood. They filled our garage to capacity, and there they rusted solid in the unheated damp, forming a massive connected structure like a coral reef. Mildew flourished on the few remaining ribbed gray plastic cases that hadn't rotted off the portable Buromarchinen Rhein Work Mattal Schreibmaschines. Sometimes I would pry one of these typewriters off the pile and reach into its guts and grab the keys and bend them in a savage twist. The keys were soft and bent very easily, which was another reason nobody wanted these typewriters, for which replacement parts were permanently unavailable. The QWERTZU instead of QWERTY keyboards made them all the more useless.

THERE IS a marvelous rubber-stamped list of names of FBI personnel to whom copies of the Kaufman documents were circulated. This was their work; this is what they got up every day to do—process this Confidential, Classified, Secret, and Top Secret information about my father. I like to imagine them, sitting at their desks, typewriters clacking and phones ringing in the background, like a newsroom. There is much to do, fresh reports on the Subject: Sidney Kaufman to pore over, there is new information gathered by SA [redacted] or reported by "[redacted], an informant who has in the past furnished us with reliable information" (or even better, information provided by the occasional "[redacted], an informant who has in the past furnished us with reliable and unreliable information"). Presumably there were reports written about these reports. Individuals must have been assigned to analyze and come to conclusions about the information that had been so painstakingly compiled about the Subject:

Sidney Kaufman. Meetings must have occurred, decisions must have been made about further interviews with informants reliable and unreliable, and all those pretext phone calls must have been scripted and scheduled. And all of the reports were typed up, copied, circulated, and filed with all the other accumulated Sidney Kaufman information.

By the late sixties, the rubber-stamped copy list had been streamlined to simple names, but I must admit to a preference for the more traditional earlier iterations, when each name is given the honorific "Mr.," and then there is the culminating, superb "Miss Gandy." This list of names reads:

Mr. Tolson	*Mr. Rosen*
Mr. Boardman	*Mr. Tamm*
Mr. Nichols	*Mr. Sizoo*
Mr. Belmont	*Mr. Winterrowd*
Mr. Harbo	*Tele. Room*
Mr. Mohr	*Mr. Holloman*
Mr. Parsons	*Miss Gandy*

I really love this list, which changes only slightly through the years of documentation of Sidney Kaufman's activities. It is a sequence of names rich in possibility, yet, seeing it repeat throughout the pages of these files, it becomes reliable and familiar, like a wallpaper pattern or a melody. The names, when seen again and again, start to have a delightful rhythm and inevitability that invite memorization, like the presidents of the United States, or Latin declensions.

The roster of FBI employees who were copied on the steady flow of classified information about Sidney Kaufman over all those years is intriguing. Clyde Tolson was Associate Director of the FBI and J. Edgar Hoover's sidekick. Lou Nichols and

Alan H. Belmont were Assistant Directors. John P. Mohr was head of five FBI divisions; he was the number-three man after Tolson in FBI hierarchy. Alex P. Rosen was the FBI supervisor on the John Dillinger case and on the Lindbergh baby kidnapping. Joseph A. Sizoo was in the Domestic Intelligence Division. E. A. Tamm was an Associate FBI Director. Frank C. Holloman was a supervisor in the FBI Headquarters in the Crime Records Section, the Fugitive Desk, Plant Survey Section, Special Intelligence Section, Informant Section, and the Records Division.

"Miss Gandy" was Helen W. Gandy, J. Edgar Hoover's ferocious and devoted executive assistant for fifty-four years. It is known that over a period of months following his death in 1972, she destroyed tens of thousands of pages of his "personal" files thought to contain the fruits of illegal wiretaps and a vast array of incriminating information about numerous public figures and government officials and their family members, as well as detailed reports from the spies Hoover maintained in every White House administration. Her devotion to the FBI and J. Edgar Hoover was that of a nun's devotion to the Church and the Pope. Their relationship was decidedly odd; Hoover never once called her by her first name. Her mother was painted by Thomas Eakins.

J. Edgar Hoover is not on this list, because just about every document in my father's files is a memo to The Director. The FBI surveillance of Sidney Kaufman, which began in 1936 and apparently ended in 1972, spanned almost the identical years of Hoover's FBI directorship.

Having opened a file on Sidney Kaufman because of a movie review on the radio deemed covert Communist propaganda by an informant (though two decades later in my father's files this informant was deemed "unreliable"), having continued to gather information about him because they thought he was a different Sidney Kaufman, and then, having been excited by his associations with known and suspected subversives, the FBI pursued my father for all those years in the hope of amassing sufficient information either to catch him in a prosecutable offense or to use his testimony in a prosecution.

The FBI did not understand my father at all. Like so many people in the course of his life, they made the mistake of taking Sidney Kaufman literally. They were persistent in their attempts to make sense of his illogical behavior, which probably invited further observation and analysis simply because it was so strange and inexplicable. Most of my father's movie career took place at the intersection of making it and making it up.

Because the FBI didn't understand the main character in their story—a novel cannot succeed if the author doesn't know what the main character wants and what he does or fails to do to get what he wants—their Sidney Kaufman story has no narrative arc. Nothing happens. It's a failure. Apparently, it never occurred to the FBI that my father's actions might be pointless or pie-in-the-sky or even just crazy, and so they were always frustrated by their unimaginative, literal interpretations of his mercurial plans, his unsubstantiated claims, his inconsistencies, and his crackpot schemes. All his life, my father gave people the impression (and was desperate to believe it himself) that he was successful, prosperous, made things happen, and knew what he was talking about. The FBI fell for his chimerical authority, too. Nowhere in all those pages of FBI intelligence on Sidney Kaufman is there any indication of awareness that most of his activity was gesture and flourish. Not once did any memo to J. Edgar Hoover suggest that maybe he wasn't up to anything at all other than being Sidney Kaufman. Because he was never publicly named in testimony or ever called to testify, my father wasn't even blacklisted by the studios. He was too unimportant.

MY FATHER took himself very seriously. Throughout his life, he believed that he was on the verge of fulfilling his intention to do great things. From his first Hollywood job at age seventeen, the summer after his freshman year at Cornell, when he hitchhiked to Hollywood from New York with a letter of introduction in his pocket to Walt Disney from a classmate's father, he had a plan to take the world by storm. When things didn't work out—and things very rarely worked out—it was never his fault, and he was always the hero, if also the victim, of the story.

My father always claimed that he went to Disney's office the day he arrived, and over sandwiches Disney offered him a job, if he would work for very little money but a significant share in Disney's fledgling company. But the scholarship kid born in the back of a grocery store in Brooklyn to immigrant parents couldn't take a job that didn't pay, plus he wanted to complete his college education (he didn't), plus, maybe it never actually happened exactly this way anyway. In later years my father always characterized Walt Disney as a fascist and an anti-Semite, and I was rarely allowed to see Disney movies. I was made to feel that my not seeing *The Absent-Minded Professor* would show Walt a thing or two about his anti-Semitism.

Instead of the phantom Disney career, my father's first Hollywood job consisted of writing subtitles for the last Hoot Gibson silent movies. The next two summers, he hitchhiked and rode freight trains west in order to work on various projects at MGM, Paramount, Columbia, or RKO, returning to Cornell by thumb or boxcar each autumn, until he abruptly left college at the start of his senior year, owing to a murky incident involving a romantic involvement with a professor's daughter and a humiliating confrontation with a dean who scolded him with the words, "But you must never forget that you are a Jew!" It is not clear if he was actually forced to leave, as he claimed, or if he was so affronted he withdrew, or if there is another way to tell this story that I will never know.

The earliest films of Sidney Kaufman's first production company, Realfilms, were industrial shorts for clients such as the New York City subway system. Among his documentaries of this period are the intriguing titles *The New South, Timing for Profit,* and *The Main Shape Arises.* (There is no record about the subject of any of these, but the last title was derived from Whitman's *Leaves of Grass.*)

My father was remarkably well-read. Neither of his Yiddish-speaking parents was ever fully literate in English, but at an early age he immersed himself in the two leather-bound sets of "literature" his father had brought home as the consequence of a barter with a customer unable to pay his grocery bill—the complete works of Mark Twain and the complete (translated) works of Honoré de Balzac. My father prided himself on his nearly perfect recall for vast swaths of poetry memorized who knows when— Tennyson, Keats, Shakespeare—which he would unfurl from time to time at moments that would seem obscure until you listened long enough to hear the line that had prompted the oration.

He did in fact rub elbows with various literary Greenwich Village characters, from Maxwell Bodenheim to Clifford Odets, with whom he shared an apartment on West Tenth Street for a few months in 1934. Jacob Sandler, a shambling, Shakespeare-quoting oddball, occasionally slept on their couch and mooched meals, not realizing that Odets was making notes about his colorful speech habits; for example, the way he called tap water "municipal champagne," or the way he exclaimed when he hit his head or stubbed his toe, "It's a cosmic frame-up!" My father would become helpless with laughter each time he described Sandler's rambling locutions. Both lines are uttered by a hapless dentist in Odets's 1938 play, *Rocket to the Moon.*

"Professor" Irwin Corey, "The World's Foremost Authority," was another babbling genius in this circle, though my father first met him in a boxcar on the way to California in the summer of 1927. Corey's comic erudition was a mockery of the very sort of self-important pomposity with which Sidney Kaufman was trying to make a name for himself.

The cover story for the November 1938 issue of *Theater Arts Monthly,* Sidney Kaufman's assessment of the coming film season in the context of the world on the brink of war, begins with characteristic grandiloquence that could have been dropped right into an Irwin Corey routine:

History has mobilized its own cast of heavies, and their shadows complicate the action that will be seen on the screen during the coming season. The shadows themselves will not appear; for the world of movies is a world of dream in which symbols masquerade in any guise other than their own. But they will be lurking presences in the atmosphere. They are the chief problem of the season. . . . Time drives a plowshare of ruin through the dreams of man; the furrow between truth and the credo of the screen has become too broad to span.

My father loved seeing himself as a rising star, someone who counted, and in these years he was especially eager to be present at events where show business and politics intersected. In

Hollywood again in the late spring of 1937, having been introduced to Lee and Ira Gershwin by his girlfriend of the moment, the German screenwriter Irmgard Von Cube, my father met George Gershwin at gatherings at Lee and Ira's Roxbury Drive house on several occasions, including a fund-raiser tea in June, hosted by Lee and Ira, at which the labor activist Tom Mooney spoke. Later that same month, when the German playwright Ernst Toller's wife, Christiane, was hospitalized at Cedars of Lebanon Hospital with a kidney infection, my father visited her and discovered that George Gershwin was in the room next to hers.

Gershwin was being evaluated for the terrible headaches and malaise that had rendered him dysfunctional and were actually symptoms of the advancing, undiagnosed brain tumor that had been slowly killing him for a long while. Gershwin was released on June 26, after three days of testing, during which time his brain tumor was not recognized. He would soon die, on July 11, after falling into a coma and undergoing emergency brain surgery far too late to save him. Christiane was very ill, and Ernst, with whom my father collaborated on two screenplays that were never produced, was anxious that she not spend time alone in her hospital room. My father spelled him, visiting her each of those three days of George's useless hospitalization, and each time he saw her, he sat at George's bedside and visited him as well. It is impossible to know if Gershwin welcomed these visits from someone he barely knew, or slept through them.

MY FATHER's devotion to pursuing women was much more successful than his efforts to produce good movies. While he was loved and admired by a series of smart, beautiful women throughout his life, his film career was a chronicle of failure, absurdity, and obscurity. Sidney Kaufman's greatest invention

was the story of Sidney Kaufman, produced and directed by
Sidney Kaufman, narrated by Sidney Kaufman, screenplay
by Sidney Kaufman (with additional dialogue by the Federal
Bureau of Investigation), starring Sidney Kaufman. By the end
of his life, my father had become the sort of man he himself
would once have derided as an unprincipled opportunist, a
poseur whose choices led him to unhappiness and destruction.
The passionate young man who taught himself English from
Balzac and Twain and had a plan to write magnificent novels of
ideas, the morally outraged Sidney Kaufman who led anti-Nazi
demonstrations in 1936—he would have mocked and satirized
the man my father became, in a story with an unsubtle moral
lesson about ambition and vanity.

Sidney Kaufman was nobody's idea of a Lothario, but fascinating women were perpetually drawn to him. He thrived
on seeing himself through their adoring eyes. He met Beatrice
Buchman in Hollywood in early 1939 at a Free Spain rally at the
Shrine Auditorium, where Ernst Toller gave a speech. In a 1982
interview about Toller, my father recalled: "That evening, I met
a woman with whom I would spend the next fifteen years. She,
at the time, was married to the head of one of the studios [Sid-
ney Buchman] and was subsequently divorced. . . . Toller used
to refer to her, he knew of this, what was at first a clandestine
relationship; he used to refer to her as the *Gran Prix*. I had really
taken the plum acquisition available in all of Hollywood, more
beautiful than any of the stars, and a very intelligent woman, a
Ph.D. in physics. . . ."

My father believed his romance with Beatrice was a crucial
element in Toller's suicide.

Toller had an extraordinary interest in this relationship
and this girl was naturally very retiring, very shy, and very

uneasy. And she didn't happen to be mad about Toller, although she was politically very aware and very active. She was one of the head figures of the Hollywood Anti-Nazi League and was subsequently persecuted by McCarthy. . . . Beatrice was very uneasy about Toller, and Toller had sort of proprietary interest in our relationship so that she came east in May of '39 and asked me not to inform Toller so that, on her arrival in New York, I disappeared with her for three days. And I returned on Sunday night, the 21st of May, to find twenty-two messages from Toller. During that weekend, he had looked for me and I had deserted him . . . and this has always been a source of extreme unhappiness to me. Of his own fabrication, he had made Beatrice very much aware of the sort of prying and invasive touch and I had assured her that I would not bring them together and took off for that weekend, not realizing Toller's needs at that time. . . . It's not important that I had to have a sequestered weekend in Connecticut when Toller was in such shape . . . the moment I knew the fact the following day that he had killed himself, it was clear to me that I should have known.

In this interview my father referred to Beatrice Buchman as "a woman with whom I would spend the next fifteen years," but my childhood nocturnal letter-reading sessions in the attic—those letters no longer exist, and it is likely that my mother disposed of them, probably unread, when she cleared the house after my father's death—provided evidence that they were actually involved for at least the next twenty-six years. Which is to say his affair with Beatrice, which began in 1939, continued through his Martha Dodd affair, his first marriage to Fran Heflin, and during the first fifteen years of his marriage to my mother.

❖ ◆ ❖

HILARIOUSLY ENOUGH, the FBI failed to take notice when, the following year, the American Communist Party commissioned Sidney Kaufman to direct a documentary about Camp Wo-Chi-Ca (Workers Children's Camp), one of the first interracial summer camps in the country. (Racial themes would be one of the few common threads running through much of my father's film career.) Operating in New Jersey between 1935 and 1954 (when it was closed by a combination of McCarthyism and fear of polio), it was a Communist Party–sponsored camp that hosted visiting artists such as Paul Robeson, Pete Seeger, and Paul Draper.

Meanwhile, from 1934 to 1941, my father was giving lectures on film at the New School for Social Research. In these years he also led a series of onstage conversations with actors and writers in Joseph Urban's new and dramatic Easter egg auditorium—Ernst Toller and Clifford Odets among them—in a format much like James Lipton's televised *Inside the Actor's Studio* onstage interviews. After the war, he was on the inaugural faculty of the New School's film department, which was created in 1947 as part of Erwin Piscator's Dramatic Workshop. A *New York Times* article that appeared on September 14 of that year described the head of this new department: "Mr. Kaufman, besides being a film critic, has had long experience as a director and producer of documentary films and before that worked for many of the large Hollywood studios as a title writer in the silent days." Other faculty for the new film department included Bil Baird, the creator of the Snarky Parker puppet films, and, according to the *Times* story, "Andrea S. Warburg, associate editor of *Film News*." (I will never know the context for some colorful vividly pornographic cartoon drawings, dedicated to my mother, by Bil Baird, which I found in her papers after her death.)

But my mother never taught at the New School or anywhere else. There is no record, either, that there was a publication called *Film News,* for which she was allegedly an associate editor, though she did work as a secretary to the head of the National Board of Review of Motion Pictures, a nonprofit organization that might have had a newsletter with that name.

The National Board of Review of Motion Pictures was created by a consortium of movie theater owners to oppose censorship imposed by the New York City mayor in 1909, though in many ways it could be said that the purpose of the National Board of Review has been, from then to now, a kind of censorship itself. My mother had no particular interest in film; she got the job through the secretarial school where she had gone to learn shorthand and touch typing (she was always very proud of her fast and accurate typing, just as she was inordinately proud of her impressive card-shuffling skills and her whistling proficiency), so she could find employment after divorcing her first husband, Justin Feldman, in August of 1945, three years into their unsuccessful marriage.

In early 1946, Sidney had meetings with my mother's boss, and he developed the habit of stopping to chat at her desk with the excuse of needing a refill for his fountain pen from her ink bottle. He would empty his pen before his appointments so as to have another excuse to stop at her desk. She never seemed to notice how strange it was that he always needed ink. His perpetual need for ink as a ploy for repeated encounters with my mother was an enactment of his Talmudic question to me about why one never buys ink. Plus, it is a perfect foreshadowing of their marriage. By the time the *New York Times* story about the New School film department appeared, my parents had been dating for a year. It is likely that my father simply added her to the roster to pad the department assets, give her a credential, and impress the *Times* writer.

The summer before, having left the OSS and returned to civilian life, when Andrea had departed New York to spend the summer with her mother, who was by then living in a house in Benedict Canyon, in Los Angeles, Sidney wrote to her from a borrowed house in Bay Shore, Long Island. He was staying there with his friend and colleague, the Hungarian screenwriter Geza Herczeg, who knew "every Hungarian in America worth knowing." They had been working together to make a movie based on the four Minsky brothers and their burlesque theaters, an abiding fascination of my father's.

Bay Shore, Long Island
27 July, 1946
My very dear,

You saw the start of the series of events that led to this weekend. Until yesterday, the plan was that Geza Herczeg and I would work here on the Minsky story. We had contracts drawn and publicity prepared—then suddenly some violence flared between the Minskys and Diamond and quite properly too because Samson [Samson Diamond, a producer] on closer inspection reveals himself an unmitigated scoundrel. . . .

The plans having been set, we came here anyway. This is a hideaway of a dame who is now in Hollywood. A wildly improbable creature, one of those exotic international tarts who has, at 24, been through innumerable marriages and amours, and built a career on swindle, blackmail, whoring, and publicity. She is the sister of Eva Gabor, a parallel character. The house is a madness of sturdy American colonial exterior, neglected grounds, and an interior that includes

pony skin rugs, ermine picture frames, large, blow-up scan-
dalous stories from tabloids everywhere in many tongues
framed in the boudoir. Here in the lady's own bed I lie as I
write you, surrounded by mementos of her triumphs, gifts,
books, hangings, all addressed to "ZsaZsa,:" and that is the
creature's name. She holds a card at the Riviera Beach Club
and we swim and dine there in fine style.

Geza has been handing me stories of his to appreciate.
Too many of them are about actresses and the deep *interplay*
between role and life. I can understand the basis of the suc-
cess of such stuff in Hollywood for it evades all connection
with reality and substitutes a profound gratification; to be a
talented, rich glamorous actress and to play with living and
to make it jibe with the part one plays—Balkan diplomacy
of yore. Today the papers carry the summaries of the Nurem-
berg trial and it seems like a ritual of primitive tribesmen
that a few Nazis are being offered up as sacrifice for the ills
of Europe. The world is terribly sick and now that the war is
over Europe is not better. The rottenness has survived and the
death of these few insects will not better it—just make us *feel*
better for the propitiatory gesture. We are so concerned that
the cultural heritage of Europe shall survive. Yet it is precisely
there that the disease is most virulent. The only wholesome-
ness in all of Europe is in the peasantry and the proletari-
ans, too poor, too simple, too degraded by the weight of their
history, to have suffered the infection. And our great ones,
our Byrnes [James F. Byrnes, Secretary of State] and Con-
nally [Senator Thomas Connally from Texas] and Vanden-
berg [Senator Arthur H. Vandenberg from Michigan] and
Dulles [John Foster Dulles, an early Hitler enthusiast and a
staunch anti-Communist, at this time an advisor to Vanden-
berg], dancing their hollow rites on this misery, muttering

more tribal gibberish. Germany where the fever ran highest is ready for health and what do we offer? Enslavement, political blind alleys, impossible nostrums covered over by names we always use to conceal swindles. The "American way of life" is the fruit of an abundant economy that we mined, a treasurehouse that we inherited when the older lands were impoverished by the burden of centuries. The Soviet Union with all its hardness and retribution offers a future, a continent organized to function—the Germans will grab at such an offer. We are angry and puzzled. For we are a people whose culture reaches its zenith in this exotic algebra, equating an actress's role with her amours. . . .

I am getting to work. I will let you know how it goes. Be easy about me. I miss you. Your friendly touch grows unnoticed, but it is dear and pervasive and becomes a strong twining in the evening hours.

For I love you
Sidney

A month later, with his work opportunities no further developed, he wrote her again, with a rare tone of unguarded introspection:

Once again, all the brave schemes and immediate hopes have vanished and I am feeling low about any prospect of immediate business or work. I shall have to resolve this soon, certainly before you return. I always revert to the same decision in the absence of choice, to get out a pencil and set to work. But it just doesn't seem to work out that smoothly for me. I have begun cataloguing all the equivocations, postponements and evasions that I use to elude this effort and some of them hold water, but most are trivial and sorry. I begin to see

*however that they constitute in themselves a good book and
they are indeed part of that novel that I have been gathering
myself for. It will come one day soon. But I am worried about
all this wasted time. . . .*

I have no reason to believe he ever wrote a word of that
novel, nor did he ever write the book he talked about intending
to write for decades, about the effect of the movie screen on our
perceptions of the human face.

WHEN HE was in his mid-twenties, my father apparently told
Clifford Odets that he wanted children. It seems an odd desire
for a young, single man to voice—not saying he wanted a wife
or a family, but specifically, children. A 1936 Modern Library
edition of Gogol's *Dead Souls* with an introduction by Clifford
Odets is one of the few books I have from my father's shelves.
It is inscribed, "For Sidney Kaufman—who is anxious for children. And the answer then becomes marriage. But who or what
to marry is a difficult question. Sidney, pick softly, easily, and
good wishes for the project. Sincerely, Clifford Odets 9/30/36."

"The project" had not gone as planned. My father had also
been married and divorced by the time he met my mother ten
years after Odets wrote his inscription. Who or what he picked,
and apparently not very softly or easily, was the actress Frances
Heflin, Van Heflin's sister. Who names their children Fran and
Van? (Harold Weisberg told me that Lee Harvey Oswald had
been arrested in a movie theater while watching Van Heflin in
Cry of Battle.) She had betrayed Sidney by being "very unfaithful"
(in the words of my mother, who never hesitated to discuss unfaithfulness wherever it occurred with the exception of anything
to do with her own marriage), and then packing up and leaving

without warning one day when Sidney wasn't there, after only a year of marriage. At least that was the way it was told.

Like my mother, Frances Heflin went to Reno for an efficient divorce, which was granted on December 20, 1945. The FBI quotes the Reno filing: "She testified she was on the stage at the time of her marriage and he wanted her to give up her occupation. He was critical and found fault. He was unpleasant to her friends and extremely unsocial."

"On the stage at the time of her marriage" is a reference to Frances Heflin having been in the original cast of the smash Broadway hit *I Remember Mama,* which opened at the Music Box Theater on October 19, 1944, five weeks after she and Sidney were married, and closed on June 29, 1946, six months after her marriage to Sidney had ended in divorce. Nancy Marquand replaced her in the role of Christine in November of 1945, so she could go to Reno for the requisite six weeks of residency before the divorce from Sidney could be granted.

I DIDN'T know about Fran, or Fra, as she was called, until I was fifteen, when I found a wedding ring in the dish on my father's bureau where he kept his cuff links. ("Where have you sequestered my cuff links?" was a question I would often hear my father demand of my mother in his usual baroque fashion— Twain or Balzac?—though it was always a silly question, since she hadn't touched them, and his cuff links were always in that dish unless he had taken them out in order to roll up his sleeves and had left them in a jacket pocket. All his shirts had French cuffs.)

The wedding ring that mysteriously appeared in that dish one day was inscribed inside, "Fra and Sidney, September 9, 1944," and I was dismayed by my mother's irritable explanation of its meaning, not having any inkling that my father had been married to someone else. I had only learned a few months earlier about her first marriage, when I was helping her in her basement darkroom and opened a cupboard while looking for a bottle of hypo, only to encounter a set of twelve dusty highball glasses with the monogram "AWF," which had precipitated the first revelation, that my mother had once been Andrea Warburg Feldman. How many other secret lives did my parents have? What would I find next?

My mother warned me never to mention Fran Heflin to my father, because it was "a bad subject." Then she told me I could see her for myself just about every day by watching the new soap opera *All My Children* on television. I could spy on my father's first wife to my heart's content: She was Mona Kane, Erica Kane's mother. Fran Heflin was now married to the film composer Sol Kaplan, my mother told me one afternoon when she caught me glued to *All My Children* while ostensibly doing homework. "Change of the name but not the letter, change for the worse and not the better," she said triumphantly. Fran Heflin's second husband had more in common with my father than a similar name; Sol Kaplan served in the OSS, and was blacklisted in 1953 for refusing to cooperate with the House Un-American Activities Committee when he was called to testify.

Although her name is always redacted, Frances Heflin is mentioned a number of times in my father's FBI records. (It is public record that they were married and divorced, so there is no logical explanation for the methodical blacking out of her name throughout my father's files, but perhaps the FBI's bureaucratic devotion to redacting the names of informants and other individuals under investigation wherever they occur throughout the hundreds of pages of my father's FBI records accounts for the nine-year delay between my 1992 FOIA request and the release of those records.)

They had no contact after the divorce in 1945, but in a 1956 FBI memo she was characterized in background material on my father: "[redacted], probably short for [redacted], was a member of the CP in Hollywood and a CP member before she came to Hollywood. The informant [redacted], interviewed in 1951 in Los Angeles, felt that [redacted] must have been in sympathy with the CP when she was in NY inasmuch as she lived with RUTH KANIN, whom EMIL THOMAS SEIDEL [an actor and informant whom the FBI forgot to redact on this page] knew to be a Communist."

My father was still teaching film courses intermittently at the New School in 1954, though Erwin Piscator's Dramatic Workshop had lasted from 1939 to 1951, when Piscator returned to Germany. (My father apparently helped himself to quantities of Dramatic Workshop letterhead, because in my baby book there are notes on how many ounces of formula [and, bizarrely, orange juice] I was given in my first weeks of life in November 1955 — I was a colicky baby, and the scribbled schedule is a diary of sleepless nights punctuated by 1½ ounces here, ½ an ounce there—all written on Dramatic Workshop stationery. Some of the drawings I made with Harold Weisberg's stolen OSS wax pencils were on Dramatic Workshop letterhead as well.)

With Bill Smith, the nightclub editor of *Billboard* magazine, my father covered a range of topics in a class called "Show Business: Work in Progress." A deadpan story by Gilbert Millstein in the *New York Times Magazine* on December 5, 1954, featured the day Kaufman and Smith—"modified hipsters"—loaded the class into a bus for a field trip to Minsky's Adam's Theater in Newark to see a burlesque show.

> Kaufman is a pleasant, pudgy man of 44, who produces, directs, and writes technical, educational, and documentary films and is involved in no fewer than eighteen corporations created to serve his various ends. . . . Kaufman handles the philosophical end of show business and Smith the practical, the pair getting along as famously as Buck and Bubbles. Thus Kaufman is in a position to declare, which he does frequently, that show business must be viewed on three levels: the artistic, the commercial, and the social.

Past guest speakers in the classroom at 66 West Twelfth Street had included Kitty Kallen, Mitch Miller, Harry Belafonte, and Sam Levenson, but on this evening at the burlesque house, Millstein writes, "the students leaned forward seriously in their seats drinking in learning. They drank in, among other things, the complicated writhings of strippers named Crystal (More Bounce to the Ounce) Starr and Nony (T.N.T. From Gay Paree); the perfunctory dancing of a buxom chorus; a spray of traditional burlesque blackouts performed by several traditional burlesque comics, and the powerful singing of an uncertain baritone. Later, they were taken on stage to participate in a post-show seminar."

IN A teletype memo to the Director and "SAC Washington Field 3" marked "Urgent," the FBI noted that.

SIDNEY KAUFMAN AND [redacted] DEPARTED NY JAN TWENTYNINTH, FIFTY-EIGHT, AT

APPROXIMATELY TWELVE THIRTY PM ABOARD
QUEEN ELIZABETH F CUNARD SS CO., LTD., BOUND
FOR SOUTHAMPTON, ENGLAND. KAUFMAN AND
[redacted] TRAVELLING CABIN CLASS LOCATED IN C
ONE NINE TWO.

A separate memo documented the different times that
Sidney Kaufman and [redacted] boarded the ship. It seems
pretty clear that the other occupant of cabin C192 was Beatrice.
In January 1958, we had been living in our Forest Hills Gardens
house for just six weeks, having moved there from an apartment
on Steinway Street in Long Island City. My brother was six, I
was two. My mother, alone with us in the new house, isolated
in this suburb without a car, had been married to my father for
less than ten years.

ONE OF my father's film projects, above all others, is exception-
ally memorable and ridiculous. Sidney Kaufman is the man
who brought the world Aromarama. The idea of movies with
aromas had been around for decades, but a feature film with a
smell track the way movies have sound tracks was something
that had never been attempted before. Mike Todd Jr. began production of a film called *Scent of a Mystery,* using a complex and
extremely costly system, Smell-O-Vision, involving the piping of
thirty different chemical scents through little jets under movie
theater seats on cue. These were triggered by special sprockets
at designated points on the sound track on the actual film reels
which corresponding to the scenes meant to be illuminated by
scent, as those frames passed through the projector. Just as certain movies depend on the music to inform an audience about
what is about to happen or has just happened on screen, the

smells in *Scent of a Mystery* were scripted into the story, as the audience was cued to recognize the presence of an off-screen character by the scent of his pipe. The movie was scheduled to open in early January 1960.

In partnership with the theater owner Walter Reade Jr., my father, who had got wind of the Todd project, so to speak, rushed a competing Aromarama film, *Behind the Great Wall,* a movie with definite smells. Using a much less complex device invented by Charles Weiss, they simply matched smells to select moments in the film. Premiering at the DeMille Theater in New York (with plans to open nationally in the Reade Organizations' forty theaters) on December 2, 1959, Aromarama beat the Smell-O-Vision debut by three weeks.

They were able to do this because they didn't write a movie and go to China to film it; they simply adapted a completed film, an Italian documentary travelogue about China that had already had some success in Italy. Chet Huntley was hired to narrate, and his script (by Sidney Kaufman) had him introduce the movie, explaining the Aromarama concept while peeling an orange. Suddenly, the scent of orange wafted through the theater. The audience loved it. That was the high point, definitely the best aroma in the movie, and there were some one hundred more to go in the ensuing two hours. As scenes of China flashed on the screen and Chet Huntley narrated, the smells wafted out of the air-conditioning vents. Audiences breathed in freshly dug soil, new-mown hay, smoke, jungle gardenia, wet straw, banana oil, the gunpowder scent of exploding firecrackers, a river, burning torches, horses, sizzling meat on a grill, incense (oh God, the incense), rain, and something that was supposed to be the scent of a trapped tiger.

"To be able to leave the theater," my father wrote in the *New*

York Times, "knowing how an opium den smells . . . will be an expansion of experience that will make this particular screening memorable."

Memorable it was. The smells didn't dissipate; they built up. They penetrated the seats and the carpets. The movie was shown four times a day. I have a vivid recollection of being taken to see *Behind the Great Wall.* I had just turned four. It was my second movie. The aroma in the theater was overwhelming, starting in the lobby, where the palimpsest of Aromarama odors was already at an eye-watering concentration. The movie had been playing for a week at that point. I remember little about the film itself, just the taste of all those scents as I sat there in the dark in my itchy red wool suit with the pleated skirt, because I was breathing through my mouth the whole time.

When I traveled in China in 2006, one evening in Guilin we went out on the Li River to see traditional sampan fishermen fishing with trained cormorants whose necks are banded so they cannot swallow the fish they catch, but must spit them out for the fishermen, who reward their slave cormorants with chopped-up bits of fish small enough to swallow past the cruel neck bands. I remembered that I had seen this before, in my father's movie. The way the cormorants didn't get to keep the fish they caught had bothered me when I was four, and it bothered me when I was fifty-one.

Audiences reacted to *Behind the Great Wall.* Some people fainted. Many others fled the theater with headaches, streaming eyes, wafting nausea, and allergic reactions. When *Behind the Great Wall* closed after a few weeks, the DeMille Theater had to be stripped down, all its carpets and curtains ripped out and replaced, and all the seats entirely reupholstered. Critically, Aromarama was also a giant failure. Noting the relationship to

Todd's Smell-O-Vision, *Variety* dubbed the rivalry "the battle of the smellies." (My father once admitted to me that the *-rama* in the name Aromarama was a deliberate mockery of Mike Todd Sr.'s Cinerama process.) *New York Times* critic Bosley Crowther hated the movie, calling it a stunt with an artistic benefit of "nil." He described leaving the theater and discovering that "the lovely fume-laden New York ozone had never smelled so good.".

For the rest of my childhood, our attic was stacked with cases of spray cans marked "freshly dug soil," "new mown hay," "jungle gardenia," "smoke," "horses," "rain," and "trapped tiger." They made excellent weapons in neighborhood skirmishes. Nothing was better than a jet of "jungle gardenia" to keep a mean neighborhood boy from bothering a group of girls playing hopscotch in the Shanleys' driveway. From time to time, during a very hot summer, a can would spontaneously explode in the attic, and the house would reek of "horses" or "trapped tiger" or "new mown hay" for a day or two.

In his sixties, for no medically discernable reason, my father lost his sense of smell, and taste, entirely. A lover of good food, he was devastated. He instructed me that the proper term for being what he called "deaf in the nose" was "snoof."

MY FATHER's film efforts shifted soon after the Aromarama debacle to dramatic features. In 1960 he produced his one truly good movie, a black-and-white production of *Macbeth* filmed for television at Pinewood Studios in England. Our time in London for nearly a year during this production was the happiest interlude of my childhood. I thought the hectic city sidewalks were a thrilling change from our quiet Forest Hills Gardens streets. We lived in a narrow rented house in Knightsbridge, on Rutland Place. Buskers (most of them tattered veterans of "the war," I was told) came around our corner playing the accordion or the violin, and I would hear them and beg my mother to let me go out onto the sidewalk to give them some of the dime-like sixpences and the thick thrupenny bits from my tobacco tin hoard. There were 240 pennies in a pound sterling! Did a pound's worth of the big pennies with King George on some and Queen Elizabeth with her flying hair ribbon on the others weigh an actual pound?

Once, when I was sorting out all my coins in satisfying stacks on the sitting room carpet, my father told me some men said "thrupenny bits" to mean something dirty about women, but I didn't know what he meant and my mother told him I was only five, for Christ's sake. One of the buskers had a monkey on a leash. The monkey wore a red outfit with a matching hat. He took my pennies, put them in a little change purse he wore around his neck, and bowed in thanks, like a wind-up toy.

WHEN ANGELA came to dinner that first time, I had been warned in advance to say nothing about her missing right arm. I was told not to stare, not to ask questions. She lost her arm in the Blitz, my mother told me, just before the guests arrived. I did not know what the Blitz was, but it sounded pretty bad if you could lose your arm in it.

Judith Anderson was one of the stars of *Macbeth,* and she came to dinner that same night, but she had two arms and she didn't make much of an impression on me, though I remember the sound of her laugh when the adults were still at the dinner table and I had been tucked into my bed upstairs. She had one of those laughs that has nothing at all to do with whether or not the person laughing thinks something is funny.

Judith Anderson had also laughed her pretend laugh all

through my puppet show after dinner, before I was put to bed even though it was still daylight, while all the grown-ups and, unfairly, my brother stayed at the table in the evening summer sunlight. We had a folding wooden puppet theater with a red curtain on a string. It was not too hard to carry it into the dining room and set it up to give everyone a show, once I had finished eating. I knew they thought I was very cute and industrious. I pretended to ignore them but was pleased and tried to be as cute and industrious as possible as I carried in the puppets and set up for my show.

All through dinner I had not said a word, but I watched Angela as she ate, using her only hand. She had long red nails, and pretty rings that sparkled. Someone must have helped her with her nail polish. She was fascinating. She was beautiful. She wore dark red lipstick. Her hair was tucked in a sleek chignon. The lipstick she could do on her own, but the hair? She wore a dark green knit suit, and a matching little hat she never took off. She seemed unaware that she was missing a body part. She cut her meat with her knife in an inexplicably deft gesture and then picked up her fork, as if this were the most natural way to eat, as if everyone ate this way. Why had my mother served roast beef, of all things?

My mother, an indifferent cook at best, wore no makeup and fussed very little over her looks. She loved her cameras, and she changed lenses on her Leica or rewound the film with a little folding crank on the side of her Rolleiflex with a deft sort of mechanical precision and competence. My mother often had headaches, though they were the kind that she treated by lying down and reading Angela Thirkell novels for hours at a time. She was habitually preoccupied with my problematic older brother. She had none of the exciting, ethereal features that made Angela almost intoxicatingly vivid to me.

The man who had brought Angela to dinner was a tall, thin Englishman named Bill, someone my father had recently met at a film studio, who made government-funded short films to be shown in movie theaters before the features about things like why, in the postwar rationing-plagued Britain, eating tinned tuna fish, something few English people apparently did, was a good idea. He called it "tunny" fish, which worried me, as tuna fish straight from the can was one of the very few things I was willing to eat, and *tunny* rhymed with *funny* and might not taste right. Bill didn't offer to help Angela cut her meat the way my father sometimes helped me cut mine. Nobody helped her. I tried to eat dinner using just my left hand, not switching the fork back into my right hand as most Americans do after cutting my bites, but just keeping it in my left hand. I didn't want anyone to see that I was imitating her, but nobody noticed. After that night, I always kept my fork in my left hand when I ate. I still eat that way.

Because we lived not too far from an elegant toy store, Hamleys on Regent Street, forays into this nirvana were a regular feature of our days, usually on our way back from walking in a nearby park. My mother, a devotee of toys and toy stores, had bought us, over a series of those visits, quite a collection of articulated wooden marionettes made by Pelham Puppets. We had Hansel, Gretel, the woodcutter, the witch, and two elegantly dressed nameless females, whom we called, inspired by their yarn-hair colors, Blondie and Brownie. There was also a prince, a cat, a dog, and a horse. These puppets were a little more than a foot high and had twelve strings each. Manipulating them was tricky. Their arms and legs were strung loosely on the strings like wooden beads. They were not knotted at the ends, and so the elements that made up the arms and legs could be slid up the strings, completely out of view of the audience, if armlessness and leglessness should happen to be part of the narrative arc in your puppet show.

My after-dinner puppet show that particular night featured a great deal of armlessness and leglessness. Most of the action consisted of the woodcutter attacking the fair maidens to chop off their arms and legs with the axe he held permanently at the ready in his right hand. The axe had its own string and I had become quite adept at developing the swinging motion to convey realistic chopping. Up the strings all the arms and legs would go, as I whisked the fair maidens offstage for a moment, and then the torsos of the victims would return to dangle helplessly while they bemoaned their sad fate, until Hansel and the prince would come to the rescue, vanquishing the woodcutter and somehow miraculously restoring the missing limbs of the fair maidens in the process. The restoration was very satisfying, because all that was involved was letting drop all the arm and leg parts which I held in a bunch, gathered up at the top of the strings where the strings were knotted through the two-piece wooden frame. The reconstituted arms and legs would slide down the strings and reattach to the bodies in an instant, but then the woodcutter would break free and start hacking away at his victims again, and the whole scenario, complete with flyaway arms and legs, would be enacted once more.

I have no idea how long my puppet show went on, how many cycles of arms and legs being chopped off and then miraculously returned were played out, before the curtain fell. It might have been five minutes and it might have been a half hour of this repetitive drama. I do recall very attentive silence on the part of my audience, except for that piercing fake movie-star laugh. After the applause, I took my bows and I kissed all the grown-ups good night, one by one, around the table, and Angela smiled at me and put her hand on my shoulder as she leaned down to kiss me good night. She wore strong perfume that lingered on me pleasantly as I lay in my bed listening to the sounds of the dinner party. It was still daylight and I wasn't sleepy. I was not reprimanded in any way, and my puppet show was never spoken of again after that night. I was in my twenties when it dawned on me what I had done.

Angela made several more appearances during the months we lived in London, at subsequent meals, on her own, without Bill of the tunny fish propaganda. Once, without my father, we met her at the London Zoo, in Regent's Park, which wasn't far from her Park Street flat. While my brother walked ahead with our mother, going to see the lions because he had become upset by the monkeys, she and I took our time visiting with the Old World monkeys and the New World monkeys, which we agreed resembled wise little old Chinese people. I had never been alone with her before. I held her gloved hand gingerly, feeling its significance as her one and only hand. I felt the eyes of people staring at her pinned sleeve as we strolled past the monkey cages. I tried very hard to avoid accidentally glancing in the vicinity of her missing arm, but I kept sneaking furtive glimpses of her face.

Her elegance was thrilling. Did people assume this dazzling one-armed woman was my mother? Did they look to see if there was a resemblance between us? Did they wonder how she coped with the one arm, or did they conclude that I was her helper? I hoped they concluded all these things, but that hope made me feel a squirmy worm of guilt wriggling inside me. Her laugh was like a tinkling silver bell.

ANGELA'S ROMANCE with my father began soon after that summer night when she came to our flat for the first time with Bill and I gave that puppet show. She met my father the same night she met me, she explained on the one occasion when I ever saw her again after that *Macbeth* year, when Nick and I met her for lunch in London in 1985, a couple of years after my father's death. So their romance was certainly in the air if not already under way by the time my mother, brother, and I flew back to the U.S. in late October of 1960, while my father remained in London for another eight months. (A letter he wrote my mother a week after our departure is signed "My very deepest regards, affection and LOVE," but in the same letter he says he is working on some unexpected opportunities for film deals that will have him traveling "most of the next three years in India, Greece, Yugoslavia, Spain, Italy, Malaya.")

My mother was stricken with a migraine on our flight from London to New York. Did she have an inkling of the Angela development? She had her way of knowing the things she didn't know. As she huddled miserably in a cocoon of Air India blankets on our three seats in the back of the plane, the sari-clad stewardesses entertained my brother and me in an empty row in the back of the first-class cabin.

I was sad on that Air India flight. Those months in London were the only extended time when all four of us had ever lived together, day in, day out—and now it was over. We were leaving something behind. Even though I was prone to motion sickness and had perpetual territorial skirmishes in the backseat with my brother, I missed being the four of us together, riding around the English countryside in our dove-gray Peugeot sedan with its cozy red plaid seats.

I refused to eat anything on the tray the stewardesses brought me—not the bright yellow rice, nor the strange curried chicken lumps, and especially not the powdery cubes of almond sweetmeats flavored with an alien spice I would recognize when I encountered it again later in life, when I was nineteen and a soon-to-be-ex-boyfriend made me odd yet consoling waffles the night my cat fell to her death from the fourth-story window of my Waverly Place apartment. Cardamom, the spice of sorrow.

AFTER *MACBETH,* perhaps inspired by the quality and success of that project, my father embarked on a decade of genuine distribution deals, with an MGM reissue program in the era before old movies were easily available to audiences via videos, DVDs, instant downloads, or cable access. There was a two-year period when one of my father's companies (was it Entertainment Events? Grand Prize Films? Entertainment Values? Splendid Films? Film Transactions, Inc.? Realfilms?) actually owned North American distribution rights to the most popular Charlie Chaplin movies.

Although he had once planned to make a career writing and directing his own screenplays, my father's only consistent success lay with completion bonding—guaranteeing completion within budget and schedule—and so his work moved from any hope of success on the creative side to the finance end of film production. One of the first movies he bonded was *A Man Called Adam* in 1966. This was a gritty black-and-white feature about a self-destructive jazz musician, played by Sammy Davis Jr., with a largely African-American cast, among them Lola Falana (making her screen debut), Cicely Tyson, Ossie Davis, and Louis Armstrong, with an uncredited Morgan Freeman in a nightclub scene (his second screen appearance, as an extra). One day, during a school vacation, my father took me to a Manhattan soundstage and told me to sit very still on a high stool at the edge of the set, where I could perch and watch the filming. At first I was excited to be there, but I was soon bored mindless by endless takes of the same talky scenes, over and over. When they broke for lunch, I was relieved, but my father didn't come back for me. Everyone disappeared. I was hungry, and I didn't know where my father was, but I didn't dare leave the deserted set.

Finally, long after the cast and crew had returned and resumed shooting, my father reappeared, having been at a lunch meeting. When he asked me if I had enjoyed "the craft services cuisine" with the crew, I nodded, having no idea what he was talking about.

Other films for which my father wrote production bonds were Martin Ritt's *Great White Hope* in 1970 and *Matilda* (based on the book by Paul Gallico) in 1978. (At the time of his death my father had in his wallet an inexplicable, un-cashed 1977 check for nearly $200,000, made out to his company, Performance Guarantees, from the *Matilda* production account, which by then had been closed for years.) These were followed by *Rabbit Test* in 1978, Joan Rivers's directing debut, which starred Billy Crystal as a pregnant man, and the final film for which Sidney Kaufman provided a production bond, *Testament,* a bleak, postapocalyptic drama starring Jane Seymour. Directed by Lynn Littman, it was originally produced for PBS television's American Playhouse series, but was then released in theaters after all, after his death in 1983.

One film in my father's motley oeuvre stands out for me for nonartistic reasons. His involvement with the 1969 antebellum not-quite-an-epic, *Slaves* (the film's publicity tag line read: "For the slave—courage knew no chains. For the master—desire knew no color in the savage world of the Old South"), which starred Ossie Davis, Ruby Dee, Dionne Warwick, and Stephen Boyd, has had a lasting impact on my life.

Shot on location in Shreveport, Louisiana, in the summer of 1968, *Slaves* was a reunion of several Old Lefties, from the director, Herbert Biberman, who was one of the Hollywood Ten (this was his first and last post-blacklist movie; he died in 1971), to his wife, the veteran actress Gail Sondergaard, who had a small role, to the film's editor, Sidney Meyers, to the producers—Sidney Kaufman's The Slaves Production Company and Philip Langner and the Theater Guild.

Eva Jessye, who was an old pal of my grandmother's, having been the choral director for the original 1935 production of *Porgy and Bess,* was among the many stage and screen veterans playing various roles, as was Julius Harris, who had starred in Michael Roemer's *Nothing But a Man.* It seems just right that a Sidney Kaufman film would be called by Vincent Canby a "pre-fab *Uncle Tom's Cabin,* set in an 1850 Mississippi where everybody—masters and slaves alike—talks as if he had been weaned, at best, on the Group Theater, and, at worst, on silent-movie titles."

My brother John, then sixteen, was given a job as a production assistant on the set. He was mostly a helper to Sidney Meyers, who edited the dailies on a Movieola set up in one of the rooms at the nearby Ramada Inn, which was taken over by the cast and crew for the duration. Nancy Weber, a writer from New York, on assignment from *Cosmopolitan* magazine, arrived on the scene to work on a story about the making of the movie (who knows what Helen Gurley Brown had in mind; the story was never published), and promptly began a romance with the assistant cinematographer, Gordon Parks Jr. (who would die in a plane crash in Kenya in 1979).

She was white, he was black, they were a highly visible and deliberately provocative couple when they went out at night in Shreveport, and very quickly the Ku Klux Klan, already agitated by the presence of so many Jews and Negroes that summer after the assassination of Martin Luther King Jr., communicated a serious threat to burn the set and shut down production. This was frightening for everyone, especially after an altercation one night at the Ramada Inn when a gun went off, though nobody was injured. The disruptions and liabilities were a headache for my father and his production bond, and he requested that Nancy Weber leave town immediately, if not at once. By the time of her departure (for another battleground, the Democratic Convention in Chicago), she had befriended my brother.

During the Christmas break, when John was home for a week from Hampshire Country School, he wanted to see Nancy, and so, having just turned thirteen, I was dispatched by our mother to keep him company (and maybe to chaperone). Off we went to see Nancy Weber the writer in her Greenwich Village apartment, a studio walk-up on Eighth Street. We took the subway from Continental Avenue in Forest Hills to West Fourth Street, a world away. Her tiny fifth-floor apartment was fascinating. Her fireplace was filled with pennies. There were fresh flowers on the low table, and a bowl of pomegranates. I spotted a cartoon drawing taped to the bathroom door, a caricature of Nancy, in curlers, talking on the telephone.

Who drew this? I asked, and she replied that her brother had. Is he an artist? No, but he studies art history at Columbia University, she explained, and then the three of us went to lunch around the corner at Shakespeare's, a bar and restaurant on MacDougal Street. When I reported on our day to my mother, she told me how much she had loved the Jumble Shop on Eighth Street, to which Gordon Heath had often taken her, before she met my father.

I didn't meet Nancy again until I was seventeen and living on my own, on Waverly Place, around the corner from her Eighth Street apartment. We kept running into each other at a Laundromat on Waverly Place, and began to meet there on Saturday mornings to play Go-Moku while our laundry tumbled.

It would be three more years, when I was just twenty, before she introduced me to her brother Nick, two days before his twenty-eighth birthday. We were married the following year, in September 1976.

Weeks after our wedding, my father underwent esophageal surgery. He had suffered from digestive distress for decades, and had for many years refused any kind of treatment for his hiatal hernia, though his symptoms caused him misery on a daily basis. Now he was really unwell.

The night before his surgery for what would turn out to be esophageal cancer (though my father concealed this information successfully from my mother and me, telling the truth only to my brother, the member of the family least equipped to handle the news, let alone keep it to himself), I saw Beatrice for the last time. She no longer shared an office with my father, and I don't think she saw him very often by then. I hadn't seen her in three or four years.

Beatrice entered the hospital room unannounced, and my mother greeted her stiffly before fleeing "for coffee." When I introduced her to my husband of two months, Beatrice took Nick's hand and said theatrically, "At last we meet." She looked older, but she was still a snappy dresser. We chatted awkwardly for a moment. She said she had begun to cut back on her editing commitments. Nick and I left so she could have some time alone with my father. When I looked back from the hallway, she had taken one of his hands and pressed it to her lips.

But it was Angela who was with my father when he died.

When we learned in July of 1983 that my father was suddenly

and unexpectedly hospitalized in London, overtaken by what were probably metastatic brain tumors as a consequence of his esophageal cancer seven years earlier, Nick offered to make a quick trip with my mother to see him. She agreed, having been gripped by a paralysis about what to do with this information, and was grateful for his offer, as she would never have even considered making the trip on her own. She was afraid, even as he lay dying, of showing up uninvited in this other part of his life. They flew over with a plan to stay just one night in London in order to assess the situation. The immigration officer was perplexed when he asked my mother the purpose of her trip and she replied that her husband was at Wellington Hospital with brain tumors.

"Ah, so you'll be staying in London for . . . a while?" he asked gently.

"No, we fly back to New York tomorrow," she replied.

"I see, of course, madam, and then you'll be taking your husband home with you then?"

"No."

THE HOSPITAL staff was equally perplexed when my mother showed up, because they had thought the devoted Angela was Mrs. Sidney Kaufman, and had addressed her as Mrs. Sidney Kaufman, and had in all ways treated her as Mrs. Sidney Kaufman, until the moment of the arrival of this odd American woman they had never seen or heard from before.

Why wasn't I there? I didn't make the trip because I had just given birth five weeks earlier, in mid-June, to our younger daughter, Charlotte, and I couldn't go anywhere without her. I didn't want to take her on this trip and leave behind our older daughter, Lucy, then twenty months old, which seemed to me potentially quite a traumatic thing to do, introduce a new baby and then go off on a trip with the baby and leave her behind without a parent. I couldn't have managed my mother and a newborn without Nick, and I didn't see a reasonable way to make this trip, under the circumstances, with both Lucy and Charlotte along, not knowing if my father would be unpleasant, or perhaps refuse to see me. Lucy and Charlotte wouldn't have been allowed to visit him. This was worse than any of those logic puzzles about crossing a river in a boat with a wolf, a lamb, and a bale of hay. Making the trip seemed impossible. But these eminently reasonable reasons not to make the trip to see my father on his deathbed let me off the hook. I really didn't want to go.

When they arrived at his bedside that first afternoon, my father was aphasically conversational and friendly to both my mother and to Nick. "I was wondering when you would show up," he said to my mother, before asking the nurse for his trumpet, which was actually a request for his "personal convenience," as the nurse called the plastic urinal. Nick had with him some photographs of Lucy and me, holding newborn Charlotte, and my father, who had been drinking tea when they arrived, first gazed at the photographs and then took them to his mouth and attempted to drink them.

Although the doctors had advised that he could live for weeks or even months, when Nick and my mother returned to the hospital the next morning for a final visit before the flight back to New York, he had deteriorated significantly overnight. He was incoherent and miserable, flailing in his bed, fettered by cloth restraints. On the occasion of her last moment ever with her husband of thirty-five years, my mother appeared not to know what Nick knew. He had glimpsed, though my mother had not seemed to notice, as they walked down the hallway toward my father's private room at Wellington Hospital, an elegant, turbaned, one-armed woman standing by my father's bedside. Just moments before they entered the room, she slid gracefully into the en suite bathroom and locked the door. Nick saw the door close and heard the lock click.

My mother spent an hour at my father's bedside, with Angela silently locked in the bathroom, and my husband hovering nervously, worried my mother might try to use the bathroom, worried that Angela would emerge prematurely, worried a nurse might look in and ask where Angela had gone. But Angela remained still and silent, and finally my mother said good-bye to my semiconscious father and they left for the airport. (Among the many questions I never asked Angela were these: Did she stand, did she sit, did she have something with her to read, was the light on, or was it dark? What did she think about? Was she calm? Was she nervous? Did she ever, even there in the bathroom eavesdropping silently on my mother's last moments with my father, feel a squirmy worm of guilt?) My father died just hours later, while Nick and my mother were still in the air on their flight back to New York.

WHEN MY father's obituary appeared in the *New York Times* (an article filled, appropriately enough, with a mixture of facts and mythology supplied by my brother), Beatrice telephoned the house in Forest Hills, where we were sorting through my father's papers, at the very beginning of what would be a decade-long process of untangling the fictions from the realities of my father's lifelong conjuring act. My mother answered.

"Uh-huh," she said, and then I saw her scowl, and then she said, "The hell with you," and she hung up the phone.

"What was that?"

"Beatrice."

"What did she say?"

"Do you really want to know?"

"Yes." I really did.

"She said, 'Kathy must feel so guilty.'"

Two days later, when my mother was staying with us in Connecticut, she and Nick took Lucy to swim in the pond adjacent to our house. On the way there, Nick spotted a grotesque corpse of a possum lying in the field, and while signaling to my mother, who also saw it and grimaced over Lucy's head, he steered them through the tall grass so that Lucy would have no awareness of the dead animal. It was a hot August afternoon and he made a mental note to go back with a shovel and move it to a more remote spot where nobody walked, before it started to decay. On their way back from the pond, within the hour, they passed the spot where the dead possum had been lying, and there was no trace of it. It was simply gone. "Like Angela," my mother murmured.

In the weeks and months after his death, I joked about Angela to my friends. When my father stopped speaking to me in a rage, it was so powerful and so sustained, it turned out, that his response to the news of my being pregnant with our first child a few months after that—I had written him that brief, uninflected note to tell him, at my mother's urging—was to change his will, cutting me out, with no recognition of future grandchildren. At the time, I shrugged this off as a meaningless gesture that had no bearing, given how little money there was anyway. Being deprived of a share of his empty bank accounts and worthless paper corporations felt insignificant to me. When I described the byzantine issues of his unexpectedly very modest estate, which was to be divided equally between my mother and my brother, a friend asked, "So did Angela get her hands on all the missing money?" My reply was a witty, *"Hand."* The elegant one-armed woman hiding in the bathroom seemed to me preposterous, like a marvelous Iris Murdoch invention.

TODAY THERE is almost no trace that Angela Lebus ever existed in the world, beyond a few obscure film production credits, numerous obvious (despite being heavily redacted) mentions in page after page of my father's FBI records, and a description in an obscure memoir by Ginette Spanier, head of the fashion house Balmain. Madame Spanier tells the story of how Angela Lebus, the daughter of a London friend, arriving in Paris for the first time at eighteen, was eager to attend the showing of a collection at Balmain, which led to Madame Spanier's employ-ment there.

This came about because when Angela was being fitted for a dress after the showing, Madame argued with the imperi-ous *vendeuse* and with Angela, who preferred a gown in black velvet trimmed with jet, while Madame Spanier thought "the little blue flannel number which was shown third in the collec-tion" was more suitable. Her astuteness about the best choice for Angela won Madame Spanier praise from a white-haired woman who had been listening to all this and who finally burst into the fitting room to declare, "Madame, it is a woman like you we need in this firm," and so Madame Spanier was hired on the spot at the House of Balmain, where she would reign as La Directrice for decades thereafter. The white-haired woman, it turned out, was Pierre Balmain's mother. It is touching to envis-age a young Angela, not yet a survivor of the Luftwaffe's bomb-ing of London between the seventh of September 1940 and the tenth of May 1941, eagerly trying on those elegant dresses.

Long ago my father told me that she came from a family of English Jews in the furniture business. Surely this would be Harris Lebus, once located in Tottenham, which closed its door after more than a century of business in 1969. Lebus was said at one time to be the largest furniture factory in the world. (It was also said, presumably apocryphally, that a notice board was hung outside the factory, "No Englishman Need Apply," because of the numbers of Jewish workers at Lebus.)

During the First World War, Lebus had government contracts to manufacture ammunition boxes, sleighs, biplanes, and the Vickers-Vimy monoplane. During the Second World War, Lebus produced aircraft, including the Albemarle bomber, the Hotspur Glider, and the Mosquito. Most intriguingly, Lebus was engaged in a Top Secret operation, supervised by Lord Beaverbrook, to build decoy Sherman tanks out of wood.

Two YEARS after my father's death, Nick and I met Angela for lunch at the Dorchester Hotel in London, with the nominal agenda of discussing the complexities of my father's tangled estate. An important loan document had been witnessed by her in a hotel room in Cannes. She had been in partnership with him on some production guarantee bonds. She might be able to resolve some of the numerous mysteries surrounding his estate. But she never did. She was puzzled by our inquiries, and couldn't understand why we were chasing across several borders after a few hundred thousand dollars borrowed by a business partner who seemed to have no intentions of repaying the estate, a sum that was surely insignificant in the greater scheme of my father's presumably immense wealth. She was disbelieving and perplexed when we told her the money we were seeking was essentially the only asset of his estate, and it was significant for my brother's welfare. I say she was disbelieving and perplexed, but there is also the possibility that Angela knew exactly where my father's money was. Perhaps she also knew of secret Swiss bank accounts he had always hinted at for which there was no record of any kind, but she clearly had no intention of telling us anything more. I will never know what she knew or what she had from my father.

Angela had possession of the 1977 Mercedes he kept in London, and she laughed at us for thinking it had any significant value, which shamed me, though we had intended to demand that she give us the keys. She may have had possession of my father's fancy Patek Philippe watch as well, a valuable object of which he was immensely proud, but it seemed tasteless to ask, though Nick had seen it on my father's bedside table just hours before his death.

I had dozens of unaskable questions swimming in my head. Even though my father was dead, I could hardly ask Angela for the coordinates and precise details of their romance. Whatever there was between them, however they had spent their time together through the years, I knew that Angela had been one of the loves of my father's life. He was with Angela in London more often than he was anyplace else, from the time they met until the day he died. At lunch with Angela, I realized that I had always felt a peculiar kind of fondness for her, a kinship, and some admiration as well. This odd, elegant woman was a working barrister most of her life. Strangely enough, she also owned the florist shop in the lobby of the Hilton Hotel. I imagined she spent much of her life alone. She had loved my father and he had loved her.

Angela looked like a somewhat faded Duchess of Windsor that day at the Dorchester. She had the same sleek, dark chignon, another elegant suit (perhaps Balmain), the red nails, the rings, the perfect lipstick. There was something almost unbearably touching when the maître d' whispered to the waiter that we should be shown to "Mr. Kaufman's table." This had been her life. She never married.

At the end of our lunch, the awkward financial inquiries abandoned, Nick suddenly asked her if she could solve another Sidney Kaufman mystery. Warily, Angela agreed to try. Why, Nick asked, given that he was always the very person last to board a flight, and always cut his airport arrival time much too close for the comfort of anyone involved in getting him on the flight, was my father always the last to get off a plane? To meet a Sidney Kaufman flight was to wait and wait and worry that he was not on the flight at all, until finally he would emerge, long after all the other passengers had passed by. Angela thought a moment and then her face lit up. "I imagine," she said, a smile playing on her lips, "that he would have been delayed gathering up all the little soaps from all the lavatories on the plane."

ANGELA DIED in 1996. I don't know if she had any family. I have no idea who places a small memorial notice in the *London Times* every May, "Angela Mary Lebus. Still greatly missed and lovingly remembered." Perhaps a nephew (does he treasure the beautiful vintage Patek Philippe wristwatch given him by Auntie Angela?). I had half hoped she would leave my daughters something in her estate, perhaps making up for the riches my father appropriated from my mother that may well have gone her way, or perhaps it was all stashed in a forever unattainable Swiss bank account—every family needs its myth of the lost fortune, doesn't it?—but all there was, in the end, was a brief note penned by her personal secretary to say she had died. Did I really need anything more from her than what I had already been given?

Not only did Beatrice think that I should feel guilty after my father's death, she also felt inexplicably compelled by news of his death to say so to my mother instead of saying it to me directly. If she felt so strongly about it, why had she not been in touch with me before then? Apparently, he had told her some version of the story and Beatrice held me responsible for my father's choice to stop speaking to me because I took him literally when he said he wanted a divorce from my mother. I believed what he said about wanting me to support her through it. It's true, I let him stop speaking to me without much of an argument. I let my father sever our relationship, telling myself, at age twenty-four, that it was in some sense a mutual decision, one that he made and I accepted. I had my own share of Kaufman self-righteousness.

But I was his child and he was my father. He made an impulsive choice and then he stuck to it for what remained of his lifetime, with no diminution of outrage and indignation (if my brother's reports and my mother's unwillingness to "get involved" in what she called our "feud" were any measure of the way he continued to speak about me).

That was all more than half my lifetime ago. As the mother of daughters in their late twenties, I find that his cutting me off as he did, when he did, is more painful for me to contemplate now than it was painful to experience at the time. What a cruel and inexplicable choice he made. I am still trying to understand what happened. I am still trying to understand him.

I doubt that Beatrice is alive today, at a hundred, though I have been unable to find any evidence of her death. I have talked to several writers with whom she used to work. Nobody has heard from her in twenty years or more, yet nobody knows what became of her. I hope she lived long enough to see my first novels in print. I want Beatrice to have read them, I suppose, out of a mixed desire to show her up and to show them off and to show her that nothing I got from her was wasted.

DID MY father want me to know Angela and Beatrice as much as he wanted them to know me? Who was being shown off to whom? Whose approval was he seeking? Was I supposed to represent my mother, or was I being enlisted in his conspiracy against her? Was I being honored or burdened by bearing witness to his other life with these women who were not my mother? My father's grand sense of himself led him repeatedly to require an audience. He needed Michael Roemer's embarrassed gaze on that honeymoon trip.

Even as my father's various rejections and betrayals of my mother throughout my childhood deprived me of the ordinary luxury of guiltless Oedipal competition with her for his affection, Angela and Beatrice both served as other mothers. They were models of successful femininity, even as they were my rivals. My perplexing, mysterious father was apparently known and understood by these two beguiling women who loved him. Their devotion was, in the end, the true achievement of his life. He wanted me to know these women and see him in the light of their adoration. This is the way to love Sidney Kaufman! He wanted my unalloyed adoration, too, and I disappointed him.

MOST PEOPLE in the film business today have never heard of my father. He's been dead since 1983. But every now and then I cross paths with someone who knows exactly who he was, and then the conversation can go either way. We once had a dinner guest, someone we had never met before, the weekend house-guest of friends, who was so horrified to be eating a meal at the table of the daughter of the man who had cheated her company of vast sums by selling them distribution rights to films to which he didn't exactly have the rights, that her first impulse was to drop her fork and stand up to leave, exclaiming, "I cannot believe I am sitting here eating dinner in the home of the daughter of that man!" though she sat back down and finished the meal perfectly graciously, considering her shock that this pleasant gathering had anything at all to do with Sidney Kaufman.

Some people in the film business have refused to explain the painful nature of their Sidney Kaufman experience. It isn't clear in these moments whose feelings are being spared—mine, or the person who declines to be any more specific than an uncomfortable, "Oh yes, I certainly remember Sidney Kaufman! How could I forget him?"

But then there are those like Lord David Puttnam, the British producer, whose face lit up with genuine warmth at the recollection of my father, whose generous wisdom and advice had been valuable to him when he was young and inexperienced. "Sidney Kaufman," he said, "was the most honest man in Hollywood."

The Memory of All That

WHEN I STARTED SPENDING TIME WITH THE MAN WHO would be my husband, I began to notice a strong and pleasing odor of coffee wafting up from his feet. Not only did his shoes smell good, they also occasionally contained a few grains of actual coffee grounds. This was, I soon discovered, the consequence of Nick having purchased an enormous and ancient coffee grinder from a defunct A&P in Vermont for eight dollars. In his tiny makeshift cabin on the edge of a forest in rural Connecticut there was only one electrical outlet wired seriously enough not to blow all the fuses every time he ground coffee, and it was in the back of his only closet. How could I not fall in love with a man whose feet smelled of freshly ground coffee?

Coffee was, if not mother's milk, grandmother's milk to me. My mother's mother, the one we called Ganz, drank coffee habitually. Her actual name, Kay Swift, seemed like the perfect, bright, peppy name for my lively and energetic grandmother. A lipstick-printed coffee cup makes me think of her still. The smell of stewed coffee (not the brilliant notes of Starbucks single-estate roasts, but the muddy chords of coffee shop java) can still take me right back to my grandmother's coffee table. It was, literally, a coffee table, and when I was a child it was just the right height for me. I would linger at the serving tray until

I was given permission to select one—just one—sugar lump, which I was then permitted to dip into my grandmother's black coffee.

In the living room of my grandmother's New York apartment, the aroma of coffee permeated the rippling scales of grown-up laughter and the jangle of her bracelets as she removed them before putting her hands on the keys of her piano. The resonance of her music vibrated through my body as I lay on the rug under the baby grand, where I could keep a close eye on her beautiful shoes as they moved over the pedals.

My grandmother played songs about love; some of them she had written herself. Mostly the music was witty and upbeat, but there were also slow, sad songs of loss. Curled under the piano, watching an elegant foot tap perfect time, I would weep discreetly, moved in ways I didn't understand by the words and music. Something about the songs, and my grandmother playing and singing in her high voice, and my mother sitting on the couch listening and occasionally singing along in a lower octave, made those moments seem, somehow, profoundly about the secret essence of life.

The coffee cut the sweetness of the sugar. There was an art to wicking up maximum coffee without letting the lump dissolve in my fingers. It was all in the timing.

WHEN I was a child, I heard the name George Gershwin invoked with such frequency and fond familiarity that I concluded he was a very close relative. I knew he was dead, but I assumed that his death was a fairly recent event, as he was still referred to with contemporary intimacy by certain members of my family.

The way he came into my consciousness wasn't only because

of the music, but the music was always there. One of my earliest memories consists of being pushed in a supermarket cart, my bare legs dangling down through those wire openings in the chromed mesh that left grooves in the backs of my thighs. The syrupy tune wafting in the air comes to an end, and a new melody begins. My mother, whose shopping list and pocketbook I hold, cocks her head in a particular focused way and leans down, murmuring to me, "That's George." Inevitably, I developed a precocious ability to recognize Gershwin tunes everywhere. By the age of seven, I could name that tune in four or five notes. It occurs to me now that the skill I had acquired was not, in fact, the ability to recognize Gershwin music, though that certainly came with time. I grew up hearing many unpublished Gershwin melodies as well as his exceedingly obscure early songs, and then of course all the standards, but my "I can name that tune!" familiarity with Gershwin music evolved later. My primary expertise starting when I was a toddler was a highly attuned ability to recognize the look on my mother's face and take it as a cue to pipe up, "That's George!" In this way I could join my mother in her secret pleasure.

WHAT WAS the pleasure, exactly? I was never quite sure, but I knew it was one of the most important things in her life. I knew she had been close to George as a child, had adored him and found him fun; perhaps the music brought back those exciting times. I knew she was devastated by his death, so maybe the music made her sad at the same time. Maybe these little moments gave us a sense of superiority over all the ordinary people around us doing their grocery shopping who had no idea what they were hearing, who had no Gershwin connection, as they wandered the aisles of the A&P on Metropolitan Avenue. I felt proprietary about George's music, the way my mother did, and loved by it the way my mother had felt loved by him—and so I loved the music back.

George was everywhere. That dog looks just like George's dog Tinker, my mother would remark, spotting a scruffy terrier on a street in our neighborhood.

"Never part your hair on the right, always on the left," my grandmother would admonish me. "George always told me to part my hair on the left because it showed my sense of humor."

THERE WERE several inscribed photographs of George around my grandmother's East Fifty-ninth Street apartment. Each time I visited her, after gazing out the window at the lacy girders of the Queensboro Bridge, playing with her miniature music boxes, examining all the little glass and silver treasures on her mantelpiece, rearranging the little wooden ladybug orchestra, which consisted of nine ladybug musicians and a ladybug conductor, peering into the intimate pink depths of the pair of conch shells that lay at each end of the mantel beneath the Dufy painting of a bowl of fruit, and studying various framed family pictures on the piano and bookcases (especially the one my mother took of Ganz with her standard black poodle, Porgy, a gift from George, taken after both George and the other poodle he gave her, Bess, had died), I would go from room to room (the ritual aspect of my devotions unnoticed by any adult) and pay a call on each of the photographs of George. I knew his face well, better than the faces of most of my relatives.

Who did I think he was? When I was very little, I wasn't quite sure exactly how George fit in. Somehow I knew that my grandmother, Ganz, had loved him, and that the songs she played were about the two of them in some way. (All the grandchildren called her Ganz, a nickname developed out of a cute mispronunciation when my oldest cousin, the first grandchild, was a baby. "Ganz" suited her far better than anything grandma- or nanna-ish ever could have. My own children called her Ganz. My husband called her Ganz.)

Ganz had loved George, and then he had died all of a sudden. She rarely mentioned her first husband, my grandfather, though I saw him and his young wife (who was my mother's age) and their children (who were my age) two or three times a year. They were our relatives and I liked them, though I always felt that my mother was anxious that we be on our very best behavior when we visited, and it was always confusing to me that she had spent all her childhood summers in the Greenwich house where they lived year round, and I knew that she deeply loved the house and the rolling landscape surrounding it, yet it was no longer hers, now that her father had his second family living there. But Ganz's preference for George over the elderly man called Pop seemed reasonable to me. My grandfather was old and wrinkled, while George, in those photos, was young and smooth.

By the time I was a little older, I understood much more. James Paul Warburg, my grandfather, had also once been young and smooth—very handsome in fact—but for some reason, as if the words to all the songs I knew were literally about them, Ganz had fallen in love with George, even though she still loved her husband. My grandmother and George had a very long romance, over ten years—and at least seven of those years were the final years of my grandparents' sixteen years of marriage.

"They had an affair," my mother had replied bluntly, provoked by my asking, reasonably, hopefully, if Ganz hadn't perhaps been married to George. She seemed so much like his widow, despite the two subsequent husbands, one of whom,

Hunter, had been very present during my early childhood. I was disappointed at the realization that whatever George was to us, there was no tidy name for it. (And I wondered, too, after my mother uttered the word *affair* for the first time, what it had to do with a certain sign out in front of a tacky restaurant on Queens Boulevard that read, "Have Your Next Affair With Us!")

Being a methodical child, I looked the word up in the dictionary. An affair was "a concern, a business, a matter to be attended to, a celebrated or notorious or noteworthy happening or sequence of events." I knew all that already, but what did it mean?

WHEN I was in second grade, I asked the music enrichment teacher (obnoxiously, I'm sure) if she had ever heard of George Gershwin. Encouraged by her familiarity with the name, I added that he was my uncle or something like that. She assured me I was quite mistaken and that I was not related to the famous composer. Embarrassed and on shaky ground, I let it go. But when I was in junior high school, I made a point of telling the music teacher that my grandmother had had a long affair with George Gershwin.

I was very adult, I thought, in my breezy reference to this celebrated or notorious or noteworthy happening or event or sequence of events. I can't recall the music teacher's name, but I can clearly remember the look of dismay that swept over his face, his visible flinch at my casual deployment of the word *affair*. He wasn't impressed—he was upset by my blitheness. We were both embarrassed and didn't speak of it again, though later in the term when the class studied a recording of the "Rhapsody in Blue," I felt him staring at me.

✧ ✦ ✧

THE FRAMED studio portraits of George in Ganz's apartment had dedications. "For Kay—with love—George" or "For Kay—Best—George" ("Best" was their secret code word for "love," a word they couldn't use freely in writing until my grandparents finally divorced), and some had a few musical bars sketched in along the bottom in his distinctive thick black pen strokes, his ink a singularly Gershwin-esque black, the same emphatic ebony of his brilliantined hair and our Steinway piano. He was a sharp dresser, a little self-conscious, a little self-important. Handsome in a brash, big-nosed way. Famous-looking, somehow. By now I knew he had been dead a long while.

When I was a child, I thought the eighteen years between his death in 1937 and my birth was a disappointing gulf. He had lived and died so long before my time. (Looking back from the present moment at age fifty-five, it is an astonishingly narrow span of time from the end of his life to the start of mine.) Most of the photographs had dates, and each time I studied them I would calculate again how many years he had left to live at the time of each portrait. Three years. Two years. (Some photos were undated but I could determine where they fell on the time line by the state of George's receding hairline.)

But the photograph of George that fascinated me the most wasn't in my grandmother's apartment; it was in my mother's bedroom back in our house. It was actually a self-portrait of George's that was also a photograph of my mother, a photograph taken and printed by George in 1934 (three years left to live), when she was twelve. Thirty-three years after the spot of time preserved in that photograph, when I was twelve, I enjoyed my close resemblance to her as a child. Some of my friends even believed me when I told them it was a picture of me with George Gershwin. I wanted to be in that picture, to have been included in this self-portrait, to have been included in the excitement of being seen so closely, the excitement of being loved so much by the man whose love changed my grandmother's life.

At twelve, the same age as the girl in the photo, I study the picture continually. Seen in a mirror's reflection, George looms out of the shadows behind my staring mother, his Leica obscuring most of his face.

"Who's the creepy guy? Is that your dad?" one less-than-impressed school chum inquires. I am furious. Of course he's not my dad, who is rarely around, has never taken my photograph (unlike my mother, who has taken far too many photographs of me), and in any case isn't the least bit like George. I might not be capable of thinking about sexual attractiveness in genuinely adult terms at this point in my life, but George, in my book, is romantic, desirable, what a man ought to be like. Not anything like my own remote father, who never, ever focuses on me in the way that George focuses on my mother in that photograph.

My father, despite his failure to dazzle the world, almost certainly dazzled my mother because he possessed certain physical and cultural traits she first encountered at a very young age in George Gershwin. Both Brooklyn boys, Jacob Gershovitz born in 1898 on Snedicker Avenue in Brownsville and Shimon Kaufman born in 1910 on Stagg Street in Williamsburg, had pulled themselves up by their own bootstraps. They shared that erudite, ambitious, New York, Jewish, confident way of speaking, a vocal and linguistic combination I have heard echoed every now and then from the mouths of certain brilliant, accomplished men of that generation, though it is a nearly extinct dialect. The publisher Roger Straus (my mother's Brearley classmate Florence's brother) spoke that way. I hear it in the speech patterns of the poet John Hollander and the screenwriter Walter Bernstein. My father was more than twelve years older than my mother, not an unseemly age difference, but nevertheless, he was significantly older, he was charming in those familiar ways, and he paid her very close, loving attention (at least he did in the beginning). Surely, for my mother, these were more than enough reasons for marrying this man who faintly resembled in these ways the irresistibly charming and talented man her mother might have married. The past does not repeat itself, as Mark Twain observed, but it rhymes.

THE PHOTOGRAPH of my mother with George is indeed a little creepy when I look at it now. My mother's stare is disconcerting. Is she pensive, or terrified? My mother wears a dark dress with a neckline far too mature for a child of twelve. Has George dressed her for the picture? There's something a little bit like a Balthus painting in the pose, in the look. He isn't standing behind her, but seems to be sitting or crouching as he frames the shot. Is she sitting on his lap? His hands are beautiful. Those long, tapered fingers, the same fingers that made such magic on piano keys, are so gracefully and nimbly cradling his Leica.

Has my mother been dressing up with her sister Kay, who appears in other photographs taken by George that same day? Is it possibly her mother's gown she wears? Are they alone in this room, and was this the final picture of the session? It is evening, and the only lighting is candlelight, something George experimented with for his portraits. What, in any case, is he doing with his lover's middle child, taking these pictures of her, spending hours alone with her in the darkroom, showing her how to develop and print, instilling in her a lifelong obsession with photography, with documenting moments rather than being part of them, her presence, her gaze so often hidden by her own Leica? She spent hours of my childhood behind the closed door of her own basement darkroom, the room she told me it was not safe for me to enter when I knocked, the room where opening the door and letting in light could expose and ruin everything.

And that wasn't just any darkroom where my mother learned printing technique from George. It was in the basement of Gregory Zilboorg's house on East Seventieth Street, which was peculiarly situated directly across the street from my grandparents' double townhouse, where my mother and her sisters grew up. Dr. Zilboorg was a notorious psychoanalyst who counted among his analysands my grandmother, my grandfather, George, my grandfather's sister Bettina (a psychoanalyst herself, for whom Zilboorg was her training analyst, which is how he was introduced to the family, and it was during that four-year analysis when he moved to Seventieth Street), my grandfather's second wife, Phyllis, my grandfather's first cousin Edward M. M. Warburg, and numerous other relations and friends, from Lillian Hellman and Marshall Field to Mary Lasker, Ralph Ingersoll, and Moss Hart, whose time with Zilboorg inspired him to write *Lady in the Dark*.

Dr. Zilboorg—"Gregory," as he was called in later years around my house, yet another mysterious quasi-relative to sort out who had been and gone before my time—was an avid portrait photographer himself, who gave George his Leica and encouraged his photography. Among the photographic portraits in the Zilboorg papers at the Beinicke Library at Yale, there are large prints of relatives of two of his long-term analysands, Ruth Field (Marshall Field's wife) and Felix Warburg (James Warburg's uncle and Edward Warburg's father). Both are signed "Dr. Gregory Zilboorg," as if these photographs constitute his professional diagnosis. George in turn gave my mother her first camera for her tenth birthday, a Leica identical to his. My mother and George spent hours together, working in the Zilboorg basement darkroom, where George had learned to develop his negatives and to experiment with photographic printing technique.

What of it? I am suspicious of my own suspicion. Is my contemporary discomfort stirred by that photograph the dismay of a mother of daughters, or the wariness of anyone who watches the news and therefore has an awareness of the rampant child abuse bubbling under the surface everywhere? Or is it the jealousy of one who has been left out of the fun? It is so easy to look from the outside at people in a complicated situation and think you know what probably happened and how people probably felt. But nobody alive today knows what happened in those private moments among these people. We only know the rough outline, we only see the artifacts.

Did anything "happen"? I have no idea what really went on between my mother and the very devoted man behind the camera with whom she was very close throughout her childhood. How exactly can we define their relationship? When someone in the story is famous, every moment of his existence has, for people who care, an aura of significance, and there will always be people with a quasi-authority who think they know things they could not possibly know, simply because they have a lot of information and curiosity and a sense of entitlement to "the truth" about George Gershwin, as if sufficient obsession and possession of a lot of verifiable facts can earn both entitlement to and knowledge of the unknowable.

My best guess is that nothing that would qualify in contemporary terms as literally abusive ever occurred between my mother and George. My mother's manipulative governess Jodie, who told the Warburg girls she could read their minds and always knew what they were thinking, not to mention her zealous administration of daily enemas, was definitely an abuser. That she had such power over her charges is certainly an indication of what today would be considered negligence on the part of their parents, who for years were so otherwise engaged that they didn't notice that a monster was minding their children. Possibly the kind of invasive care that Jodie lavished on my mother led to my mother's receptivity to other subtle violations of the boundaries, both physical and emotional, that ordinarily exist between children and adults.

I do think there was probably a covert sexual charge in the atmosphere around all of these relationships, given the complexities of the connections between George and Kay, Kay and Jimmy, George and Andrea, and George and Jimmy.

Perhaps my real question is a larger one that is just as unanswerable. How did my mother go from being the reflected child in that photo, the receptive object of George's gaze, to being the watcher, the gazing, observing, detached woman of my childhood memories, a camera masking her face at so many moments?

KATHARINE FAULKNER Swift met James Paul Warburg in the summer of 1917, when she was playing the piano in the Edith Rubell Trio, with violinist Edith Rubell and cellist Marie Romeat, classmates at the Institute of Musical Art who had banded together to travel wherever they were invited, performing Brahms and Beethoven trios. Katharine was happy to earn whatever she could this way. Katharine had helped support her mother and younger brother with whatever she had earned giving piano and dance lessons from the time of her father's untimely death at age forty-one, when she was fourteen. She had earned both a diploma and a piano teacher's certificate from the Institute of Musical Art.

Her father, Samuel Shippen Swift, had been a distinguished

music critic for a number of different New York newspapers, starting with the *New York Evening Mail* and later for the *New York Tribune* and the *New York Sun*. A sometime church organist as well, he was also, owing to family obligations, the head of the William J. Smith Company in New Haven, manufacturers of a machine tool called the One-Lock Adjustable Reamer. He made a daily commute to spend his days struggling with the business (which he ultimately sold at a terrible loss in 1910) and would then return to the city each night to go hear an opera or attend a concert for review. The Swifts were a family devoted to music, and it is evident that both nature and nurture favored Katharine Swift.

By the time she was six, having attended the old Metropolitan Opera House with her father from the age of four, she had become obsessed with opera, and had memorized many Wagner scores. It was clear even then that she had both an extraordinary memory and absolute pitch. When Katharine was seven, her grandmother Gertrude Swift (the composer of dozens of hymns) recorded in her diary that they went together to hear *Rheingold,* where she "sat with unfailing attention through the two hours and a half, enjoying it most intelligently. She has heard it once before and knew the libretto perfectly."

Katharine developed a lifelong affinity for Mozart, as well as an enduring ambivalence about Bach, whom she called "Bickle-Bockle" (she was critical of his repetitions and predictability). She was an accomplished musician by the time she was playing in the Rubell trio, having studied with Bertha Tapper, Charles Martin Loeffler, Arthur Edward Johnstone, and Percy Goetschius, in addition to her conservatory training at the Institute of Musical Art.

✧ ✦ ✧

THE RUBELL Trio were engaged to perform at Fishrock Camp, the summer home of Isaac and Guta Loeb Seligman in Upper Saranac Lake in the Adirondacks. Their daughter, Margaret Lewisohn, who knew Katharine, hired the group on the spot to come over to the Lewisohn camp (as the enormous Adirondacks lodges were called) to play for the family the following afternoon. There, the audience included Margaret's cousin, seventeen-year-old Bettina Warburg, who was enchanted by Katharine.

Bettina, in turn, engaged the Trio to perform at Fontenay, the Westchester weekend home of her parents, Paul and Nina Loeb Warburg, in Hartsdale. (Nina was Guta's sister.) There, Katharine met Bettina's older brother, Jimmy Warburg, handsome in his pilot's U.S. Naval Reserve uniform. A Harvard man who wrote poetry and rode steeplechase, he descended from German Jewish banking families on both sides. His father, Paul M. Warburg, was the distinguished banker and architect of the Federal Reserve System. Jimmy's maternal grandfather, Solomon Loeb, was a founding partner of the Kuhn, Loeb & Co. investment bank. He was named for his mother's brother, James Loeb (a Kuhn, Loeb partner before his early retirement owing to fragile mental health), who not only established the Loeb Classical Library at Harvard but was also one of the founders of the Institute of Musical Art, where Katharine Swift had been trained, which later became known as the Juilliard School of Music.

Katharine and Jimmy were attracted to each other the day they met. They met again on several subsequent occasions, as the Rubell Trio was engaged to perform for yet more Warburg relations, at Woodlands, the Westchester estate belonging to Paul's flamboyant brother Felix and his wife, Frieda. (In the Warburg family, there are many tangled relationships; Frieda was both Paul's sister-in-law and Nina's niece. The family nickname for

Paul and Nina was Panina; for Felix and Frieda, it was Frieda-flix; and for their brother Max and his wife, Alice, Malice, so for example, someone might say, "Let's invite Malice for tea.")

Katharine's friendship with Bettina flourished as well. This connection between my grandmother and my great-aunt would last all their lives, even though they didn't see each other often, and even though each would refer condescendingly to the other as "the old lady" when asking me for news. They were secretly fonder of each other than that, calling each other "Tink" in notes and cards to the end of their lives.

By the autumn of 1917, when Katharine and Jimmy were sweethearts, his parents cautioned him against committing to her. They were both young; there was no haste about such an important decision. That she wasn't Jewish may also have been on their minds, but they were enlightened people, and they were quite fond of Katharine. Jimmy proposed to her precipitously, the day after he discovered that his father's meddling had grounded him. His enlisting in the U.S. Naval Reserve Flying Corps had disturbed his Hamburg-born father (who was naturalized in 1911), who couldn't understand why anyone would voluntarily go into "the horrible business of killing people." He thought going to war against Germany would be particularly barbaric, given that there was close family on the other side. His brother Max had been appointed by Kaiser Wilhelm II to head the German Secret Service, where he served as chief financial adviser and strategic intelligence consultant. Max's son Erich, Jimmy's first cousin, had enlisted in the Prussian Field Artillery Regiment in Berlin. (By the time of the Second World War, Erich would have become sufficiently Americanized to have dropped the *h* from his name and to serve as an officer in U.S. Air Force Intelligence. He distinguished himself in the African campaign as well as during the Normandy invasions, and with his native German he led the interrogation of Hermann Göring. At the end of the forty-eight-hour interrogation, Eric took Göring's fancy badger-hair shaving brush and sent it to his cousin Eddie, who had also landed in Normandy as an Army officer shortly after D-Day, because Eddie had complained that he had lost his own shaving brush.)

Jimmy had concealed a vision defect when he signed up for pilot training, refractive amblyopia that made him nearly blind in one eye. (I was born with this condition as well, and it went unrecognized and untreated in my childhood. I was functionally blind in one eye all my life, having been told repeatedly that there was no possible treatment for the condition after the age of six, until the end of 2009, when I discovered a rigorous, life-changing vision therapy that has allowed me to go from 20/400 to 20/50 in my weak eye. This has given me, for the first time in my life, starting at age fifty-four, stereoscopic vision. I know from experience that flying with his limited field of vision and poor three-dimensional perception would have been a reckless thing to do, notwithstanding the triumphs of the one-eyed aviator, Wiley Post.)

As Jimmy waited for his overseas assignment, Paul told Navy Secretary Josephus Daniels that Jimmy's vision should have kept him from being accepted into the training program. The day after he learned that he had been grounded as a consequence of his father's communication with the Navy Secretary, Jimmy and Katharine were engaged. He had just turned twenty-one and come into a trust fund with an annual income of $4,000, and he didn't need his parents' approval. Paul and Nina did approve of Katharine, even if they were concerned about the wisdom of this step. Katharine's mother was all for it and said that her dear late husband, Sam, had come to her in a vision to tell her that Katharine and Jimmy should marry.

Katharine and Jimmy were married on June 1, 1918, an act my grandfather called in his autobiography "a spirit of revolt against parental authority," though he told me when I was thirteen that he felt he had been pressured to marry my grandmother "because of a goddamned ghost"; this was not his only revision of the history of his first marriage as the decades went by. (I have no idea how he felt about my being named Katharine Swift, given his regrets about the Katharine Swift he married.)

Paul and Nina created a trust for Katharine as a wedding day gift, almost like a dowry, with no strings attached. The language was simple; the remainder beneficiaries were designated as the issue of her marriage to Jimmy. It was an unusual and generous gesture. Were they stirring the pot just a little here, challenging Jimmy and his annual four thousand dollars, by making his charming, Episcopal, un-wealthy bride less dependent on him? In 1918, I am sure Paul and Nina couldn't have imagined that this trust, meant to give their new daughter-in-law freedom and independence, would aid her in all sorts of practical ways with her love affair with George Gershwin. Nor could they have envisioned that the trust would be her only steady source of income for the rest of her life, other than the royalties from the three hit songs she would write with Jimmy, "Fine and Dandy," "Can't We Be Friends?" and "Can This Be Love?" (Twenty years after the divorce, Jimmy gallantly gave his ex-wife his share of the copyrights of all their collaborative efforts.)

They were much less fond of my great-grandmother Ellen Faulkner Swift than of their new daughter-in-law. Paul wrote to Bettina, "I am a butterfly of gentleness and sweetness and harm-less-ness as compared to this daughter-eating woman."

Nina's brother-in-law Jacob Schiff, far more concerned about the implications for the family of this mixed marriage, sent the newlyweds a wordy telegram (as a member of the board of Western Union he had free telegram privileges) saying: "I wish you joy to your happiness but cannot refrain from telling you that I am deeply disturbed by your action in marrying out of the faith in view of its probable effect upon my own progeny."

On April 17, 1925, two days before Katharine's twenty-eighth birthday, she and Jimmy gave a party for Jascha Heifetz. When she met George Gershwin that night, she was happily married, ensconced in a fairly luxurious life with her husband of seven years. Their three little girls were then nine, six, and four. The Warburgs had a good life, with their elegantly appointed double townhouse on East Seventieth Street and their rambling Greenwich estate in rural Connecticut, which provided an idyllic summer setting for the family. There were many servants, fabulous parties. They were a charming couple who lived well and had fun. Jimmy was the youngest bank president in the country. Katharine was known for her wit and style and her piano playing. Her in-laws had been proud of her when she sat at their piano accompanying their guest, Albert Einstein (along with a cellist, Willem Willeke), in an afternoon of Mozart trios while Einstein tried out all three of their friend Felix Kahn's Stradivarius violins. Kay and Jimmy moved in glamorous and amusing, overlapping circles—the "Our Crowd" world, the Algonquin crowd of café society and *New Yorker* writers.

Pauline Heifetz, Jascha's sister, brought George Gershwin, who was leaving for London the following day, as her date to the party. The next day she wrote in her diary, "Party at the Warburgs. George goes to Europe." Next to this she drew a skull and crossbones and wrote, "Finita really," a reference to *La commedia è finite!*—The play is over!—the final line of the 1907 opera *Pagliacci*.

Katharine Faulkner Swift as an infant, with her mother, Ellen Faulkner Swift, and her paternal grandfather, Joseph Swift, 1897.

Nina Loeb Warburg and Paul M. Warburg with their children, Bettina and James, 1917.

Katharine Swift Warburg with her daughters, Kay, Andrea, and April, 1925.

Kay Swift and George Gershwin "horse riding" at Bydale, 1928.

Stars Joe Cook and Dave Chasen with the songwriting duo Kay Swift and Jimmy Warburg, aka Paul James, striking a pose during a *Fine and Dandy* rehearsal, 1930.

Kay Swift, 1931.

Andrea Swift Warburg
as a tap-dancing
Degas ballerina at
the celebration of her
grandmother
Nina Loeb Warburg's
sixtieth birthday, 1930.

Bettina Warburg
as the Mona Lisa
at her mother's
birthday fete,
1930.

Kay, April, and
Andrea Warburg
with their dog,
Inky, 1932.

George Gershwin's self-portrait in a mirror with twelve-year-old Andrea, 1934. (Courtesy of the Ira and Leonore Gershwin Trusts)

Kay Swift, wearing the antique gold cuff bracelets given to her by George Gershwin to celebrate the premiere of "An American in Paris," 1928.

Kay Swift at the beach, 1933.

George Gershwin, 1934.

Ink drawing of Kay Swift by
George Gershwin, 1935.

Mary Lasker, Kay Swift, and George Gershwin on a Long Island summer weekend, 1935.

Faye Hubbard in his "fancy duds," 1939.

Sidney Kaufman's
OSS identification
badge, 1944.

Sidney Kaufman,
1946. (Photo by Andrea
Warburg Kaufman)

Kay Swift and Hunter Galloway on their wedding day, 1947.

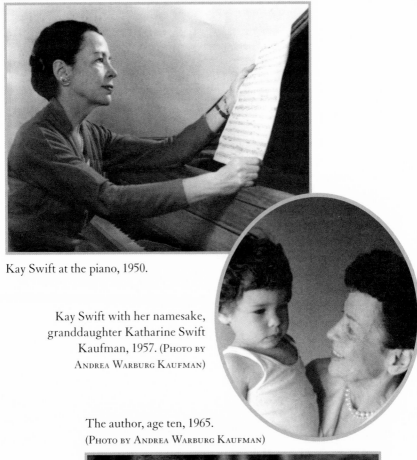

Kay Swift at the piano, 1950.

Kay Swift with her namesake,
granddaughter Katharine Swift
Kaufman, 1957. (PHOTO BY
ANDREA WARBURG KAUFMAN)

The author, age ten, 1965.
(PHOTO BY ANDREA WARBURG KAUFMAN)

By the time the Warburgs crossed paths with George again in December of 1925, at a party given by Walter Damrosch (a close Swift family friend known to Katharine from earliest childhood) after the premier of George's *Concerto in F,* which Damrosch had commissioned, the mutual fascination was already very much in evidence. Who knows what happened, or how it happened? Perhaps the Damrosch connection added meaning for Katharine, providing a link between the late Sam Swift and George. There must have been a spark, a series of sparks, between them. George's love affair with Katharine Swift Warburg, who soon began to call herself Kay Swift at Gershwin's suggestion (he also renamed his friend Vladimir Dukelsky Vernon Duke), lasted (despite the many other women) until he left New York for a stint in Hollywood writing film scores in 1936.

THE 1925 Gershwin show *Tip-Toes* featured a character called Tip-Toes Kaye, which might have been a coincidence. By November 1926, the show for which George and Ira Gershwin had written a score even before the libretto had been written by Guy Bolton and P. G. Wodehouse, a madcap froth of absurdity with the working title *Mayfair,* which then for a while became *Cheerio,* opened on Broadway with the title *Oh, Kay!* Gertrude Lawrence starred as the eponymous Kay, an English bootlegger who ends up in love with the rich American Jimmy Winter, whose opulent Long Island mansion she and her criminal brother have been using in his absence as a place to stash the rum.

Oh, Kay!, a huge hit (256 performances), was a perfect Prohibition comedy, with a flimsy plot contrived around an endless cycle of coincidence, mistaken identities, criminals dressed as servants, an easily duped, bumbling Revenue officer who turns out to be a famous pirate who hijacks the booze, an overbearing and humorless wife who is clearly all wrong for Jimmy (but it turns out conveniently that their marriage was never legal), a set of twins, a confused judge, and a wedding with a last-minute switch when Jimmy and Kay realize they love each other, which allows Kay to stay in America instead of being deported to England.

The lively tune stack, with eight of the original songs cut because they didn't fit the story line, included "Maybe," "Clap Yo' Hands!," "Do, Do, Do," "Oh, Kay, You're OK with Me," and "Fidgety Feet," but the knockout number was "Someone to Watch Over Me," which Gertrude Lawrence sang to a rag doll George Gershwin had bought for this purpose during the show's trial run in Philadelphia.

While the Gershwins didn't write this absurd libretto, they certainly influenced the elements in their shows, and there are a number of striking parallels worth noting. In addition to Kay and Jimmy W. and their opulent digs, Kay the bootlegger is English—as was Gertrude Lawrence, for whom the part was written (she was the first British performer to star in a Broadway musical)—and so, too, Kay Swift's heritage was English. Her father descended from entirely British stock, and her mother was English. Her parents met on a transatlantic crossing in 1894, when Samuel Shippen Swift was returning to New York from a trip to London and Paris after his graduation from the University of Pennsylvania, and Ellen Mary Faulkner was on her way to visit family in America for the first time.

More significantly, the action consisted of a lot of tiptoeing, subterfuge, changed identities, and the realization that the married couple didn't belong together, because a bigger love interest had come along. Constance, Jimmy's stuffy wife who is cast aside for the lively bootlegger Kay, might remind us of the demure, genteel, entirely appropriate Mrs. James P. Warburg, who hosted that fateful party to which Pauline Heifetz brought her soon-to-be-former boyfriend. By the time the curtain falls, she has been replaced by someone a lot like the effervescent, alluring, rule-breaking Kay Swift.

THOUGH I know the score by heart, I have only seen this show onstage once, at the Goodspeed Opera House in Connecticut, in 1989. Nick and I were invited to the theater and dinner with a cousin and contemporary of my mother's, one of the four Lewisohn girls who often played with their cousins, the three Warburg girls (it emerged a few years later that their governess and Jodie were lesbian lovers, which may have accounted for the amount of time the seven little girls spent playing together in the two households or in Central Park), who told me during intermission, as we discussed the show's obvious connection to my grandparents, that my grandmother and my father had been lovers. This, she informed me, was how he met my mother. It had been arranged. Sidney was one of my grandmother's cast-off suitors, didn't I know this? Everyone in the family knew this.

I don't see how this could possibly be true, but I will never know for sure. My father, despite his faint resemblance to Gershwin in certain ways, was not exactly my grandmother's type, but that didn't always keep her from romantic involvements. (The most extreme example of this being her sexual involvement with Gregory Zilboorg, with whom for some inexplicable reason she felt obligated to have sex, on the analytic couch, during their sessions, for which she paid fifty dollars each time, about whom she confided to me, "He was the only man with whom I ever had sexual intercourse to whom I was not physically attracted.") Both my grandmother and my father were capable of the subterfuge that would have been required to ensure that my mother had no clue about anything, if there was anything to have a clue about.

I don't think it happened. The dates don't work, the timing is off. Although my grandmother and my father had a surprising number of friends in common, from Kate and Zero Mostel to Madeleine and Jack Gilford, I had never heard of their meeting or even knowing of each other before my parents met at the office of the National Board of Review of Motion Pictures. Could that story contain another story about my father seeking my mother out at the suggestion of my grandmother? Or was it possible that he met her coincidentally, having once been a lover of my grandmother's? It's far-fetched. But I will never have complete confidence that there is nothing whatsoever true about my Lewisohn cousin's story, either. So there is just one thing I do know about this with absolute certainty: I come from a family in which people think it is fine to say these things to one another during the intermission of *Oh, Kay!*

MY MOTHER and her two sisters lived mostly in the large nursery on the top floor of the Warburgs' double townhouse on East Seventieth Street during the Brearley school year. They only really saw their parents for any sustained family time in the summers, when they moved to Bydale, the bucolic, rambling country house in Greenwich (at a time when almost all of Greenwich was what is now called "backcountry"), where life was much less formal, though there were many big parties that spilled out onto the vast lawns and went well into the night, the noise keeping the girls awake. Gregory Zilboorg was sometimes among the weekend houseguests. Some nights they were brought down in their pajamas to sing a few songs in close harmony while their mother played the piano, which my mother and her younger sister, Kay, enjoyed, while their older sister, April, was miserable about appearing before the partygoers in her pajamas.

George was a frequent Bydale houseguest, spending not just long weekends but also making extended visits there over the years, the first one being the entire summer of 1928, when he was ensconced in the guest cottage, writing much of *An American in Paris*. Kay's mother died at fifty-six of breast cancer in early July, which was a huge loss, but it may have relieved Kay of concern about her mother's judgments about her romantic entanglement with George. To celebrate the premiere of *An American in Paris,* George bought Kay a pair of antique gold cuff bracelets, which she wore often. (Did Jimmy notice or mind?) George didn't wear a wristwatch when he performed, and instead carried a gold pocketwatch, for which Kay gave him a gold fob, with a good-luck charm on the chain—a little golden dove which she had made for him, with a sapphire in one eye and a diamond in the other. Those were their birthstones. He carried this secret talisman everywhere.

In that same season, she and Jimmy had their first success as a songwriting duo, with two songs, "Wait 'til the Light Turns Green" and "Little White Lies" (both are sadly lost) in the score of *Say When*, a forgettable Broadway revue that ran for just fifteen performances. In the years that followed, George wrote most of his *Second Rhapsody* and some of *Porgy and Bess* in the Bydale guest cottage as well.

In Greenwich, the girls ate breakfast and lunch with their parents, even dinner at times. Life was far more formal in the city. They never sat down to a meal together. The girls ate their meals supervised by Jodie upstairs in the nursery, the bland food she selected for them sent up in a dumbwaiter from a subterranean kitchen they never saw, prepared by a cook they never met. (My mother once persuaded her little sister, Kay, to climb into the dumbwaiter and travel down to the basement, where the cook, expecting dirty dishes and not a small child, opened the door and screamed in fright, and so did Kay, because the homely cook looked to her like a witch.) If either Kay or Jimmy came upstairs to sit with the girls while they ate their supper, before going out to dinner or hosting a dinner party, it was a treat. Sometimes the girls were allowed to sit on the bed and watch their mother get ready to go out.

WHEN I interviewed the writer Madeleine L'Engle for a profile some twenty-five years ago, I asked her to tell me about her first published piece of writing, a subject most writers enjoy revisiting. She told me it was a story originally written when she was a senior at Smith College that was subsequently published in *Tanager* magazine. It concerns the very fancy household of a childhood friend, and it starts off with a vivid description of two little girls, observed by the governess, watching in silence while their very glamorous mother sits at her dressing table—her face glimpsed only in the mirror—putting on her makeup and jewelry. For no particular reason, I asked the name of this childhood friend, and discovered that she was my aunt April, my mother's older sister. The woman in the mirror was, of course, my grandmother. (It also emerged that Madeleine's husband of forty years, the actor Hugh Franklin, who had died just weeks before we met, had for more than twenty years played Dr. Charles Tyler, the husband of the Fran Heflin character, Mona Kane Tyler, on *All My Children,* which made us practically family.)

MY MOTHER's explanation to me about why her sisters didn't like George had the rhythms of a retold fairy tale. She would always tell it in the same words: The youngest sister was too young and only knew that George was a competitor of Daddy's, not to mention that George had the disconcerting habit of asking little Kay, "Don't you like me?" The oldest sister, April, was too old, and could see the threat to the family George posed all too well, because she knew what was going on and what was at risk. Only the middle sister was just right; only she was not too young, not too old, but just the right age to be accepting, responsive, eager to please, happy to have his attention. Only my mother had liked George, had enjoyed him, and he, in turn, was enchanted by her. She was probably the child he knew best in the course of his life.

In 1930, when Gershwin was conducting the premiere of the remade *Strike Up the Band,* one of the featured songs was "I've Got a Crush on You," a song for which my mother, then eight, and her little sister, Kay, then six, had worked out a soft-shoe routine. My grandmother was seated in the first row, directly behind the conductor's podium. When the moment came for that song to be performed, as he conducted the opening notes of the number, George turned around with a grin and whispered to her, "Andy and Kay!" (For some reason, probably originating with a careless assumption by the Gershwin biographer Edward Jablonski, this story is repeated in numerous books incorrectly, with George saying "April and Andy." But April had no part in the soft shoe, and it was definitely the two younger girls to whom he referred. April and Andy did sing together for company on occasion, and George especially enjoyed their harmonized rendition of the early Gershwin song "I Must Be Home by Twelve O'Clock.")

My mother, though shy, was a tap-dancing whiz as a child. In 1927, at age five, she danced one night with Bojangles Robinson on a Broadway stage as part of a benefit performance, and on a couple of occasions she was scooped out of bed and brought downstairs to a party in full swing in order to tap-dance cutely with Fred Astaire, a frequent guest with his sister Adele at the legendary parties at East Seventieth Street, and at Bydale, depending on the season. Many people learned to Charleston at those soirees. The rug would be rolled back and Kay Swift, in her elegant flapper phase, would teach everyone the steps. On other occasions, Kay and George would together play the music for dancing on the pair of baby grand pianos that graced the Warburgs' dramatically art deco, black-and-white "modern room" where the parties took place.

Ira Gershwin has described a waltz that George had written, based on the song "Tonight" from the flop 1933 Gershwin show (wonderful score, hopeless libretto), *Pardon My English*. At those two pianos, first they played "Tonight" straight through, then they played a countermelody, and finally, they played the countermelody and the melody together. Ira called this musical conversation "Her Waltz, His Waltz, Their Waltz."

My mother's little sister, Kay, was always bolder and more outgoing, but as adults, breaking into an old shave and a haircut clog step routine together in the kitchen while washing dishes after a family Thanksgiving, they both agreed that my mother was the one with the better sense of rhythm, and the better sense of pitch, too, even though Kay was always the louder, more eager performer whom my mother would elbow in the ribs if she strayed too far off-pitch.

My mother and George had a routine in those first years when he was on the scene and she was still very young: Each time they met, she would work with him on his cramp roll or his scissor steps, and he would make a point of being very serious about the whole thing, taking her advice and following little

Andy's example as if she were his teacher, but then deliberately going off-beat to make her laugh. As time passed and they grew closer, and his tap-dancing skills improved, they developed a number of their own, a shim-sham sequence they would go into at odd moments when they were together, just for a moment sometimes, often as a form of greeting.

My grandmother, who was herself a graceful dancer who loved dancing with George at parties and nightclubs, was touched by his devotion to this routine with her middle daughter. He was a man, she said, who "took joyous delight in whatever he was doing," and would often break into a tap routine at odd moments on his own; for example, while waiting for an elevator he might riffle and scuffle down the corridor and back.

At Bydale, George relished the life of the country squire as he learned to ride Denny, his favorite of the seven horses stabled there. This meant my mother had to ride a different horse, though Denny was hers, so she had mixed feelings about George's passion for riding. "Tummy in, tummy out," George would mutter under his breath, cigar clenched between his teeth, as he tried to post in rhythm with Denny's big, galumphing stride. He called it "horse riding" and Kay would gently correct him each time, "Horse*back* riding, George." He enjoyed dressing up in the riding breeches and shiny new riding boots Kay selected for him. She was a natural with horses and had what is called "a good seat," even though she had one serious riding accident that was more a story about her personality than it was about her riding abilities. When my aunt Kay, at age six, was scraped off her pony when he took her under a low tree branch as he veered off the bridle path in the woods, my grandmother reacted in a panic by diving off her horse after her. Little Kay was unscathed, but my grandmother's arm and collarbone were severely broken.

So how did my grandmother, a classically trained musician, a child prodigy with perfect pitch and a sensitive piano style, come to write Broadway show tunes? It was of course George who admired her musical talents and recognized her daring and her openness to all sorts of new experiences. In 1927, when their relationship had clearly become a complex and genuine love, he urged her to take a job as rehearsal pianist for the Rodgers and Hart show *A Connecticut Yankee,* and she did just that, leaving her luxurious household every day for a drafty rehearsal hall, being driven across town by a chauffeur in the Warburgs' gleaming Hispano-Suiza.

That year she and Jimmy, whose family tradition included the writing of multilingual, punning doggerel for every occasion, began to write songs together, starting with the revue *Say When.* George's encouragement had sparked Kay's new focus for her musical talents, but now she was off and running, her inventive composition skills meshing ingeniously with Jimmy's talents at turning a phrase. (This was not their first musical collaboration; when April was born, Jimmy had written some charming poems for her, a group he called "Tiny Songs for a Tiny Mouse," with titles such as "Doggie," "Kitty," and "Piggie," for which Kay had composed inventive tunes.)

Soon to follow were "Up Among the Chimney Pots" in *The Nine-Fifteen Revue* and then their hugely successful and still popular "Can't We Be Friends?," introduced by the torch singer Libby Holman in the first *Little Show* when she sang it to Clifton Webb. (My grandmother was a devoted and loyal friend to

Libby when, not long after that, she was indicted for the 1932 gunshot murder of her husband, tobacco heir Smith Reynolds. She always insisted on her complete innocence, but then, my grandmother also refused to believe that Libby was bisexual, despite her well-known involvements with several women, Jane Bowles among them.)

As a lyricist, my grandfather didn't use the Warburg name, because of concern about the family being publicly associated with show business, which might upset bank clients. In any case, it would definitely have signaled to his father that Jimmy wasn't respectful enough of the meaning of the family name in banking circles, and so for his pen name he reversed his first and middle names and became Paul James. If James Paul Warburg couldn't compete against George Gershwin for the affection of his own wife, maybe Paul James could.

THE CHALLENGE and fun of writing the complete score for a show was inevitable. No woman had ever written the music for an entire successful Broadway musical score before, but then neither had a banker ever written an entire show's worth of lyrics. The Crash was no obstacle; when the show's producers ran out of money and the opening was threatened, Jimmy Warburg and his friends Marshall Field and Averill Harriman became the principal backers. And so on September 23, 1930, the curtain went up and *Fine and Dandy* was born.

IN MAY of that year, while they were working on the score for *Fine and Dandy*, Kay and Jimmy wrote and performed in a lavish musical entertainment for the sixtieth birthday of his mother, Nina. The performance, in which most of the American

Warburgs as well as the Lewisohns all played multiple roles, including the children, all in elaborate costumes, took place in the garden at Fontenay, Nina and Paul's Westchester house, where the Edith Rubell Trio had performed in 1917. Hosted by Jimmy playing the part of a jocular emcee who can't quite be trusted, the script is a mishmash of typical music-hall revue routines, but the music was provided by Kay, who accompanied every act she wasn't in throughout the elaborate production.

There are numerous witty moments, beginning with Act One, when Kay, playing the part of an inebriated baby seeking a cocktail from anyone who will give her one, is wheeled onstage by Jimmy in a giant baby carriage. At another point, the music (Kay at the piano) makes a sly dig at Jimmy's preferred identity when his musical cue to enter for the next routine starts off as "Hatikvah" and segues to "British Grenadiers." The script is filled with witty high jinks, card tricks, a string quartet playing a composition credited in the script as having been written for the occasion by "K.S.W.," Bettina posing as the *Mona Lisa*, and little Andrea dressed to match a Degas ballerina breaking into a tap-dancing routine ("with encores"). The costumes were extraordinary, and the whole enterprise clearly required much preparation and teamwork from Kay and Jimmy, working together to create this loving musical celebration for his mother in which they both had starring roles, as did their three daughters. For that one afternoon, George Gershwin was nowhere on the scene.

How DID they do it? How did this unhappily married yet romantically enmeshed husband and wife manage to write music together, first the songs in those earlier shows, then the birthday fete, and finally the elegant score to an entire musical? Of course, they would never have written the score to *Fine and Dandy* if my grandmother had not fallen in love with George. The year 1930 was the halfway point in that romance. There is something poignant in banker Jimmy Warburg's willingness to pen a lyric with the lines "Yes men, press men, lawyers and bankers / Don't give me that for which my soul hankers." Gershwin's looming presence was acknowledged directly in the extra verse for "Fine and Dandy" in which all the other composers threaten to appropriate Gershwin's "themes and rhythmic schemes." One needn't be a psychoanalyst (though Kay, Jimmy, and George would soon all lie on Zilboorg's couch) to recognize the possibility that the author of these lyrics felt that something of his had been stolen and that he wanted to swipe something in return.

There are echoes, too, in "Etiquette" of Kay's etiquette instructions and sartorial advice for George, who enjoyed the finer things in life with the gusto of a street kid. She and he both grew up in modest surroundings (his background making him one of the song's working-class "Blums and Blaues and Blitzes/Steins and Lipkowitzes") and perhaps Jimmy was making a sardonic observation about the way she had taught George "the proper way to eat and talk" and (not one of my grandfather's best rhymes) "the secrets of the knife and fork" as a way of helping to join "the smartest set." George did indeed "aspire to acquire proper etiquette." As only outsiders truly can, Kay and George together relished and appreciated the deluxe amenities that came with the Warburg way of life as well as the ease and comforts and access that were a consequence of his own tremendous success.

The collaboration with Donald Ogden Stewart and Joe Cook makes it impossible to sort out who dreamed up which elements in the show. Joe Cook's insanely inventive and hilarious pointless, cockeyed machinery filled the set, inviting comparisons to the contraptions of Rube Goldberg (who had been a colleague of Sam Swift's at *The Evening Mail*). The Fordyce Drop Forge Tool and Die Company was almost certainly inspired to some degree by Samuel Swift's ill-fated stewardship of the William J. Smith Company, manufacturers of the One-Lock Adjustable Reamer. It is very likely that his adoring daughter accompanied him on a trip to New Haven more than once. They probably sang opera and Gilbert and Sullivan on the train in time with the chugging and clacking of the wheels on the rails. She definitely had familiarity with New Haven based on childhood experience, owing also to time spent visiting Milford cousins. There are numerous Fordyces in the Swift family tree as well. Whenever my grandmother took the train to New Haven to visit us, she would always exclaim, upon seeing either of the massive rock formations that bracket the city, "Now, is that West Rock or East Rock?"

Jimmy Warburg's first published economic paper concerned textile mills, which he had investigated firsthand. When you "listen to the clamor of the big trip hammer" in "The Machine Shop Opening," you are hearing a perfect moment of deep connection and harmony and love between Kay and Jimmy and the sensibility they each brought to the musical depiction of workers toiling in a noisy factory.

The title song, the ubiquitous "Fine and Dandy," was composed in the hospital room where Kay lay in traction, having broken her right arm in that riding accident. A small piano was wheeled to her bedside, and she was able to reach the keyboard with her left hand in order to work out the melody and then jot it awkwardly for later transcription. Perhaps this left-handed approach is why the song was originally conceived as a slow, lugubrious ballad, with the lyrics "Here today / Gone tomorrow." When the tempo was doubled during the first rehearsal, Jimmy quickly came up with the jaunty, upbeat, "Gee it's all / Fine and Dandy!" opener, and they were off to the races.

The score to "Fine and Dandy" is filled with many moments of personal conversation between Kay and Jimmy, if you listen for them. Their marriage would end, they would each go on to find love with other people, but at this moment, despite and because of George Gershwin, they wrote these songs, one after the other, and they clearly took pleasure in the creation, working closely together, collaborating intimately all the way through. Some people have a baby to try to save a marriage. My grandparents had a Broadway musical.

In 1932, the year George Gershwin dedicated his *Songbook* to Kay Swift, Alfred A. Knopf published Jimmy Warburg's second collection of poetry, *Shoes and Ships and Sealing Wax,* which he also dedicated to her: "To K.S. (if you can stand another one)." Both volumes of his poetry are a mix of high/low poetic sensibility, from sonnets to doggerel, the best of which is in a league with Ogden Nash and Dorothy Parker—"Hit her over the head with a hammer!/Lay her to rest without a wreath!/Do as you like with her bones, God damn her!/For she got lipstick on her teeth"—and the worst of which is sneering, racist, and bizarrely antithetical to Jimmy's contemporaneous socially conscious lyrics for "Rich or Poor" and "Starting at the Bottom"— "It's not much of a trick/To wield shovel and pick,/But it gives you lumbago./I'd hardly advise it,—/In fact you'll despise it,/ Unless you're a Dago."

The tone of this line is regrettably consistent with his lyric for one of the additional, never-published verses to "Fine and

Dandy," which eerily forecasts the assassination of Mohandas Gandhi by eighteen years:

> *Joe: Now we're in India. You be Gandhi.*
> *Nancy: I'll be Gandhi. And who are you?*
> *Joe: I shall have to be the Viceroy.*
> *Nancy: I don't want to be a colored boy.*
> *Joe: Just the same. You be Gandhi.*
> *Nancy: I'll be Gandhi. What's that to you?*
> *Joe: If I'm handy, I'll murder Gandhi.*
> *Nancy: Say, that is fine and dandy too!*

Starting in early 1929, as the economic situation in Germany deteriorated, Jimmy was abroad for extended periods on missions representing his father, Paul, and his uncle Felix to protect Warburg banking interests. (In that same time period, Felix had several conversations with Ambassador Dodd—Martha Dodd's father—seeking assurance about the safety of Jews and clarity about the intentions of the Third Reich with regard to Jewish interests.) In the James P. Warburg Papers at the John F. Kennedy Library, not only are the extraordinary demands made on him by his family obligations evident, but also the record of all his European travel (ocean crossing taking an additional five to seven days in each direction), significant time away from his family just as the connection between Kay and George was deepening.

In 1930, just days after *Fine and Dandy* opened, Jimmy sailed on a trip that lasted six weeks. In 1931 he was gone from January 3 to February 4, and he sailed for Hamburg again on June 1, returning to New York on July 10, but he sailed to Hamburg for a third time on July 25 and wasn't back in New York until October 23. The following year, he sailed for London on

March 31 and returned to New York on June 6. He left for Hamburg again that year, on July 27, returning on August 23. In 1933, after living in Washington for the first six months, he was in Europe for all of June and July. Each of these European trips had a complex itinerary that took him from Hamburg to London to Paris, or from Berlin to Vienna to London.

Without exception, every city Jimmy visited on these trips was an outpost for M. M. Warburg banking offices or interests, where he had exceedingly difficult work to do, assessing the situation and communicating daily (in a combination of letters and coded telegrams) with his father and with his uncle Felix on strategies to rescue the family bank from the profligate management by their older brother, Jimmy's uncle, Max. Although Jimmy reported to his father and uncle that the only rational choice was to shut down the Hamburg bank, Paul and Felix chose to save the bank with the venerable M. M. Warburg name by a variety of strategies, which included transfers of several million dollars directly from their own pockets, for which "Maxie the Taxi" (as my great-aunt Bettina called him) was not particularly grateful, because he thought it was his due.

Max, unlike his brothers, had spent time in London after a stint in the German army, being groomed for his banking responsibilities by training for a year at the House of Rothschild. Perhaps this was the source of his abiding fascination with titles and ranks. (Bettina was critical of the way more than one generation of the Malices "cared too much about Hons and Vons.") Max virtually memorized Burke's *Peerage* and Debrett as a way of immersing himself in the nuances of British aristocracy, and by the time he returned to Hamburg, his English was not only fluent but he had also developed a perfect Etonian accent.

Jimmy was burdened with policing the spending habits of the various members of the Malices, who were still convinced that the rise of the Third Reich wasn't a threat to their comfortable way of life. (One 1932 report to Felix from Jimmy about the Hamburg family needing vacations because of their claim that they worked under such strain includes a barbed, "If Erich needs two vacations in the course of a winter I ought to need six . . . they tire themselves out with their needless bickering.") In Berlin, Jimmy attended a rally and heard Hitler speak to a roaring crowd.

Although his father had died unexpectedly in March of 1932, Jimmy was once more on his way to London on the last day of that month. A few weeks later, his uncle Felix replied to Jimmy's report written en route between Stockholm and Berlin, in which Jimmy had urged the closure of the Amsterdam office, saying, "It might be advisable to keep it alive just in case Hitlerism makes living for the family so outrageously disagreeable that they might want to have another pied-a-terre to move to."

Soon after this, Hitlerism did of course make living for all European Jews much more than "outrageously disagreeable," but the first harbingers for the Warburgs came a few months after Hitler came to power, in May of 1933, when Nina's brother James Loeb died of a heart attack and the local Nazi authority in Murnau refused to permit the burial of his ashes along with those of his Christian wife's, who predeceased him by a few months, in the spot they had selected. The following month, the family was stunned by the news that Paul's elderly uncle, his mother's brother Moritz Oppenheim, had, with his wife, Käthie, committed suicide at their home in Frankfurt. Felix Warburg wrote: "No doubt the Hitler regime made life for them a plague and they were yearning for the end of their days."

Suicide was not unknown in the Warburg family, however. Bettina Warburg actually created a chart for herself to map

the family mental illnesses, labeling several generations of the
family tree with abbreviations signifying manic depression,
schizophrenia, suicide, alcoholism, epilepsy, tuberculosis, full
mania, general paresis of the insane, and in one case, idiot.

Bettina had been inspired to train as a psychiatrist because of
mental illness in the family, particularly the suffering of two of
her relatives—the crippling depressions of her mother's brother,
James Loeb, and the apparent psychotic interludes experienced
by her father's brilliant older brother, Aby Warburg.

A crackpot art historian whom Ron Chernow described as
"a voluble, hyperkinetic man, a brilliant little windbag, who
seemed to have absorbed, like a sponge, all of Western civili-
zation," who "gladly regurgitated his learning to any listener
for hours on end," Aby first descended into madness in 1918.
This was when he realized that he was responsible for starting
the First World War, by delving into images of pagan antiquity,
which had stirred the primitive energies that were now causing
destruction on the battlefields of Europe. His attempt to shoot
his family to spare them their fate at the hands of these un-
leashed furies led to his first hospitalization.

He was taken to Bellevue, an elegant private clinic outside
Kreuzlingen, on Lake Constance in Switzerland, where he
was treated by Ludwig Binswanger, who had already treated
both his brother Fritz and Paul's brother-in-law James Loeb for
depression. Dr. Binswanger's correspondence with Sigmund
Freud about this patient refers to "Professor V. from I." in the
"encrypted" way that psychoanalytic papers do, so nobody can
possibly recognize the patient as Professor [W]arburg from [H]
amburg. In their published correspondence about Professor V.,
Binswanger notes that the patient refused to speak with anyone,
preferring to commune only with his *Seelentierchen*—his "tiny

soulful animals"—butterflies and moths. Professor V. had become a vegetarian at Bellevue, because he was convinced that the kitchen was cooking and serving him the flesh of his own family.

In 1895, Aby, the oldest of the five brothers, had arrived in America to attend his brother Paul's wedding. From there, he had traveled west, where he stayed among the Hopi Indians, studying their snake dance rituals, which involved dozens of poisonous snakes. He would later say that he never could have fully understood Italian Renaissance art without the insights he gained studying the pageant of writhing serpents and Hopi dancers, and this formed the foundation of his beliefs in the re-iteration of pagan forms and images in Renaissance art, even as it triggered his first flight into madness, so powerful was the imagery that obsessed him.

Famously, Aby offered his brothers a deal: He would re-nounce his claim as firstborn son and step aside from the family banking business if they would agree to buy him all the books he wanted for his library. How many books could he want? Max, Felix, Paul, and Fritz accepted his offer and discovered that their eccentric brother wanted a very large number of books, some 350,000, which he assembled in a bizarre, associative ar-rangement unlike any other library in the world, corresponding to his division of all human history into the categories of Action, Orientation, Word, and Image.

Aby Warburg's private madness has become the foundation for generations of art history scholarship, and while his immer-sion in the esoteric and arcane has probably led to his being overlooked at times, many scholars recognize parallels with thinkers from Nietzsche to Walter Benjamin. Aby Warburg's greatest achievement beyond the assembly of a magnificent li-brary is probably his ability to illuminate connections between the past and the present, a theory he called "mimesis," which examined the role of the mimetic (repetition of forms) in the history of art.

Aby described his cataloguing system as *Nachbarschaft*—neighborliness—a system of organizing his library that aided creativity. In the Warburg Institute today, for example, books on heraldry, emblems, secret codes, shorthand, and the art of memory are all shelved together. Aby believed his system would lead scholars to make spontaneous new connections among these related topics. A visionary perpetually obsessed with cultural connections and exchanges through the centuries, Aby was especially fascinated by the interconnected meanings of visual images across time and space. His name for his dream of a picture atlas tool for studying these historical relationships was Mnemosyne, but it was incomplete at the time of his death in 1929, and his intentions have never been fully understood.

When Aby's brothers complained about the endless expenditures on books, he pointed out that other rich families had racing stables, but the Warburgs would have their library. Aby was for the Warburg family the equivalent of the Talmudic scholar who is not expected to earn a living, because he enriches the community while bringing honor to the family.

Removing the Warburg Library from Germany as the Third Reich ascended became a family preoccupation. While plans for a New York home for Aby's books were made (Nina and Paul's townhouse at 17 East Eightieth Street was offered for this purpose in 1935 and architectural drawings were made), it was already too late to smuggle the books under the Nazi gaze to the United States without severe repercussions for the family members still in Germany. In 1933 the Kulturwissenschaftliche Bibliothek Warburg had been packed up and moved "temporarily" from the University of Hamburg to London (which the Nazis believed would be part of the Thousand Year Reich soon enough). Now, two years later, Felix Warburg consulted Ambassador Dodd about the wisdom of moving the library to New York, and the State Department recommendation that followed was a strongly worded advisory that moving Aby's library to his late brother's townhouse at this time could trigger an anti-German uproar in New York, and the books should therefore remain in London for the time being. Felix was infuriated by this memo and scribbled "Rubbish" across it, but the New York plan, which would have been a memorial to both Aby and Paul, was abandoned. In 1941, Aby's unique and strange library became a permanent part of the University of London on the Bloomsbury campus.

WHILE NOT afflicted with any of the familial mental illnesses that led to her becoming a psychiatrist and psychoanalyst, Bettina was eccentric and difficult. Raised by parents who had fond expectations that she would follow in the traditional footsteps of Warburg women, pouring tea and doing charitable deeds between shopping trips and meeting with the cook about menus for dinner parties, Bettina had to fight to attend Bryn Mawr, let alone medical school. "You and I are alike," her mother had insisted. "We're nice, but not too bright." Girls were supposed to be handmaidens to the men in the family. Nina's pet nickname for her daughter was "Perfect," while she called her son Jimmy "More Perfect."

Nina was a generous patron of the sculptor Malvina Hoffman, who often lived and worked for weeks at a time in a cottage on the grounds of Fontenay, Nina and Paul's country house in Westchester. Malvina, who had studied with Auguste Rodin and Gutzon Borglum, was involved with a British musician and inventor, Samuel Bonarius Grimson, who was a semi-invalid, owing to his having been gassed in World War I, in the trenches of Ypres during the Spring Offensive of 1918. A brilliant violinist with a promising career ahead of him, Sam had also suffered a calamitous wartime injury, crushing the bones in his hands in a road accident on his way back from a journey to Cremona to visit the birthplace of his beloved Guarneri violin. He never performed publicly again.

From the time Bettina met him, when she was a teenager, and Sam and Malvina had not yet married (they were together for sixteen years before they married), she became fixated on Sam. As she perched on his lap and hovered near him by the hour, batting her eyelashes and gazing into his eyes, the family would joke about her innocent flirtation and tease her about her crush on the family friend who was sixteen years her senior. Malvina and Sam married in 1924, when Bettina was in medical school. (In this time period, despite her scorn for the pretensions of the Malices, Bettina had a brief romance with her first cousin Erich.) By the time they divorced in 1936 (perhaps because of Malvina's romantic involvement with the Russian dancer Anna Pavlova, whom she sculpted), Bettina was a practicing psychoanalyst in New York. Bettina and Sam were married in 1942, when Bettina was forty-two and Sam was fifty-eight. He died in 1955, succumbing finally, according to Bettina, to having been poisoned decades earlier by German phosgene and mustard gas.

It is possible that Bettina and Sam weren't married sooner because of Bettina's devotion to her work with the American Psychoanalytic Association's Emergency Committee on Relief and Immigration between 1938 and 1943, which she co-chaired with her New York Psychoanalytic Society colleague Lawrence Kubie. Working to obtain the necessary exit paperwork, booking passage on ships, and most crucially, locating sponsored jobs in America that would qualify immigrant analysts and their families for entrance visas, Bettina secretly funded most of the Emergency Committee's work herself. She also had access to the remains of the funds that had been sent to Hamburg by her father and uncle to bail out the Warburg bank. Though the bank had been Aryanized, there were sympathetic individuals there who were able to work surreptitiously on her behalf. Money was also raised by the Committee, from a variety of psychoanalytic circles, for a revolving loan fund administered in New York to aid in settling people comfortably, but it is likely that some of the repayments did not actually come from the recipient émigré analysts.

Bettina was tireless in her efforts facilitating the successful relocation of the 221 émigré analysts and other physicians who were brought out of Hitler's Europe by the Committee. She interviewed every one of them herself, often in German or French, and found some kind of work for each, even though it meant that a Hungarian neurologist would have to accept employment teaching math to high school boys in New Hampshire. She believed that it was in everyone's best interest to send as many of the analysts as far away from New York as possible (many New York analysts were panicked and threatened by the influx of this European throng of distinguished competition), and so she tried to match people who were from mountainous regions with mountains and coastal people with other, faraway coasts, probably personally funding some of those crucial sponsoring jobs herself. Many of the analysts failed to appreciate her relocation efforts and quickly migrated back to New York, which almost all of them preferred to rural Idaho or Minnesota. The impact of these émigré analysts on American psychoanalysis was profound.

✧ ✦ ✧

BETWEEN JIMMY's trips abroad, the Warburgs' social life continued as if life were status quo. In the middle of July of 1932, Jimmy went with Kay to an enormous gala benefit "circus" party at the Long Island estate of their friends Marshall and Ruthie Field. According to the *New York Times* story published on July 17, twelve hundred people had attended. Among the guests listed at Mrs. Field's table were George Gershwin, Mr. and Mrs. James Warburg, Fred Astaire, Condé Nast (whose daughter Natica was married to Jimmy's first cousin Gerald Warburg), Mrs. Payne Whitney, Mr. and Mrs. Vincent Astor, Winston Guest, Mr. and Mrs. Ogden Phipps, and Mrs. Baldwin Browne (the future second Mrs. James Warburg). The entertainment, following the circus theme, included a freak show featuring two sets of twins among the guests (the Baldwin sisters, Phyllis and Priscilla—or as they were known in the family, Phyl and Pril—were one of the pairs), and a continuous cabaret, starring the Boswell Sisters accompanied by Mrs. James Warburg.

WHEN JIMMY was once again away, this time for most of August, George Gershwin was writing the orchestral piece that came to be known as his *Cuban Overture*. It premiered at the Metropolitan Opera House in November of that year, though when it was first performed, he called it simply *Rumba*. It's unclear if Kay at any point joined the group (which included Lee and Ira Gershwin and Bennett Cerf) that had accompanied him for his two-week holiday in Havana earlier in the year. She spoke of going to Havana with George, though they might have traveled there together on a different occasion.

What is certain is that she was with him when he wrote the symphonic overture inspired by his time in Cuba, and she worked diligently to assist him with the orchestration. It was the first Gershwin piece in which he applied what he had begun to absorb from his sessions with the musical theorist Joseph Schillinger, with whom he met two or three times a week for four years, starting in 1932.

The Russian-born Schillinger, who taught at the New School for Social Research, was a pioneer in a range of musical techniques and methods, and he wrote compositions for innovative devices, from the bizarre Rhythmicon, a drum machine invented by the Russian inventor Léon Theremin for the composer Henry Cowell, to the even stranger Theremin, an electronic musical instrument that used a high-frequency oscillator which reacted to movement in its proximity. Its tones could be "played" by someone trained to make the correct corresponding hand movements. Jimmy's second wife, Phyllis, was an early devotee of the Theremin and brought one to Seventieth Street in 1935 when she moved in, where it frightened my mother the first time she walked past it on a stair landing, which caused it to emit eerie tones. (Theremin was also a Soviet spy who created a range of fantastic devices, including the eavesdropping system that was inserted into a carved Great Seal of the United States, which in 1945 was presented to the American ambassador to the Soviet Union as a "gesture of friendship" by a group of Soviet schoolchildren. It hung in the American Embassy for seven years before the bug was discovered.)

Kay accompanied George to nearly all his lessons with Schillinger, and took copious notes for him each time. She attended the *Rumba* premiere on August 16, at Lewisohn Stadium, and while the public response to the piece was mixed at the time, she would always name the piece as one of her very favorite of George's symphonic compositions.

✧ ✦ ✧

Kay and George didn't seem to mind attracting attention when they were together at parties or at the theater. In notes for a never-completed memoir, she described the night she took George to Wagner's only "lighthearted opera," as she called *Die Meistersinger*. It was one of her favorites, an opera she was eager for him to hear, and she was pleased he was enamored of the score:

> We had splendid seats in the orchestra, and like most people at the time . . . we dressed up for the occasion. Gershwin and I were rather proud of the fact that, although we always stayed for the final curtain, we were wizards at reaching the street, afterwards, ahead of most of the audience. We invariably caught the first available taxi outside.
>
> When we loped up the aisle, after this performance of *Meistersinger,* we ended up in step, rather like Astaire and Ginger when they went into their famous stride, with which they used to circle the stage before their final exit.
>
> This time, we worked up such speed that on leaving the building we were unable to slow down before loping into a heap of dirty snow that had been shoveled onto the edge of the sidewalk. Sitting waist-deep, George in his white tie, tails, and top hat, and I in a long white fur cape, we burst into a loud laugh, in which we were joined by a few fans who had recognized Gershwin. Scrabbling out of this mess, we leapt into the first taxi in sight. I remember that George muttered, "Always leave them laughing when you say Goodbye."

One can envisage them so clearly, this glamorous couple having such a good time together as they wafted through those years, flouting convention, breaking all the rules. For years I have wondered if Kay and George were an inspiration for the novelist Thorne Smith. He was a frequent guest at Warburg parties in New York and a weekend houseguest at Bydale. My mother told me of an occasion when there was a fiercely competitive croquet game taking place on the sweeping, hilly lawn, and her father sent her down to the bottom of the lawn to assist Smith, who was staggering around a wicket with his croquet mallet in evident confusion. He was attempting to sit on the grass, my mother discovered as she approached, but he was so drunk he wasn't sure how to proceed. As he struggled to lower himself, he said to her, "Do advise me, my dear. Is my boon toon on the grass yet? Do tell me when I hit the ground!"

Heavy drinking eventually killed Thorne Smith, who died in 1934 at forty-two. But in his less completely inebriated moments, he was witness to the first sparks of attraction between George and Kay in the early months of their relationship. Did Smith have them in mind when he conjured up George and Marion, the ghostly madcap beautiful couple in his novel *Topper*? It was published in 1926, so it is just possible that George and Kay might have inspired the glamorous, eternally festive and playful, champagne-drinking ghosts (as in *Oh, Kay!* and countless other novels, movies, and plays of the period, key plot elements in *Topper* revolve around circumventing the prohibitions of the Volstead Act), whose blithe high jinks haunt poor, earth-bound Cosmo Topper, a very serious banker.

KAY AND George had struck up a close friendship that was at first based on a deep musical rapport, but very quickly it became obvious to everyone that their relationship had deepened to become something much more complex. With Jimmy constantly traveling, owing to the increasing pressures and responsibilities of his banking work, George began to accompany Kay to art openings, concerts, and parties. They spent hours at the piano most days of the week. The more time they spent together, the more intimate they became, until George's presence was part of every aspect of Kay's life.

"The Warburgs led independent social lives," is how one Gershwin biographer glibly puts it. Numerous accounts refer to their "open marriage." One Gershwin biographer, Charles Schwartz, whose 1973 biography seems to have been the source for what so many writers from then to now have repeated, wrote of the Swift and Gershwin romance:

> Before long they were attached to each other and could be found together at art galleries, concerts, the theater, parties, and so on. Fortunately, James did not appear to mind his wife's friendship with Gershwin; the Warburgs were an enlightened couple who often went their separate ways without overt frictions or jealousies. Whether seeing Kay in their customary Manhattan haunts or horseback riding with her at the Warburg farm in Connecticut, Gershwin did not have to contend with a righteously indignant or jealous husband.

Writing in *The Warburgs* in 1993, Ron Chernow makes this claim about the Warburg marriage before George Gershwin arrived on the scene in 1925:

> Jimmy faced constant temptation and often submitted to it. Women were smitten by him and he had a long list of conquests. Kay was a dazzling, effervescent personality. Encouraged by the prevailing social license, Kay and Jimmy had an open marriage and neither lacked for willing partners.

This erroneous characterization was probably based on a combination of the same phrases parroted in many Gershwin biographies, the retrospective characterizations in my grandfather's 1964 autobiography, and a 1992 interview with my grandfather's widow, Joan, his third wife, whom he married in 1948 when he was fifty-one and she was twenty-five.

In *The Long Road Home* (published when he was sixty-seven and the father of the four young children he had with Joan), my grandfather wrote of his first marriage, "Neither my wife nor I realized for some time the effect on our marriage of the life we were leading during the twenties, or its influence on our children."

I believe that my grandfather indulged in some face-saving revisions of history as he looked back with chagrin and wounded pride thirty years later. He himself presumably did have numerous affairs in the twenties, but it is extremely unlikely that my grandmother had ever been unfaithful to him before she met George Gershwin. When would that have occurred, under what circumstances? Before Katharine Faulkner Swift met James Paul Warburg, she had no serious romantic involvements, let alone sexual ones. She went from being a young, virginal fiancée to being a newlywed, and then she was either pregnant or post-partum for the entirety of their married years before she met George.

Kay and Jimmy were married in June of 1918; she had her first child in April of the following year, when they were living in Washington, her second child in September of 1922, and her third child in November of 1924. She met George in April of 1925, not quite five months after giving birth for the third time in five and a half years.

So where and when and under what circumstances was she having assignations with all these "willing partners"? Of course, it is technically possible that my grandmother was unfaithful to my grandfather while pregnant or postpartum, but it is not a match with who she was and the life she was leading in those years. There has never been a shred of evidence linking her to any extramarital involvements before she met George, or during her romance with George—with the exception of her psychoanalyst, Gregory Zilboorg—while she was still married to Jimmy.

Kay's romantic preoccupation with George was far more than an avoidable complication of an "open marriage," a term and concept not even in use until the 1960s. My feeling is that there was no "open marriage," though trivializing the romance with George this way was surely a balm to my grandfather's ego, a way of revising the story decades after the fact (something his adoring young third wife wouldn't have questioned). Thus reduced to one among many, his wife's famous lover is allotted this magnanimous description in his autobiography:

> George was a fascinating but disturbing element at Bydale. His exuberant and many-sided zest for life knew no bounds.... Day turned into night and night turned into day when George was in the throes of creation. I found his visits stimulating but tiring. I liked Gershwin but resented the way in which our whole life was taken over by this completely self-centered but charming genius who was all too soon to end a brilliant career.

Jimmy Warburg was known by various family members for embellishing and shading the truth in aid of a good story, especially if the story was about his own exploits. His sister, my great-aunt Bettina, told me scornfully that *The Long Road Home* was "full of lies," including a photo of the author riding a horse over a jump in a steeplechase which she insisted was actually a photo of someone else. I believe that in looking back as he wrote his memoir at the time of his third marriage, when he was once again the father of young children, my grandfather conveniently recast the once-embarrassing Gershwin story.

Decades after the fact, my grandfather took to characterizing my grandmother's romance with George Gershwin and the end of their marriage in this way that shifted the emphasis. Now the problem wasn't Katharine's sexual involvement with George Gershwin, per se, given "the life they were leading during the twenties." His first wife's romance with George Gershwin, framed in this revised context, led to the destruction of their marriage because she was indiscreet, appearing all over town with this fascinating and important composer as if they were a couple. She let him take over their life, and she was emotionally reckless. It wasn't good for the children, the way she went overboard and got too involved with George, not to mention who knows how many others. Jimmy tried to be a good sport, but enough was enough.

If my grandfather could revise the story so that she had been promiscuous before she took up with Gershwin, then becoming involved with him would not have to be recalled as the extraordinary event that it actually was. And so, probably without much self-awareness, and one hopes without a deliberate smear campaign in mind, by the time my grandfather was married for the third time, he had developed the habit of painting his first wife and the mother of his first three children as careless, silly, foolish, selfish, and sexually voracious.

WHEN I was thirteen, I went to Florida with my mother for a month, in early spring, to stay in Deerfield Beach with my grandfather, while I recuperated from a life-threatening illness for which I had spent two months at New York Hospital. During that extremely traumatic hospitalization for a mysterious inflammation of my pancreas, my mother came to the hospital often, but my grandmother visited me nearly every day, with endless books and flowers, often accompanied by Eva Jessye, the original choral director from *Porgy and Bess* (whom I had met on the *Slaves* set), who brought me little stuffed animals and other trinkets. ("Is that your maid?" my hospital roommate asked.) I had no other visitors.

The April 1969 trip to Florida with my mother was, as it happened, not long before my grandfather's unexpected death in early June, and the only time in my life I would ever spend real time with him. Before this interlude, I had only known him as a prickly old man my mother adored whose irritability his family feared, and my only moments with him had been shy kisses hello and good-bye at family gatherings once or twice a year. In Deerfield Beach, he and I discussed books incessantly, and I was elated to feel his esteem for my knowledge and articulation. I understood for the first time my mother's obsessive devotion to her father. She was his favorite of the three girls from his "first litter." He was crazy about her.

The three of us ate every meal together, most of them in a nearby restaurant, the Cascades, which my grandfather had built and enjoyed owning, though the whole point of his wintering in Florida had been rest and avoidance of winter weather, owing to his increasingly fragile health.

My mother was as happy as I had ever seen her, away from my father, away from anxieties about my brother, having her father to herself without his other family around. The two of them were thick as thieves. One day over lunch my grandfather mentioned the house he had wanted to build for my mother as a wedding present, on the edge of Bydale, on a few acres fronting Richmond Hill Road. When they were married, he had given my mother and father a set of blueprints for the house he would build for them, but my father had turned it down, not wanting to live in what he called a "feudal arrangement" at the edge of Bydale.

Instead, when I was two, my grandfather and his sister, Bettina, had between them bought for our family our house in Forest Hills Gardens. Now I understood the thick roll of blueprints I had tried to examine up in the attic during one of my nocturnal investigations. It was so tightly furled I couldn't keep the big sheets from rolling back up, but I had glimpsed the confusing caption, "House for Mr. and Mrs. Sidney Kaufman, Greenwich, Connecticut," and I had seen the front elevations of a storybook house. What would my life have been like if I had grown up there? I felt cheated.

I NOW realize that on top of his visceral loathing for my father (whom he referred to as "Shitney")—which may have started out as a blend of snobbery and contempt for who and what my father was, along with what might have been an unconscious perception of the faint George Gershwin echo, but was also in time a justifiable dislike of the man who made his favorite daughter's life so unhappy—my grandfather had a Sidney problem.

In 1933 a counterfeit "memoir" by "Sidney Warburg" surfaced, allegedly in Holland, though no copy of the book itself has ever been documented (because the book was immediately "purged" upon publication, according to the information that accompanies the translated text, which also claims that the publisher was murdered) and only its "translation" from Dutch to German and then subsequently into English and other languages has ever been circulated. Today there are various English-language editions of *Hitler's Secret Backers* reprinted by various obscure outfits specializing in conspiracy theories and racist tracts. It originally appeared as *Three Conversations with Hitler* in 1933, having first been "translated" by J. G. Schoup into German and English; Schoup was presumably the author of the original Dutch edition published by Van Holkema & Warendorf, called *De Geldbronnen Van Het Nationaal Socialisme: Drie Gesprekken Met Hitler.*

The National Origins of Socialism: Three Conversations with Hitler purports to be a confession by "Sidney Warburg," whose identity is transparently patterned after James Paul Warburg, although "Sidney" is said to have died shortly after the book was published. In this "memoir," the author reveals that in a series of secret meetings with Hitler, he was the "cowardly instrument" of American banking interests who made payments through Kuhn, Loeb of ten million dollars in 1929, fifteen million dollars in 1931, and a final seven million dollars when Hitler came to power in 1933.

This vicious hoax of a document haunted my grandfather. His trips to Germany to deal with the family banking crisis corresponded to some degree with the descriptions of the timing of Sidney Warburg's meetings with Hitler. Finally, in 1947, he issued a careful point-by-point rebuttal to the Sidney Warburg forgery. But the details of that statement have only become the wellspring for the still-circulating literature of the so-called International Jewish banking conspiracy, which identifies the Warburg family, especially Paul Moritz Warburg and his son James Paul Warburg, among the key power-mongers who have perpetrated an insidious plot to dominate the world and enrich themselves, especially and particularly at the expense of decent Christian Americans.

In this propaganda, which flourishes exponentially on the Internet today, the greatest evidence against the family is Paul Warburg's central role in establishing the Federal Reserve System, which from the moment of its creation was never the independent and nonpolitical central banking governing mechanism he had envisaged and advocated. "The Cassandra of Wall Street," Paul forecast the market crash of 1929 in March of that year, saying that without sufficient governing by the Federal Reserve, there would be a collapse "and a general depression involving the entire country." His unheeded warning is interpreted by conspiracy theorists as everything from an encoded message to his allies so they could cash out and stay rich to a threat that was fulfilled.

Much is made of the fact that my great-grandfather was also on the board of the American chemical company I. G. Farben. Of course, the name of the German company that manufactured Zyklon B, the poison used in the gas chambers in the Nazi death camps, is a name to conjure with. But no I. G. Farben factory on any continent was manufacturing anything for the Third Reich in Paul Warburg's lifetime, when the Third Reich didn't yet exist. Paul Warburg died in January 1932. Adolf Hitler didn't become Chancellor of Germany until January 1933.

Nevertheless, conspiracy theorists and paranoiac anti-Semites parrot this "incriminating" fact about the Warburgs relentlessly. In widely disseminated speeches, Louis Farrakhan, the leader of the Nation of Islam, denounces Paul Warburg, referring to the "synagogue of Satan and its agents," the Rothschilds and the Warburgs. In a rabble-rousing speech he has made to large and enthusiastically receptive audiences on numerous occasions (various renditions can be found on YouTube and elsewhere, including a blog called WarburgEvil), he states dramatically, while the crowd roars approval, "Paul Warburg loaned money to Hitler! Paul Warburg was staying in the finest hotels in Europe while Hitler was killing little Jewish babies. If you can't call Paul Warburg an anti-Semite, don't you call *me* an anti-Semite!"

Paul Warburg is said to be the model for Daddy Warbucks in the "Little Orphan Annie" comic strip, though it makes little sense. But then there is abundant evidence that many people believe that "the Warburgs" are responsible for fluoridating the water supply, disseminating LSD, kidnapping the Lindbergh baby, and starting the American Civil War, the Bolshevik Revolution, and both World Wars. The Warburgs are said to have prevented FDR from interceding on behalf of the Jews of Europe. Warburgs are also said to have manipulated the stock market, causing the crash of 1929 in order to trigger the Great Depression. They are damned for being Zionists and also for being anti-Zionists. There are conspiracy theorists claiming there is evidence of a Warburg influence over the events of September 11, 2001. The Warburg conspiracy to establish a New World Order is widely discussed. Theories about this enterprise are usually based on Paul Warburg's role as the architect of the Federal Reserve system and as a founder of the Council on Foreign Relations, as well as James Warburg's role as a cofounder of the Institute for Policy Studies.

Paul Warburg's role as an "agent of the Rothschilds" in foisting a "German" central banking system on America was regarded with suspicion from the earliest days of the Federal Reserve, when he served on its first board for four years, from 1914 to 1918. (It is often erroneously said that he was the chairman of the first Federal Reserve board.) Although Paul became a naturalized citizen of the United States in 1911 (under which his two children were also naturalized), his German heritage, as well as his German accent, were problematic as the country waged a war with his homeland, and he was essentially forced to resign from the Federal Reserve board in August of 1918 by President Wilson, who accepted his resignation with a flowery letter, saying, "Your counsel has been indispensable in these first formative years of the new system which has served at the most critical period of the nation's financial history to steady and assure every financial process." The *Chicago Daily Tribune* story on the correspondence between President Wilson and my great-grandfather ran with the headline "Servant of U.S. Forced Out by German Blood: Letters Show Paul Warburg Victim of War Spirit."

Paul's older brother Max has long been the object of claims that the Warburg family profited by doing business with the Third Reich. In a certain literal sense, this is true. As the Jews of Germany became more and more limited in their options after 1933, Max developed a program for Jews hoping to escape Germany without becoming penniless in the process. The Nazis had fewer objections to Zionists than to the patriotic and acculturated Jews (many of whom had converted to Christianity at the turn of the twentieth century and had ceased identifying themselves as Jews) who refused to recognize that their German way of life would no longer be possible and the freedoms of the Weimar Republic had ended. There was actually a Gestapo regulation forbidding Jews from public discussion about remaining in Germany, yet departing Jews were not allowed to take their money out of Germany.

Max's Haavara Plan (the word means "transfer" in Hebrew) was an agreement he negotiated with the Third Reich that would permit Jews emigrating to Palestine to deposit all their money in specially designated accounts. After a year, they could withdraw equivalent sums in Palestine pounds. In the interim, these blocked Reichsmarks were used to buy goods manufactured in Germany, which were then exported to Palestine. Profits from those transactions were then banked for the matching payment to the relocated German Jews. Strangely enough, this flow of Nazi products helped the economy of Jewish Palestine, though it meant Palestinian Jews were in effect doing business with Nazi companies and boosting the German economy. The newly created Palestine Trust Company managed these transactions, with M. M. Warburg & Co. handling some three-quarters of the exchanges. The Anglo-Palestine Bank (now Bank Leumi) was the bank on the receiving end of this plan. Nearly 140 million Reichsmarks left Germany this way before the start of the war.

But the cornerstone for the perception that the Warburg family has a New World Order agenda was laid with the cryptic remark my grandfather made in 1950, when he testified before the U.S. Senate Committee on Foreign Relations: "We shall have world government, whether or not we like it. The question is only whether world government will be achieved by consent or by conquest."

My best guess as to what he meant by this is a prediction of a future era when world power would no longer be dominated by two or three governments but would instead depend on international cooperation and leadership shared by many powers, perhaps something akin to a more functional and effective version of the League of Nations.

A GREAT deal of the Warburg hatred circulating today has its origins in the work of the late anti-Semitic conspiracy theorist Eustace Mullins, the man the Southern Poverty Law Center called "a one-man organization of hate," whose books are frequently cited by mainstream right-wing pundits. The author of *Hitler: An Appreciation,* Mullins published his most well-known work in 1948 with the original title *Mullins on the Federal Reserve,* though it has been reissued over the years with other titles, from *The Federal Reserve Conspiracy* to the most recent *The Secrets of the Federal Reserve.* The book was commissioned by the poet Ezra Pound, who was at that time imprisoned in St. Elizabeth's Hospital in Washington, D.C., a federal institution for the insane.

The British edition of Jimmy's controversial polemic against New Deal monetary policy, *The Money Muddle,* was reviewed by Ezra Pound for the British publication *Time and Tide* in August of 1934. Pound wrote:

> It is impossible to read two pages of Mr. Warburg's book without admiring his suavity. [The first draft of this review began "It is impossible to read two pages of Mr. Warburg's book without know [sic] that he is clever as seven devils and that he will defend whatever his thesis is with all the arts of a 'silk.'"] . . . His manners, the lucidity of his style are however superior to his training in the dissociation of ideas. . . . The plain man must watch Mr. Warburg very carefully or the rabbit will emerge from vacantest possible hat. . . . The greatest swindles having often been perpetrated by the greatest authority.
>
> Henry James has remarked of one of his female characters: she put such ignorance into her cleverness. Mr. Warburg has given us a touching view of the world as seen from the banker's counter. . . . From here we have a dazzling melange: half-truth, near truth, contingencies offered as necessities, cliches, squirrel cages, vicious circles, an occasional undeniable sentence, addressed, I repeat, not to the plain

man, who can't possibly catch him. The general slipperiness of the book can be judged by his continual use of the same terms with differing meanings. . . .

Pound wrote a provocative letter to my grandfather on August 11, saying that he had reviewed the book but wasn't sure that his piece would run:

If you are merely writing devil's propganda, it don't matter, but IF you have been so clever as to get caught by yr/ own hat trick, and if you don't know WHERE and when you put the rabbit on the table under the fancy paper, I will be glad to send you a carbon of my notes. . . . I wonder if you wd/stand up to a few REAL questions?

The response came back promptly:

I gather from your letter that you rather liked my book in spite of a chronic grouch against bankers, and I should be very interested to see the review you wrote. . . . As to your question, I wonder if etc., the answer is "try and see," and I might reply with another query, "Can you ask some REAL questions?"

Pound's reply:

Better a man like yrself/ who can hear reason, than completely uninformed yawpers . . . your not a dumb bunny like some of the advocates of ideas that I happen to believe in.

And in September Pound wrote again in reply to a note from my grandfather:

If you are 40, as they tell me, I have prob/ been studying hist/ and econ/ as long as you have. And my friend Possum Eliot worked a LONG hell and bloody damnation a bloody long time in Lloyds. Who may be a bit cleverer than Barclay's?

In October my grandfather wrapped up the correspondence:

Thanks for your most amusing letter of the 26th. . . . Much as I enjoy reading your letters, I am afraid that we shall not get anywhere by correspondence. As a matter of fact, I am hoping to spend some time in Italy this winter in order to find out at first hand what a real dictatorship looks like and, if so, I shall certainly give myself the pleasure of looking you up and having as much of a knock-down and drag-out fight as you will stand for. You leave me as utterly unconvinced as I leave you.

Pound replied once more:

I come back to this correspondence, because the situation is just a joke, and you at any rate are not a complete idiot/ and ANY American with more brains than a cockroach has got to hold himself, up to the limit of his strength, respon- sible. . . . With perfect impartiality, and wanting to believe the best, I have collected, first hand, the following also IM- PARTIAL estimates of the brain trust/

Morgenthau, "brain the size of a pea"

Wallace, demonstrated repeatedly to [be]the mess/ the dregs of sub-manhood and nearly an idiot.

Perkins. Crank, no better than Upton Sinclair.

Farley. "useful" for keeping R/ in touch with old gang.

Hull, clever politician, and not an ass in private . . .

Roosevelt. Affable

Tugwell, usual vigorous fool . . . will never know he is wrong, because mechanism for registering error is lacking.

Your book was, I might say, at a pinch, a grope, and not mere camoflauge. . . . You have brains enough to dissociate several ideas, IF you set about it.

Pound recommended *The Money Muddle* to Mussolini, as a good example of confused American thinking. In his hundreds of notorious radio broadcasts from Italy during the war in support of Fascists and Nazis, Pound made frequent references to Warburgs among the Jews whose influence he denounced.

Having been indicted in absentia in 1943, Pound was arrested and charged with treason by the American government in 1945, but was sentenced to St. Elizabeth's Hospital because he was found to be insane and unfit for trial. His release from St. Elizabeth's in 1958 occurred largely through the ceaseless efforts of his pupil and admirer Eustace Mullins.

NEITHER MY mother nor my grandfather was concerned about what they said in front of me during that Florida interlude. When my mother ordered an uncharacteristic Seven & 7 cocktail before dinner one night, he dismissed it as "a whore's drink," to which she replied, "And you would know!" He recited numerous filthy limericks in front of me which entertained my mother, who relished dirty jokes in inverse proportion to her interest in experiencing actual sex, especially when the dirty jokes were uttered by her father.

The subject of my grandmother came up surprisingly often, usually after the two of them had knocked back a few of his carefully prepared martinis. Never before had I heard him mention my grandmother during our very rare family visits at Bydale. In fact, I had been coached by my mother not to bring her up in front of Pop and Joan and their kids, but now he repeatedly brought her up. He had been a gentleman about it, he told me, as if I should note the proper etiquette for future reference, letting my grandmother be the one to seek the divorce, although, he emphasized, of course divorcing had been his idea, and not hers. Arriving at the Cascades one evening, as my mother struggled to slide out from behind the wheel of his car while the parking valet stood waiting, my grandfather teased her about her maternal heritage, pointing out that she had apparently inherited her mother's habitual failure to exit cars gracefully—"That was Kay! She never could keep her legs together!"

By characterizing his first marriage as having been a casually promiscuous one in that madcap era of the Roaring Twenties, he represented what happened to their marriage as merely the consequence of the style of living that swept them up. It's a much simpler and far less humiliating way to revise the memory of all that. I think he just couldn't bear to face that at a certain point in his first marriage, his wife, whom he adored and who adored him still, was trapped by the complexity of unexpectedly finding herself also deeply in love with another man.

Although Jimmy would retrospectively minimize his bond with Kay, the Warburg marriage was viable well into 1934. They were very much a couple in June 1931, when Jimmy wrote to his father from London, during his most urgent and complex banking mission, to say that he respected the huge personal cash infusions that Paul and Felix had agreed to provide in order to bail out their brother Max, rather than let the Warburg Bank in Hamburg go under.

Dear Father,

I must say, you and Felix are a great pair of brothers to have. In your shoes I would have done the same thing, but I honestly couldn't have advised you to do it, because so far as the money is concerned, I think it's thrown out of the window in a lost cause. As I said in my memo, I don't believe that Max is capable of changing himself to the extent that would be required to give his business any kind of a chance. . . . I want you to let me do whatever scrimping is to be done on our side of the water. Kay & I are young & healthy, and my salary, even if it is reduced as might be, will be quite enough for us to live on. I am writing her by this post to consult you about starting to get rid of a few unnecessary things like horses in any case, and maybe Bydale altogether. . . . I called Kay this morning and she said you were disturbed about hearing nothing from Max. I have just phoned him to cable you. He didn't want to anticipate by thanking you for an incomplete thing & thus forcing your hand, but he should have sent you some word during this last week. He's not in the least suicidally inclined, so don't worry about that. If anything, he is too complacent and takes a hell of a lot for granted. The complete papers will be here to-morrow & I'll then shoot them off to you.

Love to you all & God bless you
Jim

Perhaps Jimmy's desire to get rid of the horses and even, possibly, sell his beloved Bydale was an unconscious wish to eliminate the very things in the Warburgs' way of life that George Gershwin enjoyed so much. It must have been a terribly painful realization when it became evident that his wife's involvement with "the self-centered but charming genius" had gone from a musically inspired mutual fascination and friendship to a profound intimacy that included a deep emotional and sexual connection. What a blow to the brash and confident Harvard man who thought the world was his oyster, a man whose life had always brimmed with opportunities and triumphs.

Jimmy Warburg had been offered a junior Cabinet post, Assistant Secretary of Commerce, when he was twenty-five, though he had turned it down, an early act of his characteristic hubris. He had published those two volumes of poetry. His witty lyrics to his wife's music were a triumph. He had ascended rapidly to extraordinary positions of responsibility at the International Acceptance Bank (by 1931, at age thirty-five, he was the president of the bank) and the Bank of Manhattan (of which he was vice chairman). His father's untimely death at the beginning of 1932 may well have been a turning point for Jimmy. Not only did he continue to carry the load of tremendous responsibilities for the Warburg banking interests that his father and uncles had placed on him, with an added sense of duty and responsibility for the well-being of his mother and sister, but with the presidential inauguration just two months after his father's death, he became a brain truster in Franklin Delano Roosevelt's presidential administration.

Although he had no official title beyond "Senior Economic Advisor to the President," Jimmy played a key role in the early days of Roosevelt's first term, and he was virtually living in Washington for the first half of 1933. FDR and Jimmy held each other in high regard. At one point, in May, reflecting on Jimmy's canny and insightful advice about strategies for a meeting between Secretary of State Cordell Hull and Dr. Hjalmar Schacht, Hitler's Minister of Economics, Roosevelt said, "You know, Jimmy, it would serve that fellow Hitler right if I sent a Jew to Berlin as my ambassador. How would you like the job?"

Just two months later, Jimmy broke from Roosevelt over the debacle at the 1933 London Economic Conference. As the head of the American delegation, he felt betrayed when he learned that Roosevelt had decided, as the conference was taking place, to take the United States off the gold standard, something Jimmy had repeatedly counseled against. He resigned on the spot, and became a vociferous critic of the Roosevelt administration, publishing several attacks on what he judged to be FDR's misguided economic policies, from *The Money Muddle* in 1933 to a series of political attacks (*Hell-Bent for Election,* 1935—which introduced to our lexicon the phrase "soak the rich"—and *Still Hell-Bent,* 1936) to doggerel (*New Deal Noodles,* published in 1936 under his then-wife's name, Phyllis Baldwin Warburg).

Jimmy sent FDR an advance copy of *The Money Muddle,* somehow expecting the father figure who had let him down so badly to accept his scornful polemic as helpful advice, and was disappointed with Roosevelt's response (a lifelong habit of Jimmy's was his expectation that people would be grateful for his guidance and his dismay when they weren't):

Dear Jimmy—

I have been reading The Money Muddle *with plenty of interest.*

Some day I hope you will bring out a second edition—but will you let an old friend make a special request of you before you do it? Please get yourself an obviously second-hand Ford car; put on your oldest clothes and start west for the Pacific Coast, undertaking beforehand not to speak on the entire trip with any banker or business executive (except gas station owners), and to put up at no hotel where you have to pay

*more than $1.50 a night. After you get to the Coast go south
and come back via the southern tier of States. . . . When you
have returned rewrite The Money Muddle and I will guarantee that it will run into many more editions!*

*After the above insulting 'advice to a young man'—do
nevertheless run down and see me some day.*

Always sincerely,

Franklin D. Roosevelt

Jimmy would return to the Roosevelt fold in 1939, soon after
he engaged in a debate with Senator Burton K. Wheeler of
Montana and John Foster Dulles at the Economic Club in New
York. Jimmy had insisted that the only way to avert a world
war was for the United States to make clear to the Axis that
any threat to France or England would be regarded as a threat
to America. Senator Wheeler saw no reason for America to
concern itself with the Axis aggression in Europe. Dulles said,
"Only hysteria entertains the idea that Germany, Italy or Japan
contemplate war upon us."

Motivated by the Nazi invasion of Paris, and recognizing
the need to make peace with Roosevelt in order once again to
have his ear, Jimmy went to the White House and wrote a note to
the president, concluding with the words, "I was wrong and I'm
sorry," which would lead to a complete rapprochement. When
America entered the war, Jimmy served in the Office of War
Information, first as a special assistant to William J. Donovan
(who later headed the OSS) and then as Overseas Branch Dep-
uty Director of the OWI, coordinating efforts with British military intelligence. There is no record that he ever crossed paths in
the OWI with his future son-in-law Sidney Kaufman.

❖ ✦ ❖

IN *The Warburgs,* Ron Chernow describes an event that allegedly took place in 1934, near the end of Kay and Jimmy's marriage, described to him by Joan, to whom it had been told by my grandfather, who might not have expected this particular face-saving fabrication about his personal history to turn up as accepted fact: "When Jimmy confronted George and told him to go ahead and marry Kay if he liked, the composer fled in panic from the offer." Nobody else who knew all of the people in this story ever reported such an encounter taking place.

There is no question that George was ambivalent about marriage and skittish about commitment to Kay, for a number of reasons. George may not have wanted the encumbrance of her children, and his attachment to my mother was counterbalanced by April's hostility. Having been unavailable as a married woman, once Kay was divorced, the issue of her Episcopal background became more prominent. George's mother, Rose, disapproved of her, first for being Protestant and married and then for still being Protestant but now a divorcée.

Rose Gershwin, my grandmother wrote to her closest friend, Mary Lasker, was the person "about whom George harbored his only completely nutty fantasy—he used to tell reporters she was 'the kind of mother the mammy songs were written about'—can you imagine that dame dashing up with a candied yam in her hand and a big smile on that tense, frowning face of hers?"

George's sister-in-law, Leonore, was remarkably similar to Rose Gershwin in certain ways. Rose and Leonore, neither of them exactly pretty, were both vain face-lift pioneers. They were both highly possessive of George. Like Rose, Lee didn't care much for Kay. Lee was competitive and jealous about Kay's closeness to George as well as her attractiveness and popularity. My grandmother believed that Lee had a brief affair with George, for whom it was only a passing fancy. In order to stay in

George's orbit, she had then pursued his more available brother, Ira, who was charmed by Lee in her early flapper days. George disappointed many women who hoped that sex meant something more to him than it did. Whether or not their affair happened, Lee's relationship with George was complex and intense. Her lifelong fascination with him was not based on her appreciation of his music. The first time Lee heard *Rhapsody in Blue,* she said, "I don't get it. You can't dance to it."

Much about Lee and Ira's marriage was strikingly similar to Rose and Morris's marriage. Father and son were soft-spoken, sweet men married to much more temperamental and demanding, powerful women to whom they capitulated. Not only would George have had pressure from Rose against marrying Kay, but he had to have noticed Lee's antipathy as well. (Ira was very fond of Kay, but he could be maddeningly diffident.) Surely these two models provided by the people closest to him would have given George a sense that marriage was an undesirable state of compromise and defeat. And of course, he thought he had all the time in the world.

In the summer of 1933, at her wit's end about her situation, being a wife and a mother with a deep involvement with someone else, Kay had hoped that she could pull her life together with a course of psychoanalysis with Gregory Zilboorg, to whom she was recommended by her sister-in-law, Bettina. At that time Bettina herself was undergoing her own training analysis with him. Within a few years, Bettina distanced herself from Zilboorg, referring to his mustache as "the lunatic fringe" and dismissing him with a scornful, "Zilly was silly," but she did not warn her brother, sister-in-law, or cousin Eddie (to whom she also recommended treatment with Zilboorg, which led to twenty-six years of costly analytic entanglement) about her loss of confidence. Eddie never forgave her for recommending Zilboorg and never revealing her subsequent misgivings.

Analysis with Zilboorg drove Kay into a deeper quagmire. Now she found herself married to one man she loved, deeply involved with another man she loved, and having a strange and unwanted sexual involvement with her psychoanalyst, who pressured her to stay in the marriage and to maintain the status quo. When after some ten months of this she told him she was determined to divorce Jimmy and simplify her life also by terminating this analysis, Gregory threatened her with exposure of her darkest secrets, telling her that if she left him, if she followed through on this plan, he would tell things to both Jimmy and George, now both in treatment with him as well, which would make both of them want nothing more to do with her and would probably also result in her losing custody of her children.

When she proceeded with her divorce plans and stopped seeing him anyway, Gregory may not have had instantaneous success with his threatened scheme of alienation. But looking back from the present moment, it is obvious that he did succeed on both fronts, manipulating Jimmy's sense of Kay, planting the image of her as foolish and promiscuous, and cultivating in her ex-husband what would become a lifelong hostility and scorn for Kay which he transmitted to his children. Although in later years Jimmy minimized his time on Zilboorg's couch as something he experimented with briefly, he actually continued his analysis for eight or nine years. Throughout this time, Zilboorg, who was also Jimmy's second wife Phyllis's analyst for seventeen years, was a fixture on Seventieth Street and at Bydale.

Kay knew how malevolent her former psychoanalyst could be, and she worried about Jimmy. Writing to Mary Lasker in

1940 (Mary was also a Zilboorg patient in the 1930s and shared Kay's loathing for the Svengali on whose couch they had both lain; their private nickname for him was Grischa), Kay asked for news of her ex-husband's ongoing psychoanalysis. "Do you have any idea whether Jim is through yet? . . . Somehow I loathe the thought of Z. having any smallest thing to do with any member of the family. It's like the buzzard passing over, in 'Porgy.'" In another letter to Mary, she referred sardonically to the "grim sight" of "Grischa's unhandsome Russky faceky peering out of a page of the Satevepost."

In 1946, Zilboorg was still very much on the Warburg scene. My father described to me an encounter with Zilboorg at Bydale, at a Sunday lunch when he and my mother were not yet married. There, a supremely uncomfortable gathering consisted of Sidney and Andrea, Jimmy and Phyllis (on the verge of divorce), and Zilboorg. Sidney and Zilboorg spoke Yiddish together over the smoked salmon, insulting their host (who couldn't understand them and probably didn't enjoy hearing Yiddish spoken by either his analyst or his future son-in-law) for his lack of bagels and *menschlichkeit.*

Zilboorg certainly went to work on George, who was in treatment with him from the spring of 1934 to the end of 1935 and continued to see him intermittently after that until he left New York for California in August of 1936 (not to mention the incessant socializing that threw all these people together in various circumstances). There is no question that Zilboorg coached George on reasons he shouldn't marry Kay.

George's good friend the publisher Bennett Cerf recalled: "Kay Swift was George's real girl. She wanted to divorce Jimmy Warburg and marry George but she had three children and

George couldn't bring himself to marry somebody who had had babies with somebody else. He blamed it on a psychiatrist. He was always being psychoanalyzed because it gave him a chance to talk about himself uninterruptedly."

In early 1934, George was approached by Lincoln Kirstein and Eddie Warburg, cofounders of the new American Ballet Company, about writing a new work of music for George Balanchine's premiere performance in the United States. The Russian choreographer, thirty, was eager to work with an American composer and had asked for Jerome Kern or George Gershwin. George couldn't take on another project at that moment, and urged them to give the commission to Kay Swift instead. Eddie, who knew and liked his cousin's wife, wrote the libretto for *Alma Mater,* a surreal fantasy based on the annual Harvard-Yale football game. Theirs was a fortuitous collaboration. *Alma Mater,* with costumes by John Held Jr. (the low-budget production utilized Eddie's own raccoon coat), was a jazzy and inventive mix of Ivy League tradition turned upside down and sideways until it segued into dramatic surrealism.

In addition to *Alma Mater,* the program for Balanchine's American Ballet Company's first public performance included *Transcendence, Serenade,* and *Mozartiana,* performed in different combinations on successive nights. The debut, in Hartford, in the Avery Memorial Auditorium at the Wadsworth Atheneum, was scheduled for December 6. The *New York Herald Tribune* columnist Lucius Beebe heralded the production, promising his readers that "the whole daffy shindig" would be "one of the most epic lunacies of the generation."

✧ ✦ ✧

WHILE KAY spent months working on the music for *Alma Mater,* meeting with Eddie, Lincoln, and Mr. B., and attending rehearsals, there is another scenario that may have been playing out in 1934, contributing to her decision to divorce Jimmy by the end of the year. In a 1940 letter to Mary Lasker, written at the end of a difficult July which had seen money troubles and the death of a beloved dog, Kay remarked that "all the prize lousy occasions" in her life had occurred in July, including her father's death, her mother's death, and George's death. She went on to note that "my choicest surgical number of recent years" was among "the July affairs—not my best month."

I wonder if she is referring to an abortion. When she was in her seventies, she told a close friend that she had always felt guilty about having an abortion, though she didn't provide specifics. It would fit. She mentions the "surgical number" following a sequence of references to deaths. Well into her eighties, when in preparation for the first of her face-lifts, she took pride in "never" having been hospitalized for anything beyond the births of her three daughters and the time she spent in traction after the riding accident at Bydale.

If she had an ordinary medical experience of some kind among "the July affairs," why would she have hidden it for the rest of her life? Why does she refer to "my choicest surgical number" with such evident irony? Mary Lasker may well have been the only person who knew at the time about the surgical number to which she referred. It would have been possible for a prosperous woman to have a discreet "surgical number" of this kind in New York (most went to Doctors Hospital), but it is also possible that my grandmother's brief trip to Mexico that summer with April, who was fifteen, was where and when she had it done.

It is clear that my grandmother was quite fertile, having had three children easily with Jimmy, and in the next chapter of her life, in 1940 and 1942, she would be pregnant twice more with babies she dearly wanted and planned for, though she would miscarry both of those pregnancies. Did she miscarry because of age (she was forty-three and forty-five at the time of those two lost pregnancies), or had she been scarred by an abortion?

If Kay discovered that she was pregnant in July of 1934, it would have precipitated a crisis. She was married to Jimmy and was still very much his wife. Although George was intermittently away from New York in the spring and summer of 1934, working on *Porgy and Bess* with DuBose Heyward, living in a little shack on Folly Beach, an island off the coast of South Carolina near Charleston, Kay and George saw each other as often as possible. They had been together during his New York interludes and when she visited him on Folly Island at least once. And then there were those unpleasant sexual encounters with Gregory Zilboorg on his analytic couch, after which (as she described it to me) she would write a check for his fee and cry. He would pocket the check and tell her to "stop the damned eye-pissing."

An unexpected pregnancy in the summer of 1934 would have forced her to confront her situation in very concrete terms, not knowing whose baby this was. How could she have this baby? What would it do to her relationship with George if it was not his? What would it do to her hopes that they had a future together if it was Jimmy's? What would it do to her marriage if it was George's? And horror of horrors, what if it was Gregory's baby?

If the "surgical number" she refers to in that letter to Mary was indeed an abortion, it would go a long way toward accounting for her apparently sudden decision to extricate herself from this impossible bind with these three men. Something in the second half of 1934 made her resolve to leave Gregory's sadistic, so-called psychoanalysis and end her marriage to Jimmy. Work on the ballet kept Kay in New York until she was finally able to schedule a trip to Reno for a divorce at the beginning of November, even though the requisite six-week residency would cause her to miss the *Alma Mater* premiere in Hartford on December 6, her first opening night since *Fine and Dandy*.

On November 6, 1934, a wire story ran in newspapers across the country:

MRS. J.P. WARBURG, COMPOSER, WILL SEEK A DIVORCE

The James P. Warburgs, known variously in Wall Street, the theater, music and literature under the names Paul James and Kay Swift, have reached the end of their romantic story. Mrs. Warburg, it became known today, has arrived in Reno to establish residence for a divorce action.

Kay wasn't alone for her six weeks in Reno; she was accompanied by her best friend, Mary Woodard Reinhardt, who was getting her own divorce from her first husband, Paul Reinhardt. Kay and Mary had known each other as teenagers, well before either of them married, and in Reno together for their first divorces, they threw their wedding rings off a bridge into the Truckee River at the same moment.

When Katharine Swift Warburg was rich and Mary Woodard Reinhardt was not, my grandmother had been very generous in a variety of ways, including a tradition of annually giving Mary last year's fur coat. When the situation reversed, which it did when Mary married Albert D. Lasker in 1940 and became immensely wealthy, for the rest of their lives, my grandmother was the recipient of Mary's graceful generosity, including Mary's cast-off fur coats.

In an undated and unfinished short story titled "Reno," about two friends, Kay and Mary, who take a train to Reno for their divorces, my grandmother, thirty-seven in 1934, calls the Kay character a "a chic, twenty-seven-year-old in a dream of a tailored suit." Her beau, who has sent a bottle of champagne to the train, is "none other than George Gregor, world-famous composer of Broadway songs and symphonic music."

The extraordinary choice of "Gregor" for the world-famous composer's surname is surely one more indication about the powerful forces that impelled this divorce journey. As they sip the champagne from paper cups, the story continues:

> Both girls are on their way to Reno to divorce their respective husbands; whether or not they will eventually marry their beaux is problematic, but each believes such will be the case. Kay, whose life with her husband... has been a series of storms, worries maternally about him, and hopes her successor, whom he has already selected, will take care of him....

On the night of December 6, George telephoned Kay in Reno to report on what she had missed—the tremendous success of *Alma Mater* and the entire program of Balanchine's opening night at the Wadsworth Atheneum in Hartford. A "Ballet Special" train from Grand Central Terminal had functioned as an opening-night party on wheels. It had delivered a glittering assortment of café society to Hartford, from George Gershwin, Margaret and Sam Lewisohn, A. Conger Goodyear, Mrs.

Nelson Rockefeller, Dr. and Mrs. Harvey Cushing, and Mr. and Mrs. Wallace K. Harrison, to Sol Hurok, Joseph Alsop, and Betsy Cushing Roosevelt and her husband, James, son of the president. Katharine Hepburn was there, as were Salvador Dali and his wife, Gala.

Though *Transcendence* was considered the aesthetic high point of the evening, *Alma Mater* won rave reviews from the audience and from the critics for its "wicked, wicked cleverness." The *Washington Post* described its "saucy, irresistible humor" and predicted that of the ballets performed, *Alma Mater* would be the most popular, for its spirit of "good mean fun."

IN HER 2004 biography of Kay Swift, Vicki Ohl writes that at the end of 1934, when my grandmother divorced my grandfather, "She had rejected the dishonesty of a loveless marriage." I think that's wrong. I think she loved Jimmy with a tenderness that never ended. I don't think it was lovelessness she was rejecting; I think it was conflict. When she was interviewed at age ninety, my grandmother said of the divorce, "I didn't like being in love with somebody else while I was married," a careful understatement.

Kay and George spent Christmas Eve together soon after her return to New York, the divorce having been finalized on December 20. They called on Richard and Dorothy Rodgers, who was bedridden with a complication of a pregnancy, bursting in together "like irrepressible magi, bearing a present that only George Gershwin could have given," as Rodgers recalled decades later. The gift of these magi was George sitting down at the piano and playing the entire score to *Porgy and Bess* while he and Kay sang.

The year 1935 brought an entirely different way of life for

Kay. She had an apartment at 530 East Eighty-sixth Street, the location of which made George complain, the first time he called at her new address, bearing gifts of the Dufy gouache of a bowl of fruit under one arm and a Coubine landscape under the other, "Why are you making this little Jewish boy walk through a German neighborhood to see you?"

My grandmother had by then begun working as staff composer for Radio City Music Hall, where for eighteen months she wrote a new musical number for the Rockettes every other week, producing a series of charming works in a happy collaboration with the lyricist Al Stillman (it was George who suggested to the former Al Silverman that he improve his name). Here she met Vincente Minnelli, who was the resident costume designer. Some of the songs they penned made witty reference to topical news, such as the Dionne quintuplets. The most enduring of Kay's Radio City songs, still used by a few magicians, was "Sawing a Woman in Half," for which, with Strobel light and costume effects, the entire Rockettes' kick line was "sawed in half."

KAY DIDN'T date other men until George left New York for Hollywood in August of 1936. Jimmy, meanwhile, was very quickly remarried, in April of 1935, to Phyllis Baldwin Browne.

Phyllis was my mother's stepmother for nearly a decade, from the time my mother was thirteen. It was a mixed experience for my mother, who did not enjoy having to dress formally for family dinners (Jimmy obligingly wore evening clothes for dinner with Phyllis and his daughters each night they dined at home), but she and her sister Kay found Phyllis smart, and attentive to them at a time when their mother was less and less present in their daily lives. They mostly enjoyed her presence as their father's wife, while my aunt April, who soon went to live with their mother in her apartment on East Eighty-sixth Street, despised her wholeheartedly. In the months when Jimmy was between marriages and Phyllis had not been available, on a few occasions April had been his date, and she resented being demoted to her previous status as a child when she was replaced by Phyllis.

In the Phyllis years, Jimmy, my mother, and my aunt Kay were listed in the Social Register, introducing the delightful terms "Dilatory Domiciles" and "Married Maidens" into the family lexicon. (When the marriage ended in 1947, their listings were each dropped.) In addition to Phyllis's twin sister, Priscilla, there were eight other Baldwin siblings. For children with only one first cousin, their mother's nephew, Shippen Swift (whom they rarely saw because his mother approved of neither Jews nor divorces), the mob of rowdy Baldwins at family occasions was an appealing novelty.

During the school year, April had been sent to Miss Madeira's School (Bettina's alma mater) as the solution to her conflict with Phyllis, though she continued to live with Kay during the summer rather than go to Bydale with her sisters, but soon enough, Phyllis decided both of the younger girls should also go to boarding school. While my mother was sent to Abbott Academy, my aunt Kay was enrolled at Phyllis's alma mater, Miss Porter's School, where she was one of two girls assigned to single rooms in the entire dormitory. The other girl rooming alone was a dwarf who had not wanted to share her room with the school's first and only Jew, so Kay was housed in a remade janitor's closet.

I knew Phyllis from my earliest childhood until she died in 1994. But I always had to conceal my relationship with her from my grandmother, who called her "the Bride of Frankenstein," and from my great-aunt Bettina the psychoanalyst, who loathed her and diagnosed her as "a screwloose from Toulouse." Phyllis attempted suicide more than once and was hospitalized repeatedly for what was then called manic depression, but she lived a long life. I always knew her by the name Phyllis Lutyens, as her third ex-husband, Robert Lutyens, was the son of the renowned architect Sir Edwin Landseer Lutyens. She liked the association to Lutyens, and advised me that if even the most tenuous of connections had value, "one must claim it!" I don't know if she claimed the connection to the writer Edward Robert Bulwer-Lytton of "It was a dark and stormy night" fame, who was Sir Edwin's grandfather.

I was instructed by my mother to keep quiet about knowing Phyllis in front of my grandfather, though I saw him so rarely this was mostly a theoretical warning. Later, I was also supposed to remain silent about Phyllis with his widow, my step-grandmother Joan, as well, on the grounds that she wouldn't approve of my having a relationship with her predecessor. I now realize this probably wasn't true; I'm certain that Joan would have recognized that my mother had her reasons for an attachment to her onetime stepmother. Joan herself had been required to tolerate Phyllis's presence at the start of her marriage to my grandfather in 1948. Phyllis was living under the same roof on Seventieth Street in a downstairs apartment, the double townhouse having been broken up into apartments shortly before. Jim retained a spacious apartment on the top floors—in the spaces that used to house the Warburg sisters' rooms, the nursery, and the governess's room—as his residence.

Phyllis told me that when she first met my father, when he was "courting" my mother, Sidney had irritated her by telling a boastful story about how, long before he met my mother, he and Jimmy had for a certain moment both been in pursuit of the same woman. The time period during which this competition was supposed to have taken place was in the same months when Jimmy and Phyllis were planning to be married, which she believed my father knew perfectly well. She didn't say the story was untrue.

Phyllis described to me a moment when she and Jimmy were on their honeymoon in April of 1935 and they were strolling on the deck of the ship taking them to Europe. She began aimlessly humming "Can't We Be Friends?" Jimmy ordered her to stop immediately and she had no idea why. "I wrote the words to that damned song, and you are tormenting me with it!" he replied. Based on my own experience with the crafty and manipulative Phyllis, I find it hard to believe that she didn't know he had written the lyrics for this hit song. I can well imagine her pretending that she had no idea and humming the tune to get a rise out of him.

For most of 1935, Kay worked tirelessly on *Porgy and Bess,* doing whatever George needed her to do. She often made musical notations for him, having an attractively legible hand. Scattered throughout the original score of *Porgy and Bess* are sections of music in her handwriting—for example, the first sixteen measures of "I Got Plenty o' Nuttin'," and the "Crown-Robbins fight fugue" at the end of the first scene in Act One, where there are seventeen pages in her hand. Ann Brown, who played the original Bess, told me she saw Kay at every casting audition and every rehearsal. She said that Kay could give notes with so much flattery and enthusiasm that you hardly realized she was correcting you and making suggestions for changes in your performance.

After the first performance, of *Porgy and Bess,* at the Colonial Theater in Boston, George was pressured to make numerous cuts in order to tighten up his four-hour folk opera. Kay was more reluctant than he to accept this. She did her best to persuade him to refuse, knowing how hurt he was by this compromise. They walked the Common all night, with the show's author DuBose Heyward, director Rouben Mamoulian, and composer Alexander Steinert, one of the vocal coaches, arguing back and forth about what to cut. By the time the sun rose, a quarter of the score—an hour—had been eliminated.

In 1976, when *Porgy and Bess* was produced in its four-hour entirety by the Houston Opera Company, my grandmother was consulted by the producer, Sherwin Goldman. She agreed to consult if he would promise her that if the production toured, it would play the Colonial Theater in Boston and she would be invited to attend the premiere. The tour was scheduled, and *Porgy and Bess* was booked into the Colonial Theater, even though the production was complicated by changes that had been made to the theater, which meant that the orchestra didn't fit into the pit until some box seats were temporarily removed. Why the insistence on the Colonial Theater? Goldman explained to Hollis Alpert, author of the 1990 book *The Life and Times of* Porgy and Bess: *The Story of an American Classic*:

> Kay . . . told me what seats she wanted on opening night. She wasn't quite sure exactly which ones, so I blocked off several. They were toward the back of the house. When we came to the theatre she remembered the seats and we sat together. "Now you've given me my gift," she said. "So many years ago I sat with George in these seats. I was in tears because of all the cuts that were being made in his work. 'George,' I said, 'they're not going to hear and see what you wrote.' He told me, 'Someday, Kay, you'll sit in that same seat and you'll hear what I wrote, I promise you.'"

In 1935 the hybrid nature of the score satisfied neither the classical nor popular taste of the critics, who had been harsh about many aspects of the opera's form and content. Perhaps the greatest scorn for Gershwin's masterpiece was voiced by Virgil Thomson, who sniped in *Modern Music,* "I do not like fake folklore, nor fidgety accompaniments, nor bittersweet harmony, nor six-part choruses, nor gefilte fish orchestration." (Thomson subsequently hid his anti-Semitic jab, editing his review when it was reprinted with other criticism by changing "gefilte fish orchestration" to "plum pudding orchestration.")

WHEN GEORGE traveled to Mexico for four weeks at the end of 1935, he went hoping for musical inspiration. He was exhausted by the mixed response and controversy surrounding *Porgy and Bess.* He was ready for something new, and it was precisely this sort of trip that had borne fruit in the past. Not only had he spent that time on Folly Beach in South Carolina to soak up the Gullah rhythms and dialect when he was writing *Porgy and Bess,* but in 1928 he had been stimulated by Parisian taxi horns to write *An American in Paris,* and the 1932 sojourn in Havana had inspired the *Cuban Overture.*

This trip was different, though. George's companions included neither his lyricist brother Ira, nor Kay, nor anyone else involved in his music. His entourage consisted of Gregory Zilboorg and two fellow analysands, Marshall Field and Eddie Warburg. George returned from this trip musically uninspired and disappointed not to have made any discoveries of intriguing indigenous music. But his interest in collecting art, as well as his growing fascination with his own potential as a painter, had led him to seek out the well-known Mexican artists Diego

Rivera and Frida Kahlo, Miguel Covarrubias, and David Alfaro Siqueiros.

The trip had many discomforts for George. Zilboorg, who had fled Russia in the 1917 revolution, claimed to be paranoiac about a potentially Bolshevik political climate in Mexico, so he carried a loaded pistol at all times. He also went out of his way to speak Spanish with the painters in order to exclude and embarrass George, who had confided to his analyst his fear of being left out in precisely this way. Worst of all, Zilboorg conducted analytic sessions early every morning with each of his three patients and then presided over breakfasts during which he often made humiliating references to their private matters.

George struck up a friendship with Siqueiros. (In fact, the visit by the four travelers was a turning point in Siqueiros's career; all bought canvases by him and brought him wider recognition in the United States after returning home with the works.) And when the Mexican painter traveled to New York to teach a workshop in early 1936, George commissioned him to paint his portrait. In his memoirs, Siqueiros wrote that the painting was conceived as a simple portrait head, but that as he began to work on the painting in George's New York apartment, George decided he wanted a full-length portrait. Siqueiros started over with a larger canvas. Then George changed his mind again: Now he wanted to be shown in concert at a piano. An even bigger canvas was brought in.

Finally, when Siqueiros thought he was done, the painting showed Gershwin alone onstage in a vast hall somewhat resembling the Metropolitan Opera House, where Gershwin had performed in a benefit concert in 1932. But now George suggested that the audience include little portraits of the people most important in his life, and he chose with great care where each of them should be seated in the first rows. He had recently bickered with Oscar Levant (whom Vernon Duke called a "professional sourpuss"), and there is a story that George put him in the second row for this reason. Siqueiros filled the rest of the hall with an overflowing audience of a faceless public that he called "a theater of the masses." He painted the front-row portraits from life and from photographs, many of them George's own striking photographic portraits.

Morris Gershwin, George's father (the man who called "Fascinatin' Rhythm" "Fashion on the River"), had died in 1932, and George's closest friend, orchestrator William Daly (no one knows why Bill Daly and George called each other "Pincus"), died as the painting was being finished. But just as the Dutch Masters painted arrangements of flowers that could never have actually bloomed simultaneously, George was able to transcend the sad limits of reality and assemble for this fantasy concert his perfect dream audience of the friends and family—and Gregory Zilboorg—most significant in his life. In the front row, Kay is seated beside Zilboorg. The finished *George in an Imaginary Concert Hall* had been hanging in George's New York apartment for only a few months when he left for Hollywood in August 1936. He never saw it again.

IN 1936 the Gershwin brothers were offered the opportunity to write the score to an Astaire-Rogers film, *Shall We Dance?* Zilboorg seemed to delight in emphasizing the significant trauma for George of the tepid response to *Porgy and Bess.* After this huge letdown, George should make a big change in his life, Gregory counseled. He had been so badly misunderstood, and had not received the recognition he deserved. He should leave New York. It would do him good to go to Hollywood for fresh opportunities to work on motion picture scores—and above all, he should take time out, test a separation, and get far away from Kay Swift.

Kay recalled their departure in an interview with Robert Kimball and Alfred Simon for their 1973 book, *The Gershwins*:

> I didn't see him for the final year of his life. He went to California in August 1936 and I never saw him after that photograph of him standing on the step of the ramp at the airport. And he had a mark around his head which was a deep groove from a straw hat that was too small for him.
>
> George left his apartment all furnished, and Emily Paley and I went afterwards and arranged to have everything packed up and stored. When he left, he did not know how long he was going to be gone—he went for one picture and another one came up afterwards and he stayed and did it. He and Ira went to the airport separately. George and I went in a taxi. [George asked Mabel Schirmer to accompany them, so that he did not ride alone with Kay, which would have led to one more final weepy and emotional farewell that he wanted to avoid.] We had decided we were not going to see each other or write and see how it went and see if it would be a happy arrangement. We kept everything cheery and bright. He laughed and talked about the picture. We said goodbye and he walked up the ramp. And I knew for sure I'd never see him again. I didn't know why, but I knew that was all, that was it. And he stood at the top of the ramp and he waved the hat and all I could see was the groove that went around his head like an Indian headband.

Despite her later assertion that she somehow knew on that day that she would never see him again, friends and family were told that they had agreed to take time off, and their romance was on hold for the duration of his Hollywood commitment. They both began to see other people, and though they had agreed to the mutual silence, they both confided to close friends their understanding that their relationship was unfinished business. Those who knew them could see clearly that this was intermission, with a final act to follow.

The score to the Astaire-Rogers film *Shall We Dance?* was completed, and work for *A Damsel in Distress* was nearly finished when George Gershwin died in July of the brain tumor that had been plaguing him with symptoms for months, according to most thinking, or years, according to a new study. Although it has long been accepted that he was killed by a hopelessly lethal tumor that could neither have been diagnosed nor treated adequately in 1937, several Gershwin scholars have disputed this, and the evidence against that diagnosis has grown. Most recently, the psychoanalyst Mark Leffert, M.D., has delved into the case, and his 2011 paper "The Psychoanalysis and Death of George Gershwin: An American Tragedy" reports on these devastating discoveries.

First, there seems little doubt that Gregory Zilboorg, brilliant and accomplished as he may have been, misrepresented his European training as a medical doctor when he arrived in the United States, and was in fact not just a fraud in the sense of a false personality or a duplicitous, immoral Svengali (he was those things, too), but literally a fraud. Zilboorg finessed certain requirements with false and sometimes contradictory claims of prior training, experience, and medical degrees in Germany and Russia before arriving in America. On the basis of these dubious credentials—each of which Leffert has meticulously investigated and demonstrated to be, at best, misrepresentations—he was admitted to and graduated from the Columbia College of Physicians and Surgeons. But Gregory Zilboorg, M.D., was never licensed to practice medicine for the entirety of his professional practice in New York, from 1931 until he stopped treating patients in the 1950s.

Leffert has also examined every scrap of the medical record that exists today concerning George's brain tumor, which has long been considered an incurable, deadly glioblastoma multiforme about which nothing could have been done, even if it had been diagnosed by Zilboorg and other physicians in the final weeks of his life, when George was suffering from increasingly acute symptoms, including blinding headaches, episodes of confusion (there was a bizarre incident of his smearing his torso with a box of chocolates, and on another occasion, he inexplicably tried to shove someone out of a moving car), depression, olfactory hallucinations of bad odors (a classic brain tumor symptom), and a general weakening and loss of ability to function.

Most Gershwin biographers perpetuate the characterization of their subject as a hypochondriac. (Edward Jablonski calls him "a notorious hypochondriac.") It is true that Gershwin was obsessed with his digestive system, and would often tell his friends more about the state of his bowels than they cared to know. His various digestive problems, Zilboorg persuaded him, were all emotional, which was why he referred to his problems as "composer's tummy." My great-aunt Bettina told me with unprofessional glee that Zilboorg long ago disclosed to her that "George's only real romantic feelings were for his enema bag."

Because he was perceived as a neurotic hypochondriac by Zilboorg and by his closest family members on instruction by Zilboorg, when George was hospitalized for testing at Cedars of Lebanon Hospital from June 23 to June 26 (when Sidney Kaufman visited him in his room next to Christiane Toller's), although a neurologist who examined him had recommended a spinal tap (which was not performed) to rule out a brain tumor, George was discharged with the diagnosis "most likely hysteria."

There are many sad and troubling stories about George Gershwin's final days, when he was, in retrospect, clearly in significant distress and floridly symptomatic, yet Lee and Ira Gershwin, with whom he was living in their house on Roxbury Drive, seemed strangely complacent and insufficiently concerned. Lee told more than one person to ignore him when George did things like try to put his fork in his ear instead of his mouth, or when he lay disconsolately on the sofa and refused to speak or even play the piano. They minimized their reports on his condition to most everyone who inquired about George, including the three women closest to him—Kay Swift, Mabel Schirmer, and Emily Paley—all on the East Coast and unaware of his terrible state. Years later, Lee would tell her nephew that she had deep regret about having taken Gregory Zilboorg's advice on how to treat George's behavior.

George's final days are horrifying in retrospect. He was listless and depressed and could barely function. He dropped and spilled things at the table, which irritated Lee, who at one point simply ordered him up to his room. Attempting to live normally, George accompanied Lee and Ira to lunch one day at Chasen's Restaurant, which was owned by the comic performer Dave Chasen (who had played Joe Cook's sidekick in *Fine and Dandy*). After lunch George collapsed on the sidewalk in front of the restaurant. "Leave him there," said Lee to Ira. "All he wants is attention."

When Lee heard that Yip Harburg's nearby house would be empty, with Harburg in New York working on a Broadway show with Harold Arlen, she arranged for George to move there, which he did, on July 4, accompanied, at this point, not only by his "man," Paul Mueller (who had previously worked for Paul and Nina Warburg before Kay got him the job with George), but also by Paul Levy, a male nurse dispatched by George's new psychiatrist, Ernest Simmel, to keep a close watch on George.

Years later, Mueller said that Lee had "exiled George" to Yip Harburg's house. When old friends such as Lillian Hellman, S. N. Behrman, and Oscar Levant saw him that summer, they were all shocked at his condition. Behrman said "the light had gone" from George's eyes. George was now sleeping in the daytime, and was rarely without the unbearable pain he said was behind his eyes. He was often stupefied by phenobarbital, and he spent his days isolated and alone, apparently on advice of his psychiatrist, who didn't want him to be overstimulated or agitated by visitors. "All my friends are leaving me," George said more than once. He continued to deteriorate, and on July 9 he fell into a coma. He was hospitalized, but surgery was not immediate, as there was an attempt to locate and fly a specialist from the East Coast, but then it became apparent that George's situation was dire, and shortly after midnight, on July 11, he underwent surgery for the brain tumor that was now beyond obvious. He never regained consciousness, and died a few hours later.

Leffert has concluded that George Gershwin exhibited symptoms of temporal lobe epilepsy, not for a few weeks or months but for at least fourteen years. The lesion in his brain causing these symptoms, he argues, was a very benign and long-term pilocytic astrocytoma, not a deadly, fast-growing glioblastoma. Further, contradicting the received wisdom that nothing could have been done for George at any point, Leffert writes:

I would suggest that Gershwin's tumor herniated sometime on July 9, resulting in his gradually falling into a coma.

Further evidence was seen in the post-operative elevations in body temperature, respiratory rate, and pulse rate that all pointed to brain stem damage resulting from that herniation. It is important to recognize that Gershwin did not die of his brain tumor. The tumor itself was small and most likely benign. He died from the mechanical effects of the rapidly enlarging cyst on his brain; compression followed by herniation. It seems possible, one cannot be sure of course, that Gershwin's life and talent might have been saved had surgery been done as late as the morning of July 9; he certainly could have been saved if it had been done at the time of the first Cedars admission, June 23–26.

On July 11, my grandmother was in New York, attending a concert of piano music with April. When a piece ended, she stood up abruptly, saying to her daughter, "George is gone, I feel it, we have to go home right now," and they hurried back to Kay's East Eighty-sixth Street apartment, where the phone was ringing as they walked in. It was Leonore Gershwin.

"Kay—George is dead," said Leonore.

"Oh, no!" said Kay.

"Oh, yes!" said Leonore.

On August 3, Kay received a condolence letter from George Pallay, a Paley cousin and a friend of George's since 1917. Pallay was a bit of a shady character. It was said that he had Mafia connections. A stock promoter and investor who had changed his name from Abramson, he was often part of George's entourage, someone who arranged the tickets, knew the right bootleggers. He was the friend who would get the girl for George and then get rid of the girl for George. Pallay was singularly devoted to

George, and no one had been more vigilant during the final days.

Pallay had played a key role at the hospital during the surgery, having been stationed at a desk just outside the operating theater, along with George's agent, Arthur Lyons. As the operation progressed, the doctors would tell Pallay what was happening, and then he would relay the latest update by telephone to the four family members—Lee and Ira, and Lee's sister Emily Paley and her husband, Lou, who had just arrived—waiting on another floor.

At first the news had seemed good, and Pallay informed the family that a cyst the size of a grapefruit had been discovered and excised. This seemed to be good news, and the doctors were momentarily optimistic. The news was relayed to the family. Then the surgeons discovered that in fact there remained an embedded tumor. At this point, George's brain was swelling uncontrollably. The outlook was grim.

This terrible update was relayed by Pallay to the family, via Lee, who chose to keep this news to herself. And so when George's surgery was finished, and she and Ira left the hospital at 6:15 in the morning with Emily and Lou, three of them thought that George had a good chance of full recovery. The moment they were back home on Roxbury Drive, Emily sent a telegram to Kay, telling her the good news. They went to bed, after this sleepless night, all but Lee feeling relief and hope for George.

Kay's telegram to Emily in reply, sent at 11:04 New York time, reads:

DEAR EMILY THANKS A MILLION FOR THE GOOD
NEWS STOP MY BEST LOVE TO YOU TWO AND
LEE AND IRA STOP CANCELLED PLANE PASSAGE

AND WILL HOPE FOR REPORT OF FURTHER GOOD
PROGRESS FROM YOU JOYFULLY = KAY.

It seems likely that in the aftermath of George's death (he
died, entirely alone, thirteen minutes after the telegram was received at Western Union in Beverly Hills) my grandmother actually forgot that she had made the decision to fly to California
and see George. She never mentioned the booked and canceled
flights in any discussion of the days surrounding George's death.
She never voiced bitterness, and preferred mockery to any other
form of grievance, but only when it was far too late did she learn
to what extent she had been kept in the dark about how sick
George actually was, right up to the end.

Kay's reply to George Pallays letter of condolence:

Dear George,

   *Since our best friend is gone, no word from anyone ever
has been any help to me except your letter. Nobody knew so
well what we've been to each other,—and no other person—
except you, and me—has ever been wanted by George in a
time of illness.—He often spoke to me of how wonderful you
were to him that other time, in 1931, when he had flu in
California; and it comforted me to feel that at the last he had
you with him.*

   *The past year was so terrible for both of us; it seemed,
when he left, that all I could ever do for him was to leave him
free for the choice he never was able to make either one way
or the other. But I have often wondered what he'd have done
if I just called up and said, "I'm coming out,"—even though
he seemed to accept my leaving him, as I finally had to or go
crazy watching the mail. Thank you, George, for your very*

extra splendid letter, which was a help. And, good luck to you
always!
 Kay

A month after George's death, Kay wrote to Ira (on World's
Fair stationery, as by now she had left Radio City Music Hall
to become Director of Light Music for the 1939 Fair, for which
preparations were well under way), to tell him that she had
been unable to bring herself to attend the memorial concert at
Lewisohn Stadium the night before, but had gone instead to the
rehearsal, where she found the selections from *Porgy and Bess*
"shatteringly beautiful and the performance too good to be easily borne."

In this three-page letter she talked about how seeing him
had been "the only comfort since George's death; it brings him
nearer and reminds me of so many happy and funny incidents
that get lost along the way otherwise." She also wrote about
making plans for the two of them to work on George's music,
reminding him, "there are many fragments I can recall on sight
and harmonize as George did. I long to get at it and feel sure
you can assemble quite a lot of material." At the very bottom of
the last page there is an afterthought that feels as if it had been
on her mind when she began the letter but she could only blurt
out before sealing the envelope: "Please destroy my pictures and
letters."

Ira honored her request, and she herself burned every letter
and photograph in her possession of the two of them together.
She didn't believe in saving letters. "My mother always said letters are for today," she would say as she read her mail and then
tore it up and dropped it in a wastebasket.

When George died, she wrote, many years later, "A great

many people not only felt sad but bored. He loved every aspect of life, and made every aspect of life lovable. People thought they could never sense that special joy again."

THEY NEVER lived together, and they only had fleeting times of a certain sort of ordinary quotidian intimacy that some of us love. She preferred the drama of a romance conducted this way, intense encounters followed by solitude. She wanted to perpetuate the mystery, and she thought it was preferable for the man to go home instead of staying over and lingering awkwardly the following morning. She deplored the things men tended to do if they were still around by daylight, like read newspapers in bed. A surprisingly modest person in some ways, she liked her privacy for ablutions and all other bathroom activities. Her description to her friend the composer William Bolcom of her preference for romance conducted on these terms and her claim that she was glad she and George never got to the tedium and exposure of "toothbrush time" led him to compose, in 1979, with lyricist Arnold Weinstein, a song of that title, sung by a woman who despairs that a man has spent the night and "now he's crashing round my bathroom, perusing all my pills, reviewing all my ills."

OVER THE years, Kay wasn't entirely consistent about the way she talked about her romance with George. When asked if he was the love of her life, she replied tartly to one friend, "Well, I was the love of his!" When she was in her eighties, she told another young friend that with George she had "the best sex" of her life. But in her seventies she had confided to her last lover (a talented arranger and trombone player with the Guy

Lombardo Orchestra who was thirty-five years younger than she) that while George was well endowed, he was perfunctory in bed, and this was one of the reasons she had never really been jealous of his other women, because sex wasn't the basis of their deep connection. In her letters to Mary Lasker in the 1940s and '50s, she wrote often about her dreams about Jimmy, her awareness of phantom anniversaries with him, and her sense that he loomed larger in her thoughts about the past than did "anyone else."

At various times she told people different versions of George's messages to her in the weeks before he died. She described to one interviewer an exchange of telegrams with George when she heard that he was in the hospital in June, his reply to hers saying, "I'm going to get well for both of us and will come back." Immediately after his death, both George Pallay and Paul Mueller reported to Kay that George had said that he loved Kay and planned to return to her in New York as soon as he got over this illness. In her old age she said more than once that George himself had telephoned her several times in his final days, from his seclusion in Yip Harburg's house, and that he told her he was "coming back for both of us."

She did once admit to me that if George had lived, she imagined they might indeed have married, but in time they might also have divorced, which is to say that perhaps there was the ring of sad truth to Oscar Levant's nasty yet prescient quip when he saw Kay and George arriving at a nightclub at the height of their romance: "Look! Here comes George Gershwin with the future Miss Kay Swift."

Emotional Problems in Pants

I got a great bang out of my New Year's Eve—the first non-nostalgic one since 1926 for me . . . from 5 to 6, instead of being in a hair-dresser's getting a last-minute going over, prior to going a round of parties, I was in the barn shoveling manure. Former years found me with a new dress in the closet and orchids in the ice-box, while some emotional problem in pants waited to take me out. Here I wore blue jeans—plus a bulky pair of cotton pajamas underneath, for warmth. Also, dear, 3 sweaters, 2 pairs of socks and fishing boots. Pretty seductive, what?—I did a lot of shoveling (the Indians were out on their binge) and then returned, took a drink of TEA (no drinks for either of us) and went to bed by ten. Old man Nostalgia, all Ninsky aches, were gone.

—KAY SWIFT, *letter to Mary Lasker from the*
Faye and Kay Ranch, Bend, Oregon, January 1940

WHEN GEORGE DIED IN JULY OF 1937, KAY HAD BEEN dating Ed Byron, a versatile radio actor, writer, and producer whose greatest successes were a radio drama called *Mr. District Attorney* and a quiz show called *Ask Me Another.*

My mother always mentioned that he was handsome and "a big drinker" whenever his name came up, and more than once she said of him, "He clearly wasn't Mr. Right for Mother, but he was certainly Mr. Right Now."

Although they had been seeing each other for a few months, when word came of George's hospitalization, Byron, separated from his wife but not divorced, broke off with Kay abruptly, recognizing that for him, this had been a casual, lighthearted fling with nowhere to go. Kay was charming and amusing and had feelings for him, but if she was about to plummet into mourning over the loss of George Gershwin, the fun times were over and he didn't want to be stuck nursing her through the devastation. It was a terrible blow that came at a very low time for her.

By the spring of 1939, she had begun to see Charles Wertenbaker, a brilliant journalist and author of several novels who was the foreign editor at *Time* magazine. Kay's affair with Charles was so discreet that nobody in our family has ever known about it at all. I learned about the Wertenbaker interlude only when reading the hundreds of pages of my grandmother's frequent letters to Mary Lasker, all written between 1939 and 1948, while Kay was living out west and the two close friends maintained an intimate correspondence in lieu of their usual telephone calls and frequent lunches.

Charles Wertenbaker was a fascinating character. Just a few years after their involvement, he would land on Normandy Beach with Robert Capa. Together, they would follow General Leclerc's Jeep into Paris in August 1944 for the liberation, and accompany Hemingway to the liberation of the Ritz Bar. After the war, he remarried and went to live in Basque country, where he and his wife had children (one was the playwright Timberlake Wertenbaker), but a terminal cancer diagnosis in 1954 led to his decision to take his own life, assisted by his wife, Lael. Her 1957 book about this, *Death of a Man,* was made into a film starring Henry Fonda.

When Kay took up with Charles (or "Wertie"), he had been married to the novelist Nancy Hale for only three years, but they were already on the verge of divorce. The romance was brief and tempestuous, and by autumn of that same year Kay was married to her second husband, Faye Hubbard, a rodeo cowboy ten years younger than she whom she met at the World's Fair. They eloped after a three-week courtship, and she went to live with him in Bend, Oregon, on his hardscrabble ranch, renamed the Faye and Kay. Looking back at the New York life she left behind from her Bend kitchen table in the spring of 1940, Kay wrote to Mary:

> *This has surely been a terrific year of upheaval for you, and me too. It's just about a year—less about 10 days—since your cocktail party, where I met Charles, your horrible beating over Fiend [their nickname for a married lover of Mary's] and mine over Byron. . . . Think of all the vicissitudes!*
>
> *I read a story of Nancy Hale's last night,—the second since I came West that had Charles in it. I think she's a pestiferous gal, with whom I am basically out of sympathy; but I believe she's profoundly in love with Charles, and question whether either one will ever get the other completely out of mind. It gave me quite an odd sensation to read of his little sayings and expressions. I think that marriage was so scarring that it couldn't be thoroughly erased, and would have been a shadow between Charles and me, particularly as there's a child. I guess the whole Charles affair, which saved my reason at the start, when Byron (whom I really loved ten times more) left, was the most violent and upsetting I ever had. Those*

horrible nights of fighting, just as you and Fiend had them, almost drove me nuts. The only person I ever dream of—and I do, often very homesickly—is Jim. He seems to mean more to me, and be closer to me in my mind, than any of the others, just now, at this distance from everything. Perhaps because of the marriage pattern, which recalls early married life with Jim; I don't know. Faye is ever more of a dear, and more of a grand person, than I knew. . . . I am negotiating with my trustees to promote enough cash to get the house fixed up.

In 1943 they moved to a second Faye and Kay Ranch in Van Nuys, California, the same year she published a "novel" about her life as a rancher's wife called *Who Could Ask for Anything More?* She would divorce Faye in 1946 (answering the question of her book's title), and marry for the third time in 1947, returning to New York with her new husband, Hunter Galloway, in 1948. Once Kay and Mary were reunited and resumed their frequent lunches, the very personal, confiding, intimate correspondence ceased.

IN THE autumn of 1942, Kay wrote from Bend, thanking Mary for sending her Nancy Hale's newest novel:

Youse were a dear to send me the books—specially the Nancy Hale one, which is really an important job. She has only twice as much talent as her handsome ex-husband, and now adds marvelous workmanship to it, and sensitivity as keen as Katherine Mansfield's without that poisonous defeated quality and that fragility that gripes me in K.M.'s oft-touted masterpieces. Several conversations I had with Chas. Wertenbaker were duplicated word for word in Nancy's book, which showed all too plainly that his pattern is such an uncomfortable one at close quarters that any female extant would suffer hideously therefrom.

It is really rather astonishing the way Nancy and I crossed each others' paths at various times. I see many autobiographical features in her work, some of them recounted to me by Chas., and believe she really went through a great deal of hell. He was evidently the love of her life, and she was undoubtedly his, yet they hurt each other every minute. . . . She had been so crazy about Jim, long ago, I remember well how mixed-up I felt about her. I am sure she knew and resented Charles's fling with me though the divorce was under way at that time,—indicated by the fact that she gave the name "Evelyn Swift" to a character who had a brief affair with the husband of one of her 3 heroines,—all of which heroines are Nancy in various aspects.

She is now, I firmly believe, in a class with Edith Wharton and Willa Cather as a novelist. Tops.

Three years ago today we got married, Faye and I. Seems strange, as I look back at the neurotic setup that led up to it over a period of several years. I certainly fell on my feet; if Charles had been free at that time, I might have married him, which would have been disastrous, and if Byron had been able to marry and we had done so, I'd probably have been through another divorce by now. All very something-or-other to look back upon. Faye is such a dear, I am lucky to have him.

When Kay Swift eloped with Faye Hubbard in 1939 (one gossip column headline read "Rodeo Romeo Romances Kay Swift"), it was a graceful if surprising exit from her New York life. Being swept off her feet and carried west by a big, handsome (by some standards, if not others), semiliterate rodeo cowboy of simple means and taste, who boasted that he had broken every bone in his body at least once, was for her a welcome change.

In her 1943 roman à clef, she described "Chris" (the book is dedicated "to Faye Hubbard, otherwise Chris") as someone who "gave the immediate impression of being resolved, like a number reduced to its lowest terms. He had that something which numberless people I know—myself included—have raised heaven and earth to acquire, a simple, happy adjustment to living. To be with him was, from the beginning, a refreshing, tonic sensation."

After only a couple of years on the ranch, the idea for the book, and the hope of making some money with it, had Kay writing every moment she could find. She sent chapters to Mary back east, and depended on her response as she wrote, explaining at one point that she had sent nothing recently because "All mumpsy chapters were so tumpsy they had to be scrapped." ("Mumpsy" was a term my grandmother used for things that were inauthentic, cloying, or twee.)

Although transformed into a series of amusing anecdotes in her book, life on the ranch was actually quite primitive and challenging, especially before she pried loose some of her Paul and Nina Warburg trust money for extensive upgrades, which included heat and running water. Faye had two little girls who came to live with them, and for the first time in her life Kay was involved in the daily needs of young children. Her three daughters never got over her mothering of the Hubbard sisters in ways they themselves had never experienced, especially since it came at a time when she had exited their lives to such an extent that she would not be present at any of their weddings. Even so, Andy and Kay did make several visits to the Faye and Kay, some of them lasting months.

Although the family's way of talking about Faye Hubbard—"the cowboy"—has been to treat him as a passing fancy, a phase, just another of the madcap situations my grandmother got herself into and out of, the truth as revealed in the pages of all the letters to Mary Lasker is that she not only truly loved him and thought she had found her perfect match for life, but also that she was hoping to have his child. She was pregnant twice, at forty-three and forty-four. Faye was ten years her junior but she had told him they were the same age, and it isn't clear, even when she talks about trips to the doctor's office in Portland and descriptions of her feelings about the pregnancies, as well as Faye's anxiety about her health, that he ever learned her actual age.

The first baby had a due date of April 2, 1941, but she miscarried sometime after four months. The second pregnancy, the following year, which had been achieved under the medical supervision of Goodrich Schauffler, M.D., in Portland, was lost in the second trimester as well. She had written to Mary that she might have the baby in New York, delivered by Mabel Schirmer's brother Norman Pleshette (who would deliver me in 1955), if a job should come through. She wouldn't mention her pregnancy to Broadway producer Cheryl Crawford just yet, because she didn't want to lose the chance to be considered as musical supervisor for a show with a Gershwin score. Dorothy Fields had worked on a show while seven months pregnant, she noted. The second miscarriage, however, ended hope of what Kay had referred to in her letters to Mary as "an exciting eugenics experiment." (She had other dealings with Dr. Schauffler, because, as the letters reveal, during her years in Oregon, my grandmother was enlisted by Mary Lasker to conduct a number of covert "b.c." missions, disseminating birth-control information among the Native American women.)

Cheryl Crawford was in fact keen to produce this musical

with a score by the Gershwin brothers, with Kay Swift as musical supervisor. The project never got off the ground, most likely because of Ira's ambivalence about creating a score from George's unfinished melodies. But in December 1942, Crawford wrote to Ira Gershwin to rave about Kay's performance the previous week (during a Christmas visit east), for her and S. J. Perelman, in Rose Gershwin's living room (an uncomfortable venue for my grandmother, one that was probably required because of the preciousness of the musical scores), of many of the unpublished Gershwin tunes Kay and Ira were working together to organize and number. In her letter to Ira, Crawford pitched the show, with a book by "Sid" Perelman, and stars she hoped would tempt Ira—Ed Wynn, Frank Sinatra, and Libby Holman. She also added that Ira should tell Lee that "Kay's cowboy behaved himself quite nicely," beyond his first line on being introduced to Crawford, which was "Where's the crapper?"

THE FAYE and Kay was mostly devoted to raising and training horses for use in Hollywood in an era when hundreds of low-budget shoot-'em-ups crowded the screen. In addition to the horses, there were cows, pigs, chickens, goats, a pair of sheep my grandmother named Happy and Trudge, and at any given moment some of this livestock might be in the house. Marauding cougars were a genuine menace to the ranch, and Faye slept with his gun at the ready, one ear always cocked for sounds of nocturnal attacks on the stock.

When Kay was bedridden with a bad case of mumps (actual mumps, not just a mumpsy illness) acquired from one of the Hubbard girls, Faye brought her a treat which she couldn't possibly want. As she lay in her bed of misery, with eyes tightly closed she said a feeble "No thank you" to what she thought she had heard him offer: a "cinnamon bun." When he didn't leave and asked her just to open her eyes to take a quick look, she finally obliged, and discovered that he had brought to her bedside a Cinnamon *Bear,* a cub whose mother he had just regretfully shot.

ALTHOUGH THE move from her New York existence to life as a rancher's wife in the wilderness might seem like a completely alien choice, lighting out for the Territory ran in the Swift family. Her grandfather Joseph Swift, born near Philadelphia in 1843, had spent two years in the Wild West, having been sent at age eighteen in 1862 to work on a ranch in the dry Montana desert as a cure for his tuberculosis. He found work in the Idaho Territory, in Bannack, Montana, a boom town that had come to life in 1862 owing to the discovery of rich deposits of placer gold on the banks of Grasshopper Creek.

In Bannack, Joseph soon became acquainted with a boarder on the ranch, Henry Plummer, the highly regarded sheriff of the Idaho Territory. They became good friends. When Plummer was married, Joseph Swift was his best man. After the ceremony, the wedding party feasted on a Bannack delicacy, a baked buffalo hump.

Joseph looked up to the older man with enormous admiration. Plummer was a gentleman with impeccable manners, the epitome of a law-abiding citizen. By all accounts, Joseph was completely oblivious to Henry Plummer's secret life as the head of a gang of road agents responsible for a seven-month spree of vicious murders and robberies of gold shipments. Plummer led two lives: law enforcer by day, murderer and thief by night. By some estimates, in a single four-month period in 1863, the

Plummer gang murdered more than 120 gold miners. Their M.O. was grisly. After killing the men and stealing their gold, they would hack up the dead bodies into small pieces, which they scattered for the buzzards and coyotes.

In January of 1864, the citizenry of Bannack could no longer tolerate the rampant lawlessness flourishing in their midst, and a local vigilante group of about fifty men was formed and sworn in. Their pursuit of road agents was successful, and some twenty criminals were apprehended and hanged on the gallows at Hangman's Gulch, which had been erected and used by Henry Plummer in his duties as sheriff. One of them, in his confession before the noose was placed around his neck, identified Henry Plummer as the leader of "the Innocents" gang.

On January 10, Plummer was apprehended at his home by the mob and they marched him to Hangman's Gulch. He made the vigilantes an offer: If they would give him two hours, and a horse, he would return with his weight in gold, which they could share. His plea was ignored. Before the noose was placed around his neck, he took off his necktie and said, "Give this to Joseph Swift . . . he may have it to remember me by."

When he got word that Plummer was being hanged by the posse, Joseph Swift hurried to the gallows, but there was a mob of men surrounding the scaffold and he couldn't penetrate the crowd. When Plummer was hanged, Joseph threw himself to the ground, crying in despair that his innocent friend had been murdered so unjustly. He was regarded with suspicion by some of the vigilantes, given his devotion to the leader of the Innocents, but nothing ever came of it. It was estimated that Plummer's gang had been responsible for the murders of some three hundred men whose gold they robbed, gold which was estimated to have been worth millions of dollars. It has been widely believed from then to now that Henry Plummer held all the gold the gang plundered from their victims, and buried it in the Montana hills surrounding Bannack. People are still looking for Henry Plummer's gold.

In response to Joseph's letter home telling of the vigilante hangings and what happened to his friend Henry, his father, Samuel, wrote back to say, "These matters as far as you are concerned personally have given me no uneasiness, always confiding in your good star. After such a purgation of villainous rascality perhaps things will go on better."

There is no clear record of Joseph's return east from Bannack, but by December of 1864, his lungs presumably clear, he was back in Pennsylvania, superintending oil well drilling for the Sugar Creek Oil Company. He had *saved two thousand dollars in gold* in his two years working as a ranch hand in the Idaho Territory. Apparently, this astonishing thrift was never questioned. The following summer he went to work with his brother William at the family business, Swift and Courtney, in New Haven, Connecticut, a safety match company that later merged with the Diamond Match Company, which bought out Swift family interests, alas. He lived the rest of his life in the East, in Philadelphia and then Wilmington, having married Gertrude Horton Dorr, who was not more than four and a half feet tall to his unusual height of six feet, seven inches. They had twelve children, of whom six survived—five girls and one son, Samuel Shippen Swift, who was Katharine Swift's father. (The Shippen family name was handed down through the generations in alternating form, with a Samuel Shippen Swift followed by a Shippen Samuel Swift. Margaret Shippen, the grasping Tory wife of Benedict Arnold often blamed for his traitorous decision to side with the British during the American Revolution, was my grandmother's first cousin, four times removed.)

For the rest of his life, Joseph Swift did not like to speak of the fate of his good friend Henry Plummer. If the delicate subject did come up, the careful language the family always used was "Joseph's friend Henry died very suddenly when a platform gave way at a public event."

GERTRUDE SWIFT's nephew John Van Nostrand Dorr, who became Katharine Swift's stepfather in 1924 when he married his first cousin Sam's widow, had also lit out for the Territory. Having been chief chemist in the Orange, New Jersey, laboratory of Thomas A. Edison, C.J. (for Cousin John) spent two years in Deadwood, South Dakota, as an assayer and chemist at the Delaware Smelter there. Although there are family stories about his having driven the Deadwood Gulch stagecoach, the historic record for that remains silent.

Subsequently, he was the manager of a small cyanide mill at Fantail Gulch, before working in mines in Colorado and Arizona, where he invented his apparently renowned "continuous counter current decantation process." His work in those mines led to dozens of inventions that are today still known and used throughout mining and chemical processing, from the Dorr Thickener to the Dorr Classifier and the Dorr Floculator. He returned east and had several extremely successful businesses, the last one being Dorr-Oliver.

C.J. died at ninety, in 1962; I met him at my grandmother's several times when I was little. I didn't understand that he was her stepfather, but he was family anyway, as was explained to me—he was my first cousin three times removed! She always regarded him as her stepfather even though her mother's death had come in the fourth year of their marriage. His third wife was the photographer Nell Dorr (whose work my mother dismissed with a faintly competitive tone as being "naked pictures of mothers and babies"). I heard nothing about C.J. having worked for Edison or about his time in Deadwood, but I knew he was important because he was the man who invented the white line at the side of the road.

His *New York Times* obituary notes this, describing the first test of his theory, in the 1950s, that white lines at the sides of the road would prevent highway accidents at night, when limited visibility forced drivers to follow the line in the middle of the road, leading to collisions. The first white lines were painted on a stretch of the Merritt Parkway near Greenwich, and it was such a success that by 1954 the Merritt Parkway became the first highway in the nation with white lines at the sides of the road.

DID MY grandmother feel an atavistic connection with the Wild West? Was this why something about Faye Hubbard in his ten-gallon hat and his fancy boots and his big belt buckle and his colorful rodeo shirt felt just right?

In 1943, Kay wrote to Mary from Van Nuys, shortly after a Thanksgiving at Ira's. She reported that "Dot Parker and Lewis Milestone were there," and that she and Faye "and two other cowboys" had attended "in cowboy clothes." She went on to muse about her marriage to this unlikely man:

> *You know how strongly I believe in that old number, pro-*
> *pinquity, and once two people really get the habit of being*
> *together it's amazing how obstacles can be melted down to*
> *a thin gravy. Look at Faye and me, for example. He simply*
> *stuck around, knowing I was profoundly attracted to him,*
> *until finally everything that had looked insurmountable fell*
> *away. He couldn't have started out at more of a disadvantage,*

either. Charles in the No. 1 spot, no dough to offer, inconve-
nient geographical setup, etc. . . .

Life is so completely—not to say wildly—different than
formerly has been the case I can hardly believe this is Swift.
Yours for bigger and better contrasts, more refreshing than a
drink in the desert . . . Faye couldn't be more fun, more con-
siderate, or generally more satisfactory to me. That feeling
of peace and comfort, that his very personality and size and
devotion gives me, is stronger than ever—and I realize how
goddamn miserable I've been so much of the time before. I
find even my brain works faster and more clearly without
that extra load of anxiety it used to carry. And that sex num-
ber—always particularly necessary to me—used to bring
such a long chain of practical difficulties and miserable little
concealments in its train that just waking up in the morning
here and knowing that a knock at the door need not make me
jump up and rush into a bathroom gives me no end of a kick.

"Who could ask for anything more?" is of course a Gershwin lyric, a line that occurs in two very different songs, both "I
Got Rhythm" and "Nice Work If You Can Get It." When Kay
wrote to Ira asking if he would mind her using the phrase for
her book title (a courtesy, as he had no legal claim on the words
if appropriated for a book title; Ethel Merman also used it for
the title of her 1955 autobiography), his reply was an indifferent
approval, but with it came the nasty and not serious suggestion
that she consider "My Man's Gone Now" (from *Porgy*) for her
title. (DuBose Heyward, and not Ira, was the lyricist for that
song.) I am pretty sure this snipe was suggested by Ira's personal
secretary at the time, Lawrence D. Stewart. Lawrence, who was
to co-author *The Gershwin Years* with Edward Jablonski, the

1958 book that is the wellspring for much of the published minimization and trivialization of Kay Swift in George Gershwin's life, was one of the very few people in the Gershwin world who really disliked my grandmother, and he typed the letter. But Ira did sign it.

Who Could Ask for Anything More? was published in 1943, with blurbs from George S. Kaufman and Ilka Chase, among others, to nice reviews. There was a flurry of media attention, and many interviews in print and on the air ensued, most of which brought up Kay's relationship with George Gershwin. The demands of all the publicity were a challenge to Faye, who didn't want his wife to travel or spend time away from him.

The book was made into a 1950 movie, *Never a Dull Moment,* with Fred MacMurray as the cowboy and Irene Dunne as "Kay Kingsley." Although she wrote a full score, words and music, for what was originally planned as a musical (Lerner and Lowe's not unrelated *Paint Your Wagon* was a Broadway hit a year later), Kay was disappointed when only a few songs were used in the film. By the time the movie was out, of course, it had become apparent that Kay Swift could ask for anything more, having divorced Faye Hubbard in 1946 and having married for a third time the following year.

Faye's drinking and his nearly insane jealousies had become a lethal mix. Even in the first years of their marriage, his drinking was a problem. In a letter from the Faye and Kay in Bend, Kay lamented to Mabel Pleshette:

> *Why does John Barleycorn play, directly or indirectly, a part all through my life?—I am now on the wagon for a year (up next Xmas) because the drinking problem is one Faye can't seem to cope with unless I go dry.—He likes to drink & always has, harmlessly enough—but the trouble is that in*

this state you can't get it at any public place. So you have a permit & buy a bottle, & bring it home & drink it exactly the way people drank in prohibition, Faye likes his liquor in the morning, like all cowboys. The trouble is that for the past 15 months he's been drinking for 2 or 3 days at a time steadily, then stopping for a fortnight. And I find him hard to deal with when he's really tight—the only time he hasn't an angelic disposition. He is perfectly pleasant then, <u>unless</u> I disagree or refuse to do something he wants. Then he confuses me with his mother or first wife—both poisonous—But it's difficult to handle, and he'll say anything that comes into his head on such occasions—generally before the children.

I've tried being Old Patient and also You Godamn Son of a Bitch, and conclude the only thing is never to drink myself, as I get so damned mad I'm afraid of rushing off or doing something silly.—Isn't it funny how my life is tied in with drinking problems? I always got into such a scene with George after too many—and Byron you know presented problems, in that respect.—Sometimes I think Jim & I would have done better minus alcohol.—The hell of it is, it's <u>fun</u>. Faye and I can have such fine times & good laughs when drinking—but then when he gets over the edge I've got to be cold sober to save the bacon. Then I can see that it's all a reversion to childhood, by Faye.

And no matter how mad I get, and am happy that he clutches for me, is scared to death of losing me.—Poor lamb, he often can drink just mildly—but the awful times when he doesn't are really pretty tough.—I hate to have him go on the wagon entirely (he did recently, but fell off)—so many contacts & jolly sessions with the boys would be out for him.—At any rate, I'll ask him to do it while I'm in N.Y., as I am doing it too. . . . All this under your hat, <u>please</u>."

Faye became so possessive and controlling of his wife, so unhappy first about her travel to lecture on *Porgy and Bess* in 1942, and then about her desire to travel to promote her book the following year, that he finally smothered the marriage. The tipping point, ironically, was the effect of the success of this book about their wonderful life together. Ira Gershwin admitted to Kay only after her divorce had gone through that there had been a time when the two of them were working together on the trunk of unfinished Gershwin songs and he had been terrified when he spotted Faye surreptitiously following them when they left the house on Roxbury Drive and went out to lunch.

WHEN I was eighteen, my cousin Betsy and I spent a strange couple of days with Faye Hubbard at a racetrack outside Spokane, Washington. John Wayne would have been better casting. He was worn out but he was still a powerful man, an old sixty-seven with very few teeth, and he was living in his pickup truck with a horse trailer, both of which had been painted with a flat pink house paint. He introduced us to some of his cronies, saying, "These are my two granddaughters from New York! After the show, I'm going to take them down to the Double Clutch and dance hell out of them!"

He was moved by how much Betsy and I resembled our mothers, Kay and Andrea, at roughly the same ages, when he knew them. He called me "Little Fart" a few times, and over fried chicken at the Double Clutch—which Betsy and I paid for out of our winnings, because Faye had told us which horses to bet on in the last three races and each horse had come in exactly as he knew it would—he told us about the young nurse he was seeing who sometimes "wanted sex so bad we just pull over behind a billboard on the interstate!" He carried a tattered copy of *Who Could Ask?* in his truck so he could win bar bets, he said, that he "had a book wrote about him."

The day after our visit, he telephoned my grandmother at our urging, and they spoke for the first time in more than twenty years. She reported to me that he had been worried that he had behaved crudely with us, and when I asked her what she thought he meant by that, she said he had been worried that using a toothpick right in front of us at the table after our fried chicken at the Double Clutch could have made a bad impression.

Three years later, perhaps encouraged overmuch by that phone call with his ex-wife, and a few subsequent ones as well, Faye showed up in New York. My grandmother was visiting April in Rome and wasn't due back for a few days. In Connecticut, where Nick and I were living in a rented house for the first year of our marriage, our phone rang at six a.m.

"This is Kathy's grandfather from out west!" boomed in Nick's ear. "It is imperative that I see Kay! Do you know where she is? It is imperative that I see her before the meat goes bad!"

He had made the trip from Spokane in a truck, surely not the pink truck, with a Styrofoam cooler filled with chunks of meat, game animals he had shot and butchered himself along the way, he said. There was deer, bear, elk, rabbit, and who knows what else. This was his love offering to the woman who had once loved him. He left the cooler with the doorman, who kept it in the courtyard of the building. When my grandmother returned from her trip she summoned Nick and me to New York to deal with it. By the time we picked it up, there was a pool of blood leaking out. She kept avoiding Faye, perhaps aware that he would detect the truth about her age, and finally, the day he was scheduled to leave New York and head back west, she saw him briefly, with an apartment full of other people, sidestepping any possibility of real conversation or anything else he might have had in mind.

My GRANDMOTHER's third husband called himself Hunter Galloway, choosing to name himself for a region of Scotland. Coincidentally, in the Swift family tree there are actual Galloways, though ironically and coincidentally, he had been born with the name Samuel Kaufman, the same name as my paternal grandfather. Hunter was twelve years Kay's junior. When they married in 1948, it was only a few months after she had written a rambling letter to Mary from her house on Yoakum Drive in Beverly Hills, where she lived after leaving Faye, saying:

> *Funny to reflect that it's nearly a year since I walked away from home on October 6th. I have seen nobody who strikes me as at all possible for me to wish to marry; perhaps I shall never find the man anyway, and if I get along as well as this without one, I shan't mind it. It seems odd, at times, and of course I miss Faye—and even, still, Jimmie. But not so much as I'd miss being free to do what I want, I think.*

Hunter had a theater background. Both his parents were actors, and his first role on Broadway was what he called a "carry-on," as opposed to a walk-on, in a Holbrook Blinn production when he was three years old. He worked on film sets, and was an office boy at the Paramount studio in Astoria. In 1929, when he was twenty, he had a role in *Kibitzer* on Broadway, with Edward G. Robinson, credited as Hunter Kaufman. He was also a stage manager for the road production. Over the next few years, he had a variety of small roles on the screen and stage, and was back on Broadway again in 1938 in a flop called *Censored* that ran for nine performances.

Hunter had more success in radio, and acted in a number of serials and dramas, *Gangbusters* among them. He also had numerous roles in programs in two educational series produced by CBS Radio, *Columbia Workshop* and *American School of the Air,* before entering the Army. He spent most of his time in the Persian Gulf, running the American Expeditionary Station in Tehran, where he directed live dramatic and music programs.

When he met Kay, the war had just ended and Hunter was working as a civilian for the Armed Forces Radio Service in Hollywood, producing programs. She was a guest on a show. They had a whirlwind courtship and married in her garden on May 19, 1947. He never held a job again.

The following year, they moved to New York, and Hunter began to function as his wife's collaborator and manager, which goes a long way toward explaining why the work prospects dried up for Kay Swift from this point on. She had one more big success after this, the score to the one-woman Cornelia Otis Skinner show *Paris '90,* in 1952, which had a good run at the Booth Theater and then toured, with Kay at the piano in the pit for some of the run.

As a child, I adored Hunter. He pulled quarters out of my ears, and could juggle five lit flashlights in the dark. I thought he was handsome. I thought he looked like Superman on television. He was gallant, always rushing to pull out a chair or offer his arm to a lady in a way that verged on the dramatic.

My mother didn't like him. She was critical of how untroubled he was about being supported by his wife's modest income.

(This was, in fact, what she would call, if she had observed this pattern in someone else, pot and kettle talk.) For many years, Hunter's mother, a retired vaudevillian with the exotic name Minerva Stanley, was also dependent on Kay Swift's kindness for her rent and other living expenses. She was the widow of the stage and film actor Edwin Stanley, who appeared in dozens of British comedies, but apparently no royalties or pension came her way.

My father told me Hunter was a parasite. He also told me that Hunter's real name, Kaufman, meant "shopkeeper." Who knows how many people were renamed for their trade when they passed through Ellis Island? He was certain that Hunter was not a Kaufman relative of ours.

Ganz and Hunter always arrived with presents, and I loved spending the day with them in the city, on my own, without any other family. Once, after a Saturday-night sleepover at their apartment on East Fifty-ninth Street, I went to church with them. They belonged to something called the Church of the Truth, which had services in Carnegie Hall. The minister was named Ervin Seale. Sometimes they listened to him on WOR instead of going to hear him speak in person. I thought it was a special religion for theater people. When my mother found out that I had attended church with Ganz and Hunter, she was furious. Adding to the trouble, Hunter had bought me a pair of bright red patent-leather shoes with pointy toes, which I had come home wearing. The shoes pinched my feet but I didn't care, because I thought they were incredibly glamorous. So that was two escapades in one visit.

My mother relished her disapproval of Hunter. When Ganz and Hunter stayed with my brother and me in our house in Forest Hills for a week while our mother made a rare solo visit to her father, who was staying in a rented house on the Cape after a heart attack, there was an incident. Hunter, who always liked to fix things, which made Ganz very proud, was tightening a loose bolt on one of the legs of our swing set. As he knelt on the ground, my brother scuffled some dry dirt near him that went into his face. Hunter erupted, shouting in a terrible voice that he was going to kill John. Ganz was in a frenzy over Hunter's loss of temper, and also over the consequences. She begged us not to tell our mother that Hunter had shouted at John. She gave hush money to our housekeeper, Kitty, whom I had run to for comfort, and who had witnessed the shouting.

The following week, however, Kitty told our mother what had happened, and Hunter was banned from our lives forever. Perhaps my mother's decision was influenced by having just spent an unusual amount of time with her father. Much conversation with him could include a carving up of every family member not present in the room, and she may have been freshly exposed to his acid remarks about his first wife.

Did she really think Hunter could have hurt one of us or would hurt one of us in the future? Was Hunter really what she said, "a powder keg ready to blow"? It was a completely uncharacteristic and decisive action on my mother's part. Hunter had lost his temper and shouldn't have shouted that way at John, and Ganz shouldn't have tried to bribe Kitty, but my father shouted the same way at her. Why this disproportionate punishment now?

IN 1961, Ganz rented an "office" two blocks away from her apartment, on East Fifty-seventh Street, a simple studio with a spinet and a fold-out couch and a galley kitchen behind folding doors. From now on, this was where we saw her, and I even had sleepovers with her there. It strikes me now as odd that my grandmother would accept this bizarre partitioning, which required her to choose between her husband and her grandchildren at Christmas, or Easter, a holiday she loved. But she never protested the exile, and she never brought it up to us. Was this a massive displacement through time, thirty years later, of my mother's desire to control her parents? Was Ganz's dignified acceptance of this effacement of her husband from our lives some sort of penance for everything that happened with George?

Hunter's behavior, while offstage from my life, grew erratic. There were purchases of jewelry for Miss Venezuela, whom he claimed to be dating. In her perpetual need to raise cash, Ganz sold an early notebook of George's musical notations for a few thousand dollars, only to see the dealer turn around and sell it for five times what she had been paid. (Twenty years later, the notebook set a record price for a Gershwin manuscript at auction.) She had by then also sold her beloved Fauve Derain painting, *The Charing Cross Bridge,* which she had inherited from her mother.

On Thursday, October 26, 1967, Hunter attended an auction at Parke-Bernet Galleries on Madison Avenue. It was a sale of "Highly Important Impressionist & Modern Paintings & Sculpture." The auction began at eight o'clock. By the end of the evening, he had been the high bidder on ten paintings for a total hammer price of nearly half a million dollars. Among the paintings Hunter had bought were a remarkable Cezanne, the first known portrait of his father, for $250,000, another Cezanne for $40,000, three Chagalls, a Vlaminck vase of flowers, and other paintings by Diego Rivera, Manzù, Rouault, and Raoul Dufy. The catalog for the sale, which he marked up before, during, and after the auction, contains notes on the hammer prices of the paintings he failed to win, including a Cezanne *Tete D'Enfant,* about which Hunter noted, "OUTBID, SHOULD HAVE BOUGHT IT. I LOVE THIS PICTURE." Beside the paintings for which he was high bidder, he made a big check mark and wrote his initials, HG, as if signing an important document.

The *New York Times* front-page story, "Art Buyer 'Sorry,' but He Can't Pay $467,775 Bill," explained that the "Mystery Bidder Who Doesn't Have the Dough" had planned to sell some of the paintings at a profit in order to raise the money to pay for them. He had not realized that payment was expected so quickly.

In order to cover the cost of the settlement agreement with Parke-Bernet, Ganz sold her two Foujita cat drawings, and was grateful that her name was never connected to the story, which continued to play in the *Times* and many art magazines. Auction houses developed new rules for registration of bidders after this catastrophe. Hunter moved to "the office." I saw her apartment again for the first time in seven years. The mantelpiece seemed lower; I no longer needed to drag a chair across the rug in order to climb up to see all the familiar objects. Everything was in place, from the little enameled box with "A Trifle from Ashby" on the lid and the ladybug orchestra to the iridescent conch shells she and Hunter had brought back from a Caribbean holiday in happier times. Her only remaining valuable work of art, the Raoul Dufy gouache of a bowl of fruit which George had brought to her on Eighty-sixth Street, was still on the wall over the mantel.

When Hunter was served with divorce papers, he became deranged with remorse and he begged her for reconciliation, promising he would get a job. After a few difficult encounters, Ganz came to our house in Forest Hills to stay away from the apartment for a few days so he could take all his things. One afternoon, when my mother had gone out for groceries, Ganz told me that if the phone rang, and it was Hunter asking for her, I should tell him I didn't know where she was. To make it true, because she didn't want to ask me to tell a lie for her, she would run out of the room, and run to another room in our house, and I wouldn't know which room it was, so I would be telling the truth if I told him I didn't know where she was, but he didn't call.

On Valentine's Day in 1969, Ganz was visiting my aunt Kay and her family in Evanston when the New York City Police telephoned there to say that Hunter Galloway had been found dead in his apartment. His suicide did not surprise her, but in later years she took to calling herself a widow, although they were divorced when he died.

The memorial service for Hunter was held in the vast living room in Mary Lasker's house. "We're all here for love of Hunter," intoned Ervin Seale, beginning his eulogy. "Balls!" declared Ganz's double first cousin, Lucy Faulkner.

Ganz

GANZ WAS A LOT OF FUN IN A NERVE-RACKING SORT OF WAY. She found joy everywhere, but she misplaced theater tickets, or went on the wrong night. She over-tipped wildly and walked so fast down the street it was hard to keep up with her. She was known to buy entire extravagant bunches of balloons from the vendors in Central Park, decades before balloons were commonplace, inflatable greeting cards.

Perhaps because of her English mother, Ganz abbreviated in a Bertie Woosterish way, toasting at celebrations with several glasses of "champers," telling taxi drivers to go to "Mad Ave," or greeting friends on the phone with "How are things in Gloc?" (She herself called these word shortenings her "abreeves.") Her cocktail of choice in her later years was a "vod ton." Once, walking on the street with me, she spotted the open shirt of a hirsute construction worker and then asked me if I agreed with her that "H.C." (hairy chests) were unattractive. She praised a friend by telling him that he was one of the "G. P. of the W." (great people of the world). I have a hunch that her penchant for abbreviations charmed and inspired the brothers Gershwin as they composed the verse to their song "'S Wonderful," which was introduced in *Funny Face* in 1927:

> *Don't mind telling you, in my humble fash*
> *That you thrill me through, with a tender pash,*

When you said you care, 'magine my emosh
I swore then and there, permanent devosh

She regularly uttered stunning bon mots, whether it was naming Judy Garland and Vincente Minnelli's apartment "The Minnellium," or murmuring to me as we passed an inexplicably crowded Szechuan restaurant that we had both found disappointing, "Szechuan à son goût!"

When I was a child, going out in public with Ganz felt like a high-wire balancing act of pride and embarrassment. I was a mortified twelve the night that Ganz, needing to attract a waiter in a restaurant, half stood, waved her napkin high in the air, and called out, "Yoo hoo! Waiterkins!" (At a certain hour in the day, the perpetual cup of coffee was generally replaced by her perpetual "vod ton.") She once introduced me at a party at a gallery to celebrate an exhibition of paintings by Zero Mostel (whom I had last seen the night of the roll-licking) to Ring Lardner Jr., whose writing I admired, and in fact I had recently read his novel *The Ecstasy of Owen Muir,* as "My friend Kathy," because she just could not bring herself to admit that she had a granddaughter of sixteen.

Though her picture was on the wall at Sardi's, in her later years Ganz was famous only to the cognoscenti who had heard of her, and it pleased her immensely when she was asked for her autograph when she went to hear her friend Bobby Short, who sometimes sang her songs and fussed over her at the Café Carlyle.

Like most eccentrics, she was largely oblivious to her own eccentricities. Our only serious argument, ever, occurred when I was in my twenties, and it was on the subject of her wish to provide diction lessons for the dim, unsophisticated fiancée of one of my cousins. I insisted that she refrain, that the offer would be offensive and insulting; Ganz ultimately conceded, wondering at the same time if the poor dear girl might not at least like to be treated to some electrolysis.

When I think about it now, it strikes me that my grandmother was astonishingly available to me as a child for someone so narcissistic and onstage all the time. She was much more fun to be with alone than out in public. But she had a genuine warmth under all the showbiz hoopla. She knew the names of my stuffed animals. She loved to play Hearts or Casino or Gin, on the floor, though she cried real tears over her Monopoly losses. (That, my mother explained to me, was because her hopelessness with money was all too real. After a certain point we were actually forbidden to play Monopoly with Ganz.) She was also a champion reader out loud, often from books on my shelves that were from her childhood library and had the name Katharine Faulkner Swift on the flyleaf in her child's handwriting, recognizably hers, but rounder and simpler.

When I was very little, she would push me on the swing in our backyard and tell me stories about the Swing Fairy. She wrote loving songs for each of her grandchildren that made reference to specific experiences and elements in our lives. Mine was about balloons in Central Park. Ganz took me to countless Broadway shows, often shows she had seen before, more than once, and so instead of watching what was onstage, she would watch my reactions, to make sure I was enjoying the performance. If there was a particularly funny moment in the show, I would know it was coming, because I would feel her gaze shift so she could watch me enjoy it when the joke landed.

I was taken to numerous stage doors where we were welcomed in the dressing rooms of Ethel Merman, Beatrice Lillie, Ben Vereen. She was usually greeted with a fond and deferential "Come right in, Miss Swift!" by the men guarding the stage doors. I wish she had taken me to the opera, her childhood passion, and I don't know why she didn't, but it is possible that my mother turned her down, on the grounds that she herself hated opera, a subtle sort of rejection and rebellion. My aunt April was the one child who shared her passion for opera. Though it was April's intention to sing opera professionally, and she was apparently quite gifted, once she married her voice teacher, she never pursued a professional career.

Ganz and I played a window-shopping game, where we would take turns picking out the very worst thing in a store window display and then she would try to sell it to me, or I would try to sell it to her, playing the part of an obsequious sales clerk. "Oh, Modom, these little dickenses just say you you you!" she would say, holding up an imaginary representation of the hideous flowered undergarment in the shop window.

At times Ganz gave off sparks, she was so nervous. She had manic tendencies, perhaps, and she drank too much coffee, for sure. But she was an enjoyer. Her enthusiasms were sometimes vague and careless, and she was often so eager to agree with you that you just knew she hadn't been paying close attention to what you were saying. Some of her enthusiastic "Yes! Wonderful! Marvelous!" or "Terrible! Awful! The shits!" exclamations were nonsensical interruptions, but she meant to be responsive and engaged above all. When I told her how much I had enjoyed a day with Jackie Onassis, among other reasons because I found her to be possessed of a rare ability (even if it had evolved as an understandable defense) to be utterly interested in you and your details without needing to talk about herself or bring it back to her own interests or experiences in any way, my grandmother replied, "How marvelous! That's exactly the way I am!"

Ganz assumed that I, too, believed that life was filled with potential wonderfulness—an intriguing and sometimes confusing contrast to the chaotic and mostly depressing atmosphere in my own childhood household. My mother dwelled in the past, and talked a lot about her glorious childhood. The things most important to her seemed to have taken place before my time, and I had missed them. She spoke so poignantly about a certain moment on a summer day, when she looked out the window at Bydale and felt complete happiness, yet she knew at that same moment that it wouldn't last, and she recognized even then, at age seven or eight, that she wouldn't be allowed to stay in that moment, that she would have to grow up and leave Bydale and live her life. By the time I knew her, my mother had spent decades looking back, with a terrible longing for that lost moment.

MY FATHER was on a perpetual quest for love, or something like it, but nothing he had was sufficient, and he was always in pursuit of more, perhaps proving the rule of life that you never get enough of what you don't really want. My mother loved the past more than anything else. Ganz loved to love. She loved being alive. She celebrated the experiences of daily life. She was always focused on the present moment and was always keen to make the most of it. For all her nervous energy and complications, she was always completely present with me. My father wanted to see himself in me. It didn't occur to him that I might have needed something more or different from him than very occasional invitations to enter his world on his terms. My mother dwelled in her lost childhood, while counting on me to be far more mature and responsible than was reasonable, and she, too, had only a small awareness of my experience beyond the ways it reminded her of her own childhood. Neither of them was equipped to recognize me as my own person. In a simple and essential way, from my earliest memories, I always felt very loved and seen and known by Ganz.

✧ ✦ ✧

MY GRANDMOTHER was nearly eighty when Nick and I met. I introduced Ganz to him early in our courtship—it seemed essential to me that they should know each other, because it was a way for each of them to know me, and because I knew they would adore each other.

My mother's family was, in those days, still populated by numerous elderly women whose preference for men over women was remarkably transparent. They were, themselves, of course, exempt from their beliefs that men were essentially superior. In their eyes, my acquisition of a fine male specimen like Nick was probably my greatest accomplishment. Nick understood this (which is to say he understood what they believed, and he understood how much it annoyed me), and he also enjoyed basking in their approving glow from time to time. Nick was my gift to them, and they were my gift to Nick. Meanwhile, with the comfort and security of this alliance, instead of that perpetual feeling some of these old ladies gave me, that I was like a steerage passenger attempting to mingle with my betters in first class on the upper decks, I could begin to laugh about their archaic hierarchies. (Bettina always cheated ferociously at croquet, to ensure that Nick won, she came in second, and I finished last.)

Nick's bond with my grandmother was instant and profound. He was no doubt caught up in my intense devotion to her, but he says now that he was instantaneously moved by what he saw of me in her and of her in me. Our romance made my grandmother happy for me, but I think something about us as a couple also made Ganz happy in a vaguely narcissistic way, too. She compared us to her parents often. She admired their marriage, and she adored her father, the man who died so tragically at forty-one, the handsome man in the oval photo that always hung by her bed all her life.

Though I am more unlike her than like her in my nature, I bear a certain physical resemblance to her, and am, after all, her namesake. Perhaps my alliance with Nick felt to all of us like an idealized redoing of the past, a better version, in which nobody dies and the couple gets to live happily ever after.

Nick and I spent quite a lot of time with her in our first months together. When we would go out to dinner, Ganz often asked that we provide her with an escort from among our friends. ("What if there's dancing?") When we told her we were getting married, Ganz was very excited and pleased—"And he has blue eyes! All of my husbands had blue eyes!" she blurted. (George had golden brown eyes, an unusual topaz tone shared by our daughter Charlotte, but of course he was never one of her husbands.) We went out to lunch with her that day, and she ordered "champers," instructing the waiter to take away the water glasses, because we certainly didn't need water at the table. "Think what it does to your shoes!"

Ganz told me she knew Nick was "the one" the first time she met him. Maybe she did. I love my husband for many reasons: his kindnesses, his passions, his humor, his intense devotion to our daughters, Lucy and Charlotte, his sensibilities. But I don't doubt that the coffee in his shoes was truly an element of my early attraction. He smelled right. Why do we like the things we like? Psychoanalysts smile knowingly when we say something "just feels right" or is "the most natural thing."

We were married at Bydale, then as now my grandfather's widow Joan's house, owing to the kindness and generosity of my step-grandmother, a very good sport who certainly had no obligation to host our wedding. I was twenty and had no sense at all of what I was imposing by making that sentimental request.

Why did I want to be married there? It felt right. It was the most natural thing. The ceremony took place outside, in front of the millpond, in sight of the guest cottage where George had stayed so many times, the guest cottage where George spent that summer of 1928 writing *An American in Paris,* playing with the Parisian taxi horns in various keys for which he had shopped in Paris with Mabel Pleshette Schirmer. (She gave us a ladle for a wedding gift, which we still call Mabel.)

The music played right after our wedding ceremony, the recessional, was an eccentric arrangement my grandmother wrote for us, for flute and trombone, of "Love Is Here to Stay," the last song George finished before he died. *Our love is here to stay* are the words inscribed inside our wedding rings.

When, a year later, we bought the ramshackle eighteenth-century Connecticut farmhouse, the one that made my father vanish that day, Ganz speculated that we might consider building a guest cottage somewhere on the land. "A guest cottage can be very *convenient,*" she told me. As I write these words I am in the studio that is in fact across the lawn from the house, which we built just a few years after my grandmother's death. I regret she didn't live to see how I followed her advice. But I don't follow her example.

Nick and I have been married now for thirty-four years and she's been dead for eighteen years. When you've been married for a long time—this was something I didn't particularly anticipate when I was young, and my sense of time and personal history was very different—you become a repository, a private archive, of memories of your spouse's friends and relations and history as well as your own. Love is loving some or most of the people your partner loves, and then it is mourning and sharing in remembering them when they have died.

I cherish the way my husband loved my grandmother. He really had her number, too. Once, after spending the night in the small guest room of her Fifty-ninth Street apartment, in order to get to an early meeting in the city, Nick sent her flowers with a card that simply read, "From the man who spent the night." Ganz was nearly ninety by then. She was so delighted with his flowers and card, her housekeeper Mattie revealed to me, that not only did she display them on the table in the entrance foyer just inside her door, for maximum exposure, but after they wilted, she replaced the flowers several times, each time putting Nick's card back into the arrangement.

GROWING UP, I missed George Gershwin without ever knowing him, because two people I loved, my mother and my grandmother, loved him and missed him.

He doesn't haunt my dreams, but I often think about the way he changed my life. It is probable that the inheritance of wealth in my mother's family would have gone in different directions had my grandparents not divorced as they did, when they did, and under those circumstances. Writing to Mary Lasker, my grandmother said of her psychoanalysis with Zilboorg, "I wonder now why I took such a lot of unadulterated bull from him, and conclude that he simply made a whip of my own sense of guilt and beat me with it on all occasions." I think that guilt is why she accepted poor terms in that divorce, feeling perhaps that punishment was appropriate. Unfortunately, her children were also punished.

My mother might have led a happier life, made a better marriage herself instead of settling for Sidney Kaufman, a poor simulacrum for George Gershwin, if the territory of her own childhood had been less occupied by the powerful, intoxicating presence of George Gershwin in her mother's heart.

For the rest of her life, my grandmother dedicated much of her musical energy to preserving the Gershwin music that was still in her head, all those melodies that lingered on. In her mid-eighties, she was still jotting down fragments of Gershwin pieces not known to the world, with careful notations about working titles and original keys.

Someone else in her situation might have simply claimed the Gershwin tunes known only to her as her own work and gone on to publish any number of successful hits, but she would never have done that. As it is, I think she always suffered, while gracefully retaining her dignity, when people made the inevitable comparison, insisting on either a Gershwin influence on her work or even suggesting the outrageous possibility that Gershwin helped her write her most successful songs. More knowing musicologists familiar with the work of both can identify possible influences going the other way.

If anything, the Gershwin music in her head obstructed and overwhelmed her own production at certain times in her life. For a songwriter of her caliber, she has a very small catalog. It is very obvious that the gap in her productivity in the years after *Fine and Dandy,* when she produced little work, corresponds to the periods when she was particularly active in her advocacy for George's work. Her support of *Porgy and Bess* was ceaseless, from 1935 to the 1980s.

It was agreed before *Porgy and Bess* even opened that she would travel the country giving talks about it in the hope of stirring greater interest and acceptance. She often spoke from a piano so she could illustrate her lecture with examples from the score. She had the entire 559 pages committed to memory, and could have, if asked, played the uncut, four-hour opera flawlessly. This was true well into her eighties. On October 10, 1935, the night *Porgy and Bess* opened in New York at the Alvin Theater, she hosted a spectacular party at Condé Nast's thirty-room Park Avenue penthouse. The next morning, after two hours' sleep, she took a train to Philadelphia for her first lecture on the circuit, at the Art Institute. After George's death, she spent years keeping the *Porgy and Bess* candle lit, traveling extensively to lecture on both the 1942 and 1952 revivals.

It was probably a solace to both Ira and Kay to work together with George's music as they created the posthumous Gershwin score to the 1947 film *The Shocking Miss Pilgrim,* which starred Dick Haymes and Betty Grable. They also spent a great deal of time together identifying and completing a number of unfinished Gershwin songs, based on a combination of extant fragments and her spectacular memory for anything George had ever played for her.

She would dearly have loved to collaborate with Ira herself, and it seems like a logical next step that ought to have occurred, but Leonore was very likely the chief obstacle to any possibility of that songwriting alliance. My grandmother dropped numerous hints about this wish in her letters to Ira over the years, and he always deflected her. Ira, while very fond of Kay, would never have fought for something that displeased Leonore. He may have had his own reasons to demur as well.

Kay was consulted on various Gershwin recordings and revivals until she was in her late eighties. Even as she began to lose some memory, she was a valuable resource for writers and for performers of the American Songbook, and she could still speak with authority about original keys or tempi for George's music. She influenced Michael Feinstein, whom she first met when he was Ira's assistant, long before he became a performer. She taught Bobby Short a number of obscure and unknown Gershwin songs for his 1973 *Bobby Short Is K-ra-zy for Gershwin* album, playing the second piano obligato for the song "Hi-Ho," which George had written for *Shall We Dance?* before he left New York, though it wasn't used in the film. Over the years she advised Bill Bolcom and Joan Morris, whom she adored, and she valued their friendship as much as she admired their musical talents.

AT THE end of 1992, when she was ninety-five, I moved my grandmother to the Alzheimer's Resource Center in Connecticut. She had required constant care for a couple of years, and now that she no longer noticed her surroundings, it was time to take her out of her Fifty-ninth Street apartment, where she was isolated with round-the-clock helpers. I furnished Ganz's room with a few familiar things, wondering if I was doing it for her or for me. She had a roommate named Olive, but each of them seemed completely unaware of the existence of the other. There were two nameplates beside the door to their room, one over the other. One afternoon when I was visiting her, Ganz and I walked the halls briskly, as was her habit, and then she veered toward her room, though it wasn't clear to me that she knew where her room was until that moment. She had only been willing to play "Pop Goes the Weasel" when I had led her to the piano in the dayroom. As she went through the doorway, she pointed at her nameplate, which was over Olive's, and exclaimed triumphantly, "Look! Top billing!" and then grandly proceeded into her room.

✧ ✦ ✧

WHEN MY grandmother began her long affair with George Gershwin in 1925, she was twenty-eight, the wife of a banker, and the mother of those three little girls. I have to admit she was a truly terrible mother. The life of many parties, she was mostly absent from the daily lives of her daughters. And she was punished for that in certain ways in later years.

Of the three Warburg daughters, only my mother, the middle one, remained really close to her mother as an adult, both emotionally and geographically. Consequently, I had the opportunity from my earliest childhood to form my own relationship with Ganz, a gift from my mother for which I am profoundly grateful. While I may have been told too much, too soon about Ganz, nothing was presented to me in sufficiently judgmental terms that would prevent the kind of relationship we had. Otherwise I might well have grown up as distant from my grandmother as some of my cousins, whose mothers, my two aunts, were a little angrier and less forgiving.

MY COUSINS all loved Ganz, as she loved them, but they didn't know her quite as well as I did. She was in my life from my earliest memory. I saw her all the time, and spoke with her on the telephone several times a week, from childhood until she lost her ability to enjoy a telephone conversation at age ninety-three.

She was exciting and fun when she visited my cousins, I am sure, but she was a phenomenon, someone they only saw on occasion. She was painted by my two aunts as a flighty, irresponsible Auntie Mame, a silly person apt to be out of control, apt to drink too much and misplace things. While she did those things, that's not who she was. Not much was ever said by any of her daughters to her grandchildren about her work as a composer. They were reluctant to take her seriously, which might have had to do with their own professional ambitions (in one case) or lack of ambitions (in the other two cases). My mother loved her mother's music, but at the same time there was something faintly judgmental and condescending about the way she regarded her mother's professional hopes and disappointments. It is true, Kay Swift's career faded considerably in the 1950s, when her talent and drive certainly didn't. She could have had many more successes if only just a few of the shows and television projects that she worked on and pitched for decades had come through.

She had a lot of bad breaks. Cheryl Crawford was always on the verge of committing to one show or another that never happened. There were scripts for stage musicals or television shows by Frank Sullivan, George Oppenheimer, Robert E. Sherwood, and Marc Connelly. There were high hopes for a *Fine and Dandy* movie, which probably failed because the writer Donald Ogden Stewart was blacklisted and had left the country. There was a musical based on a Rumer Godden novel that fizzled. She spent decades hoping to make a new musical comedy based on an opera by Puccini, and she was never able to get traction on a project to make a musical out of a series of children's books by the British writer P. L. Travers about a magical and eccentric nanny named Mary Poppins.

A play by W. S. Gilbert (the playwright half of the Gilbert and Sullivan team), *Fogarty's Fairy,* written in 1882 and never scored by Sir Arthur Sullivan, inspired her for decades, but she could never get the backing. There were pitches for more shows and television programs, and then she was reduced to writing music for industrial shows. She wrote superb songs about Elsie the Cow, Clairol products, the Campfire Girls, a theme for an American Medical Association celebration.

Her daughters regarded her ambitions with a subtle sort of exasperation and contempt, as if she were being unrealistic to want attention, and yet her daughters also judged her for not accomplishing more. And so her grandchildren, and I include myself, were not given a sufficiently nuanced sense of her artistic accomplishments and talent. But then, in any family, how often is anyone ever given a sufficiently nuanced sense of their relatives?

My grandmother's affair with George Gershwin has defined something for me about love and loss. I have never really understood completely how she came to make that dangerous leap, but her having done so was always an essential part of her, and a central aspect of my family's sensibility. It is something that defined her privately as well as publicly.

Maybe the bittersweet consequences of her infidelity are why I have always been so committed to the vows of my own marriage. Looking back, I have often calculated at various points in my life what my grandmother's life was like when she was my age. It is almost always unfathomable to contemplate what she was up to in contrast to what I have been up to. Her choices are appealing and might even seem inevitable when measured in terms of glamour and excitement and passion, but her choices remain unfathomable for being emotionally unsupportable. She loved two men at the same time and she didn't want to choose one over the other and then she lost them both.

The heart wants what the heart wants, as that Gershwin connoisseur Woody Allen has so famously observed. What's hard to take in even after all these years is that my beloved grandmother's heart led her down such a complicated and destructive path that changed so much.

NICK AND I share a dependence on strong coffee every morning to begin our days. We are writers, it's our necessary drug, and it's one of life's pleasures that we can't give up. The vintage A&P coffee grinder has a special cabinet of its own in our kitchen.

Lucy and Charlotte were twelve and ten when Ganz died in January of 1993, and now they are adult women living their lives. It's hard to believe that it was longer ago than that when we could still take our daughters on enjoyable visits to see their great grandmother, diminished but as warm and loving as ever, in that same apartment facing the Fifty-ninth Street Bridge where I made those childhood pilgrimages.

When Charlotte was six, she and Ganz would sit at the piano together, and Ganz would give her a note to play, just the way she would give me a note to play when I was little and would sit beside her on the piano bench while she played one song after another, and I would play my note in time with the music. When Charlotte was eight and had been taking lessons for a while, she sat down at the piano with Ganz and played a very simple version of "Fine and Dandy," which she had taught herself. By that time, Ganz had lost most of her memory, and it was heartbreakingly evident that she didn't recognize this tune, her most popular and enduring melody, known the world over. But she began to play along with Charlotte, following her tentatively at first, then adding harmonious chords with her sure and graceful touch, even though her ninety-four-year-old fingers were knotted with arthritis, augmenting this unfamiliar tune with an increasingly complex countermelody, surrounding

Charlotte's simple rendition of her melody, ending with a grand glissando flourish and a happy laugh.

On a lazy Sunday morning soon after that visit, Nick and I were lying in bed together with coffee and newspapers, thinking the girls were still asleep, when we heard the first few bars of "Love Is Here to Stay" come drifting up from the piano in the living room. Charlotte had been working on it for a week, and now she had really got it. It was a moment that felt just right.

Scattered at Sea

G ANZ DRANK HER COFFEE BLACK, WITH ONE EXCEPTION. When we went to the counter at Robert Day Dean or Schrafft's and she would have an iced coffee, it would be served with a little beaker of milk. It was always my delightful task to pour the milk into the coffee for her. I would hold the beaker over the coffee and ice cubes, and tip it very slowly, so that the thinnest stream of milk would drizzle down and swirl into the coffee, with no splashing, and we would watch the milky cascading ribbons as they unfurled through the murky brown coffee, gliding around the ice cubes, now sliding down the side of the glass, curling like smoke and joining the coiling helix forming in the bottom of the glass, and we would watch together for the moment—that's what we called it—the moment being the instant just before the milk and the coffee became one thing.

When we walked down the street holding hands and swinging our arms, if someone or something came between us, we would let go and she would sing, "Bread and Butter, Bread and Butter!" Sometimes she would sing, "You're the cream in my coffee/You're the salt in my stew/You will always be my necessity/I'd be lost without you," and I loved it when she sang those particular words, "You will always be my necessity," and gave my hand an extra squeeze.

✧ ✦ ✧

In her will, Ganz said she did not want a funeral, and that she wanted her remains to be cremated, and if possible, scattered at sea. When I went to settle the bill at the funeral home I had employed for the cremation, I asked the man there what my options were for scattering at sea. He said they offered this service, and I asked how they did it. He told me he waited until he had maybe ten cremains (that word! Ganz would have loved hating it) to scatter, and then he would take them out to sea on a friend's Boston Whaler, out on Long Island Sound. Maybe they would drink a few beers and fish for blues when they were finished with the scattering.

Ganz's ashes were in a tin container like a tea caddy on the table between us. You want the scattering service? he asked me, reaching for the tin. No problem, we can take care of that for you. I snatched it up, and found it surprisingly heavy as I cradled it in my arms protectively, although until that moment I had not really thought of the contents of the tin sitting on that table as my grandmother. I said I would figure something out.

Not one of my blood relations has ever asked me what I did with her body. She died in 1993, and I suppose I should stop waiting for someone to ask.

The sea where I could scatter her ashes in a way that felt right to me was off our own coastline in the village in Ireland where we have a cottage and spend as much time as possible. It's the village where we spent our honeymoon in 1976 in Moura Budberg's dacha. The process of smuggling her tin of ashes on the Aer Lingus flight was comical, especially the moment when we had to open duffel bags and repack them on the floor in Terminal Four at Kennedy Airport, because one bag was too heavy, so there was Ganz's tin of cremains on the cold tile floor next to the books and hiking boots we were rebalancing.

Nick and I went out in the rowboat on a beautiful afternoon. Sometimes Glandore Harbor is rough, and the water is the color of slate, and the tide beats on the rocks. Other days, when there is no wind, and the sun is shining, it is like a tropical lagoon, and you can look down deep into the water and see a school of mackerel swimming far below the surface, and you can see the tide ripples in the sand. This was one of those days.

Nick rowed us out of the cove and around the point, staying near the cliffs, and we rowed just past the tilted rock formation called the Shelves and then Nick stowed his oars and helped me pry open the tin. We bobbed in the swells and everything around us was perfectly still. Her ashes were in a plastic bag, and I opened that, and then I tipped it out over the side of the boat in one motion.

Until that instant, I had felt sentimental, and sad, and I had also felt some resentment and bitterness about the two living daughters (one of them my mother) of this flawed, loving woman who had closed off part of their hearts to her a long, long time ago, leaving me to take care of everything they didn't or couldn't handle in Ganz's final five years, up to and including this. So I was satisfied with my efficiency and creativity about honoring my grandmother's last wish, getting it done, and done well. But I hadn't planned for the feelings. And I wasn't expecting the moment.

There it was. The moment just before two things become one thing. I poured her ashes over the side of the boat into the sea, and something happened. Those particles of cascading bone matter reconstituted into a form, a quiddity, suspended in the crystal light under the water, an entity wearing the most gossamer, ethereal negligee of smoke. The dust that was my grandmother hung there in the water just below the surface, staying present for a long moment, and then it dissolved into the sea.

Credits

About the Author

KATHARINE WEBER is the author of the novels *True Confections, Triangle, The Little Women, The Music Lesson,* and *Objects in Mirror Are Closer Than They Appear.* She lives in Connecticut with her husband, the cultural historian Nicholas Fox Weber. Visit her at www.katharineweber.com.